Distant Voices Drawing Near

Distant Voices Drawing Near

Essays in Honor of Antoinette Clark Wire

Marvin L. Chaney
Robert B. Coote and Mary P. Coote
Mary Therese DesCamp
Joanna Dewey
Elisabeth Schüssler Fiorenza
Barbara Green, O.P.
Holly E. Hearon and Linda M. Maloney
Hisako Kinukawa
Archie Chi Chung Lee
Eung Chun Park
Gina Hens-Piazza
Richard L. Rohrbaugh
Luise Schottroff
Herman C. Waetjen
Hugh Wire, with Robert B. Coote and Mary Howland
Ruth Ohm Wright
Sojung Yoon

Holly E. Hearon
Editor

M
G

A Michael Glazier Book

LITURGICAL PRESS
Collegeville, Minnesota

www.litpress.org

A Michael Glazier Book published by the Liturgical Press

Cover design by Ann Blattner. Photo of the ruins of the ancient city of Corinth, dominated by the remains of the Temple of Apollo.

| 1 | 2 | 3 | 4 | 5 | 6 | 7 | 8 |

Library of Congress Catalog-in-Publication Data

Distant voices drawing near : essays in honor of Antoinette Clark Wire /
    Marvin L. Chaney . . . [et al.] ; Holly E. Hearon, editor.
      p. cm.
    "A Michael Glazier book."
    Includes bibliographical references and index.
    ISBN 0-8146-5157-7 (pbk. : alk. paper)
    1. Feminist theology. 2. Bible—Feminist criticism.   I. Wire, Antoinette
Clark.   II. Chaney, Marvin L.   III. Hearon, Holly E.
BT83.55.D58 2004
230'.082—dc22

                                                            2003020581

Contents

PLACING THE TEXT IN CONTEXT

CROSS-TEXTUAL, INTERTEXTUAL, AND INTER-MEDIA READINGS

Foreword

⟋⟍

The title of this volume, *Distant Voices Drawing Near*—language borrowed from Anne Wire's book *The Corinthian Women Prophets*—is intended to evoke the values that inform Anne's scholarship. First and foremost it represents Anne's commitment to giving voice to those whose voices have been obscured and marginalized, most especially, but not limited to, women. It also reflects her commitment to hearing these voices within their own contexts. In terms of scholarship this translates into attention to the social, cultural, and historical distance that distinguishes voices in the past from those in the present as well as persons and cultures in the present. Ultimately it describes her dedication to bringing these voices together in conversation around shared values, the central value being recognition of how God is present in the world, challenging the limitations of our visions and calling us to take delight in God's good gifts for promoting the well-being of humankind.

The contributors to the volume represent persons from across the spectrum of Anne's career. Each of them has, at some point, worked with Anne in a shared endeavor. The contents of their essays reflect, in various ways, the values cited above. The volume begins with a biographical sketch, written by Anne's husband, Hugh Wire, assisted by a colleague at San Francisco Theological Seminary, Robert Coote, and Anne's older sister, Mary Howland. This essay offers insight into how the unusual and distinctive character of Anne's early years has informed her scholarly commitments. While many introductions focus exclusively on the individual's scholarly development, the authors here seek to bring to light the intersection of *praxis* and scholarship in Anne's life.

The essays that follow are gathered under four subheadings: Women and Christian Origins, Placing Women at the Hermeneutical Center, Placing the Text in Context, and Cross-textual, Intertextual, and Inter-Media Readings. The section titled "Women and Christian Origins" opens with an essay by Elisabeth Schüssler Fiorenza in which she argues for the need for feminist reconstructions of Christian origins. Acknowledging the dangers inherent in any attempt at historical reconstruction, she contends that it is critical for those who reside at the margins to be able to identify and trace the "roots of historical struggles for emancipation." The result, she maintains, is not the creation of a "myth," but a narrative of "possibility" that challenges the assumptions that inform reconstructions rooted in kyriocentric paradigms. The essays that follow represent two such narratives of possibility. In a study of Romans 16:1-2, Sojung Yoon argues that descriptions of Phoebe as a helper, servant, or patron are inadequate. Following an analysis of the titles assigned to Phoebe, she concludes that Phoebe may have exercised administrative oversight of the church at Cenchreae. She goes on to demonstrate how Paul downplays this aspect of Phoebe's role in his letter of commendation, an indication, Yoon suggests, that Phoebe's authority may have represented a challenge to the authority of Paul. Holly Hearon and Linda Maloney combine their research efforts to produce a double-chapter in which they describe ways in which women were actively engaged in giving rise to, shaping, and transmitting traditions in the early church. This reconstruction calls attention to the integral relationship between theology and social experience, and reveals that the formation of traditions in the early church took place in the context of struggle.

The three essays in the section titled "Placing Women in the Hermeneutical Center" are striking examples of how different tools and approaches serve to bring the women in texts into focus. Gina Hens-Piazza uses the New Historicism as the lens through which she reads the Abraham-Sarah tradition in Genesis 18. By examining the "cracks" in the narrative structure, Hens-Piazza reveals the climax of the story to be the moment of Sarah's laughter, a moment in which God's presence is disclosed. Mary Therese DesCamp employs cognitive linguistic analysis to demonstrate that the use of three contradictory variations on the biblical metaphor "Israel is God's flock" in Pseudo-Philo's *Liber Antiquitatum Biblicarum* reflects the skill of the author in characterizing the foreign woman Jaʾel as among the chosen people. Finally, Luise Schottroff, in her study of 1 Corinthians, argues that purity describes all aspects of life, not only those associated with sexual expression, and references the whole life of the community rather than individuals. On the basis of this definition she examines issues of purity and impurity and their impact on the lives of women in the Corinthian community from the perspective of a feminist hermeneutic, noting the intersection of holiness and justice as believers draw near to God.

In the section titled "Placing the Texts in Context" the five authors turn to social and historical contexts to illumine the content of their chosen texts. Marvin L. Chaney undertakes rhetorical and social-scientific analyses of Hosea, on the basis of which he proposes that Hosea's "wife of promiscuity" serves as a "sarcastic trope for the male urban warrior elite of Israel and for the land whose agricultural priorities and techniques they increasingly dictated." Herman Waetjen examines the "correspondence between content and context" to shine light on the enigmatic parable of the Ten Virgins (Matt 25:1-13). He proposes that the parable subverts dominant cultural paradigms and invites hearers to "scrutinize their discipleship within the eschatological reality of God's reign" at the same time that it opens up a "new possibility of world." Employing a postcolonial hermeneutic, Hisako Kinukawa uncovers the power dynamics at play in the story of the Syro-Phoenician woman recorded in Mark. Through a careful analysis of the cultural and historical context of Tyre in relation to Galilee, she demonstrates how these dynamics inform the exchange between Jesus and the woman, and offers insight into Jesus' words, "it is not right to take the children's bread and throw it to the dogs." Richard Rohrbaugh argues that the story of Nicodemus (John 3:1-21) is best understood in the context of anti-language and anti-societies. In this context Nicodemus' encounter with Jesus is not intended to clarify, but to obscure, in order to establish "distinctiveness, distance, and boundaries" within the Gospel of John. In the concluding essay of the section Joanna Dewey challenges the historical and theological basis for interpreting Jesus' death as a blood sacrifice. Following a description of the cross-cultural characteristics of blood sacrifice, she traces how Christianity, which early rejected blood sacrifice, began to turn to sacrifice as an interpretive lens for understanding the death of Jesus. The effect, she observes, is to enshrine victimhood, a result that is harmful to both men and women.

The final section, "Cross-textual, Intertextual, and Inter-Media Readings," includes essays that embody Anne's commitment to bringing voices together across time and cultures. Archie Chi Chung Lee employs a cross-textual hermeneutic, bringing the biblical text *Lamentations* into dialogue with the Chinese poetic book, *The Lament for the South,* in order to explore how each text understands the role of Heaven/God in relation to the calamities experienced by humankind. Barbara Green traces a shared thread through the Wisdom of Solomon and the Gospel of John: the narrative of the life, death, and Life of an innocent just man. Green observes ways in which this narrative addresses fundamental problems dividing each community, and points to the crucial role of Sophia in each text for articulating the capacity of God to offer life. Robert B. and Mary P. Coote offer a counterchallenge to recent studies arguing that the Gospel of Mark is dependent on the Homeric epics for plot development and characterization, by presenting evidence pointing toward Mark's primary dependence on the Jewish Scriptures. The section closes with two studies on the *Acts of Thecla.* Eung Chun Park examines the *Acts of Thecla* in relation to the Platonic idea of *hagneia* (chaste love) as the sublime form of *erōs* (carnal affection). He proposes that the story of Thecla traces her movement from *erōs* to *hagneia,* as described by Plato, but with the result that the anti-social message of *hagneia* is transformed within the story of Thecla into one of empowerment for women. In a cross-media study, Ruth Ohm Wright brings together recent findings from the discovery of a fresco in Ephesus (featuring three main characters from the *Acts of Thecla*) with literary remains to pose questions concerning the audience addressed by the story of Thecla and how the story was received.

This volume represents a labor of love on the part of many people. I wish to express my thanks to each of the contributors for the collegial spirit they have brought to the project. In addition, I wish to express my appreciation and gratitude to Peter Rehwald and Maureen Maloney of the Graduate Theological Union (Berkeley, California), along with Hugh Wire, for their timely assistance in getting the project underway; to Carla Bradley and Lorna Shoemaker of Christian Theological Seminary (Indianapolis, Indiana), whose skill and expertise during the final stages were critical for the completion of the project; and to Linda Maloney, whose support and commitment have been unfailing and without whom this volume would not be possible.

H. E. H.
Indianapolis, Indiana
July 2003

Introduction: A Biographical Sketch

Hugh Wire, with Robert B. Coote and Mary Howland

ॐ

Antoinette Clark Wire began teaching New Testament at San Francisco Theological Seminary in 1973. She is now the Robert S. Dollar Professor of New Testament at SFTS, and a member of the core doctoral faculty of the Graduate Theological Union. She is the author of two major studies, *The Corinthian Women Prophets: A Study in Paul's Rhetoric* (1990) and *Holy Lives, Holy Deaths: A Close Hearing of Early Jewish Story Tellers* (2002), in addition to numerous articles and booklets. She has been active in the Society of Biblical Literature and the Pacific regional Society of Biblical Literature/ American Academy of Religion, served on several commissions of her denomination as well as the World Council of Churches Plenary Commission for Faith and Order, and has traveled to China a dozen times to research songs created and sung by rural Christians. Most recently she taught New Testament for a year at Nanjing Theological Seminary in Nanjing, China, one of the first two western scholars, along with Old Testament professor Carolyn Higginbotham, invited to do so since the 1950s. She is married, has two married children and one grandchild.

Anne was born in China in 1934. "We were more than usually close because the family moved every year from place to place, thanks to the Japanese and the Presbyterian Board of Foreign Missions in Philadelphia," Anne told an audience in 1996. From a mountain retreat where Anne was born after her missionary mother had gone there to escape the summer heat, the family returned to Changsha for three years, where her father was ministering under the Presbyterian Board to Chinese university students, and then moved to Kunming in southwest China when the faculty and students went to seek safety from the Japanese. Shortly after the youngest sister, Jean, was born, the mother and her three daughters were sent to Burma (in 1940) by their father. As the Japanese closed in on Burma they boarded a clipper plane across the Pacific, leaving every morning before dawn and landing before dusk, from island to island.

The girls attended grammar schools in Seattle, El Cajon, Manhattan, Berkeley, and Pasadena, moving always to the next place where their mother would be speaking about China. Their father's letters from Kunming came from China in code until 1944 when he came home in a ship zigzagging across the Indian and Atlantic Oceans to miss submarine torpedoes. "Mother provided the security behind all this. What did it matter if the people outside our house changed faces every year and the mountains moved around?" Her mother provided not only security to these daughters but formed their image of what a human being can be. Anne's ongoing research in China over the last fifteen years could be seen as an effort to retrace her mother's image in the confidence in God she finds in the songs of ordinary Chinese Christians there, particularly the women.

Anne's mother, Antoinette Black, had gone to China in 1925, called by her sense of mission and supported by her Seattle family and their Conservative Baptist congregation. She met her future husband, William Harold Clark, in the language program for new missionaries in Nanjing, just up the Yangtze from Shanghai. In 1927 she responded to her family's urging to come home, her brothers even sending their mother to China at a time when warring Chinese armies were closing in on the cities. When Hal Clark returned to the United States on furlough in 1930 they courted and married. An issue that took time to resolve with her family was whether their Baptist faith would be compromised in their daughter's marriage to a Presbyterian. The couple went back to China, where Tony Clark gave birth to the three daughters, Anne being their middle child, and managed the household of a missionary family while her husband went out to his work with students and later in support of Chinese pastors and mission-funded middle schools.

Education was central to family life. Anne remembers her father's intense interest in geography, places, and plants, about which he taught his daughters. Though Anne went one term to a mission school for Chinese girls, the Clark girls were taught for the most part by their mother. Mary Howland, Anne's older sister by one year, recalls that when she learned to read at age six she had to focus on the task lest Anne learn first. As refugees in Burma the girls attended their first school, which was not only British but Baptist. The girls were teased unmercifully because their dresses were too short. On their return to China in 1946 the girls continued to be taught by their mother with the help of a correspondence course. Writes Mary, "Anne felt less and less motivated to do all that work for a factotum in Baltimore, Maryland. I went to Shanghai to high school after a year in Kunming, but she was home with our younger sister Jean for two years. Though I had forgotten how, she would rather play. Our parents were actually concerned about her academically until they finally sent her off to Shanghai when she was in 9th grade, and she immediately, with competition in the classroom, reverted to form." As a result of the 1949 Liberation/Revolution and the family's subsequent relocations Anne would ultimately attend four high schools. "Academically she sailed through, but friends were lost," Mary notes. "When she arrived at Pomona College she immediately made intimate friends, who have remained so not just for her four years there, but for life."

It was in a seminar on Kant taught by Gordon Kaufman that Anne became acquainted with her future husband, Hugh Wire. Hugh recalls: "In that Kant seminar the passion of opinion mixed with the sparking of our hormones to generate an energetic intimacy that Kaufman later would recall as 'transcendent.' Anne was one with opinions to wrestle with. She was confident, and her ideas were interesting and grounded." In philosophy courses students read the primary texts unaided by secondary sources except the professor's introductions and questions, and were challenged to discover for themselves the truth of the ideas and then write, admonished by Pomona's Fred Sontag, "saying more than the obvious." These were approaches Anne would one day use with her own students. She took art history classes that she relished, and studied poetry and creative writing, areas in which Pomona excelled. Hugh still remembers her short story about a single mother, told with uncanny authority.

Anne participated in intramural women's sports, was a leader in the women students' organization, sang in the college choir, was moderator one year of the college church, and spent a summer as a church volunteer on a Navaho reservation. She was reader to Ved Mehta, who complained that she omitted the bloody details of Homer, studied so hard one year during finals that she complained that she was seeing two moons, and with Mehta graduated summa cum laude. Her strong sense of herself drew around her a small circle of devoted friends, mostly women, several of whom have indeed remained friends for life.

Anne came to college choosing to major in both history and philosophy. But, she told the Pacific Coast Theological Society in 1996, in a paper on her theological autobiography, "I took everything I read into a think tank that was incorrigibly theological. The teachers would write, 'A very interesting paper, but is this philosophy, or perhaps theology?'" She was after something more than her critics understood. "The thread of reflection is not understanding but searching to understand," she told that audience. "In our family this meant talking about God. On our return from China the family discussion that led to our buying a Chevrolet was theological. Sometimes Dad would get didactic about God's will, but we had discovered by now that he could be wrong and that his own arguments could be mobilized to question him. Both Mom and Dad had graduate degrees, she in English Bible at New York Theological Seminary in its earlier years, from which she went to China on her own, he at

San Francisco Theological Seminary in 1923, followed by an Edinburgh church history dissertation on Calvin's social teachings. So the family theology was biblical and the criticism historical." In her senior year Anne discovered Kirkegaard—"at last, someone else plagued to think theologically. He too was torn between ethical responsibility and aesthetic fascination. And he knew that religious reflection was more important than either. A comfort to find I wasn't as strange as I'd thought, but unnerving considering his early end."

After graduation Anne attended Bonn University on a Fulbright scholarship. Nine weeks that summer at Middlebury gave her usable German. At Bonn she heard lectures from Helmut Gollwitzer, was enamored of the ambition of German students to find their way intellectually and personally in the austerity of postwar Germany, came home with the complete set of Barth's *Dogmatics* in German, and with Greek learned in German. Hugh adds, "and even less tolerance for my American liberalism." Paul Shubert, who knew the German university system, examined her lecture notes and secured for her full academic credit for that year when she came afterward to Yale Divinity School.

Anne joined Hugh for her field work in the Wider City Parish, New Haven's sister inner-city ministry to the East Harlem Protestant Parish, where she led Bible study groups in a public housing project. When she and Meredith (Jerry) Handspicker were sharing leadership in one group, she said each would kick the other under the kitchen table to get a word in. Anne and Joan Forsberg, one of the founders of the parish as well as Anne's supervisor, challenged Connecticut laws against birth control by ferrying inner-city mothers from New Haven to Planned Parenthood clinics in Port Chester, New York. Anne also taught a Bible class in an African American Baptist church. Hugh comments, "When I complained after a visit that the preacher had just stood up there doing nothing but a monologue that finally trailed off into sound and rhythm, she said, "No. He says first what the people think and then he answers it back with what the Scripture says. He's really doing what you want."

One Sunday after Anne had asked her class in this church what the first of Matthew's beatitudes meant, she remembers how a woman had heard the Word spoken to her, "The poor of spirit are us, we who do not know what to pray." With several seminary classmates also involved in the parish, Anne met weekly in a Bible study group that struggled with the personal meaning of Scripture and theology. Hugh remembers Anne finally becoming exasperated with his self-doubting. "You are so busy judging yourself you leave no room for God to get to you." Asked at a faculty reception when she had become the newest faculty member at San Francisco Theological Seminary to explain the focus of her doctoral work, she presented her thinking in a way that caused one colleague to blurt, "My, you are a theist." Says Hugh, who was present, "He was another one who stumbled over how this woman, though she thinks about things critically, works from faith."

Anne and Hugh married in 1959. Although friends considered this step inevitable, agreeing to marriage was a traumatic step for Anne. While Hugh finished seminary in the following year she audited courses and with a group of graduate student and faculty wives, including Joan Forsberg and Vi Lindbeck, worked through issues of vocation and marriage. The vision that seemed to give them a hold on the future was to see themselves aiming toward two careers, somewhat sequentially.

Anne and Hugh went to Springfield, Massachusetts, in the summer of 1960 to follow the model of the Forsbergs, living in Springfield's poorest neighborhood and doing a ministry of learning and service supported by Protestant congregations in the local council of churches. Hugh steamed the wallpaper off the walls of their third floor walkup while Anne painted them and the pressed tin ceiling, and made curtains for the windows. At first unsure about having their daughter living in the midst of the inner city, Anne's parents quickly adjusted themselves with the thought that she, too, was following a mission calling, as they had.

The core of their work was forming home Bible study groups with African American families in their neighborhood and creating programs with children. In addition, they established social service projects with Puerto Rican neighbors and their storefront Asemblias de Dios congregation. Although Anne cut back on her ministries after the first child was born, Annette, the fifth in the line of Antoinettes in her family, she organized with a Panamanian social worker an English learning and friendship-building program between Puerto Rican women in their inner-city neighborhood and English-speaking women from the suburbs. She also began, with the willing support of the Girls Club up the street, a cooperative play school for preschoolers involving the families. And with an eye toward a different future eventually, she began Hebrew study in classes for women in a local Conservative synagogue, where the focus was not on translation but simply on being able to read along in the services. She says she began her practice of Hebrew while in the rocking chair nursing her second child, Joseph.

Visions of working for empowerment of common people, black and white together, led Anne and Hugh in the fall of 1964 to Atlanta, where seminary colleagues found them a place in Mennonite House, an intentional, integrated Christian community conceived by Vincent Harding, located within walking distance of Ebenezer Baptist Church. Their two preschoolers occupied Anne, while Hugh looked for ways to be usefully involved with some white counterpart to the awakening in the black community. Before Christmas they moved into a low-income private, white rental housing complex, surrounded by small black-owned houses. As Hugh began earning money doing construction work, all the while wishing he was doing something for the cause, Anne saw a need close at hand, and with another woman met at Mennonite House began organizing a cooperative preschool for the area. Because federal funds were available, the preschool would be integrated. Resistance to the idea emerged, and the apartment management put up a chain-link fence between the white rental housing complex and the black homes. But a downstairs neighbor with preschoolers of her own, a non-churchgoer from the red hills of Alabama, told Anne, "They all got souls, don't they? Anyway, all schools are going to be integrated." Hugh says of this story, "When she sees something concrete she can do about human need, she acts." Once, while representing the Presbyterian Church (USA) at a World Council Faith and Order event, she helped mobilize the Reformed delegates scattered across languages and cultures without the kind of ecclesial focus offered Anglicans, Lutherans, and Roman Catholics by their bishops present. After a caucus she instigated, the Reformed family found ways to have voice in the assembly.

Before the Atlanta preschool project got fully underway, Anne and Hugh left for the mountains of western North Carolina, to live up a hollow eight miles outside of Boone. They paid extra to bring the telephone line up to their house. It was a lonely place after Hugh had left for the day and often an evening's work in the local poverty program. Anne "grew a good garden" and made special friends with some of the other lonely women up that hollow. She also organized in their tiny upstairs attic a morning preschool, with Montessori-inspired activity for their two children and three others. During the summer she taught the junior highs in the summer vacation Bible school in one of the Baptist churches in the hollow where once, Hugh remembers, "I saw the delight in her class when a junior higher playing Potiphar's wife chased another junior higher around the room." And he adds, "Since she could deal with preschoolers and junior highers like this, I knew when the time came, getting grownups involved would be no problem for her." Seminary colleagues would later acknowledge her attention to non-traditional methods and collaboration with pastors, artists, and other colleagues in order to help seminary students become engaged with texts.

When a young Israeli woman turned up to work for a year as a "reverse" peace corps volunteer, Anne and Tami Dothan had regular sessions together in Hebrew. And the following year, with their older child now getting on a school bus every dawn to go to first grade, Anne took their younger child with her into Boone, where each went to school for the morning, Anne to graduate courses in counseling at the state college, which permitted her to be a teaching assistant in the religion department, he to preschool in Boone's First Methodist

Church. In spring of 1968 Anne and Hugh came back to California, where they settled in Los Angeles, and Anne began full-time preparation for her "second" career, that fall commuting fifty miles each way to Claremont Graduate School. She later told the Pacific Coast Theological Society, "I chose doctoral work, I told people, because to be accepted in ministry in our world a woman has to be doubly qualified. But in fact I wanted to study as long as I could get away with it. Since I had never seen a woman lead a parish or teach theology, why not aim for teaching? I chose Biblical Studies, where history and theology come together, figuring that if Christians are going to understand God differently and make a different history, it would have to begin here."

In this pursuit of understanding she was recapitulating the career of her scholar-missionary/pastor father. He had earned a doctorate before going to the mission field. He had intently absorbed the culture and history of China even as he was teaching Chinese about Christ. He had taken advantage of every opportunity to see more of the world and take his family too, while preparing himself by studying beforehand what he might see. In retirement in the late 1960s—at a time when there was little contact between the Chinese church and the West and much resentment toward China in the U.S. politically—he would write his reflections on the church in China, seeking to see what was promising for the Chinese people in the work of the Communist Revolution in spite of what he deplored about it, and painting a picture of a church that could survive suppression, whose spirit he was sure would not be quenched.

Bob Coote observes how Anne engages others in this pursuit of understanding: "Students and colleagues know that Anne, rather than making statements, more often asks questions, but this seeming diffidence and indirection masks firm conviction and intention. The questions have barbs—they are not so much arrows as hooks. You see them coming and greet them eagerly, even when they are aimed at you. They are full of surprises, abruptness of metaphor and twists of expression. A good example of such surprises, here in the form of a statement, can be found at the conclusion of her short article on Romans, where she states: 'Paul's genius should be characterized . . . by his willingness . . . to take the risks necessary to liberate Gentiles, including women and slaves, from their role as the contrasting foil for God's people.'[1] You find yourself acquiescing, as veterans of the Friday afternoon hikes into the Marin County watershed can attest, in excursions whose end is never in sight, knowing there will be good talking and listening to sustain you on the way."

---

[1] "Paul and Those Outside Power," in Richard A. Horsley, ed., *Paul and Politics: Ekklesia, Israel, Imperium, Interpretation. Essays in Honor of Krister Stendahl* (Harrisburg: Trinity Press International, 2000) 226.

xviii   *Introduction: A Biographical Sketch*

When Hugh became pastor in the fall of 1968 of a small Presbyterian congregation in a racially changing neighborhood in Los Angeles, the old timers were not sure at first that they were happy with a pastor's spouse who was occupied elsewhere. Anne sang in the choir and started a women's circle that met in the evenings around concerns of the other younger women in the congregation, frustrating some older leaders because the group was separate and pleasing them because there was a group at all. Her graduate work at Claremont involved translating documents in the Nag Hammadi Library. While Hugh wondered whether his congregation might consider her work with this Gnostic material heresy, Anne introduced a close look at some of these texts for those in the congregation who might want it. They found them, as she did, a fascinating door to the faith of these people. Anne would continue involvement in the lives of small congregations near wherever they lived, becoming ordained as an elder in 2003 at Calvary Presbyterian Church near her Berkeley home, where worship is in both Chinese and English.

After five years in Los Angeles, Anne, now an ABD ("all but dissertation"), secured an interview at San Francisco Theological Seminary. She began teaching at SFTS during the fall of 1973 as instructor, and completed her dissertation during that first year of teaching. In 1981 she began the first of many trips back to China, finally in her sabbatical year in 2001–2002 teaching New Testament at Nanjing Union Seminary in buildings where her parents had once studied English.

Reflecting on Anne as a faculty colleague, Bob Coote observes that one of her strongest and most appealing characteristics is her common sense, that is, her sense of common reality. Her ability to perceive the impact of decisions and events on ordinary people pervades her life even as a professional academic. It is evident, for example, in faculty discussions: when it was announced that SFTS was selling its Berkeley housing, Anne accurately predicted that this would result in a significant decline in students' willingness to make the trip from San Anselmo to take courses there, and have an effect on racial-ethnic recruiting. While these observations seem obvious in hindsight, Anne was the only person to voice these concerns at the time of the decision.

This sensitivity to the experience of ordinary people leads to the articulation of what Bob refers to—and often—as the "Wire principle" for understanding the nature of texts. Bob recalls, "Anne attended a regional SBL meeting at the University of Southern California where two books were being considered, Burt Mack's *Myth of Innocence* and my *The Bible's First History.* After some academic exchange, Anne spoke up and said they were good books, yes, but there was one problem. In each case, dealing with both New Testament and Old Testament, the authors prided themselves on discerning how clever and inventive and innovative the biblical writers could be in creating writings their hearers and readers would accept and preserve. The trouble, she observed, is that people aren't like that even now—at least outside of academia—and certainly weren't then. We scholars imagined that these writers had created something that was ninety percent new and ten percent old and gladly received as such. In reality, said Anne, to be convincing a writing had to be ninety percent old and only ten percent new, at most. How did she know? Because she had been listening to normal average people telling stories all her life!"

Listening to people's stories has indeed been Anne's life work and the subject of most of her research and publication. Anne's most recent book, as Bob observes, is characteristic of Anne in many ways. She translated nearly all the texts herself, and paid very close attention to the particularities and peculiarities of the wording of the text itself. Her intellect and writing are lucid, compact, penetrating, vivid—often metaphorical—concise, methodical, and respectful. This, along with the book's interest in commoners' storytelling, resonates with Anne's history of interacting with nonacademic people, often poor and illiterate, all her life. Similarly, Anne's interest in storytelling and her concern for Paul's rhetoric are of a piece. *The Corinthian Women Prophets* reflects her great interest in the way people communicate with one another, in all directions. This is how Anne envisions life: in terms of people trying to be heard. This becomes apparent in the way she focuses not only on the ways in which Paul himself is communicating with people, but also on how Paul's rhetoric provides insight into—indeed was shaped by—the claims, assertions, and arguments of the women of Corinth who did not write. Giving voice to women speakers who did not or do not write is perhaps Anne's prime interest throughout her career as a woman who both speaks and writes. Anne has intentionally spoken and written for more than herself, on behalf of women whose voices are liable to go unheard. Anne's interest in rhetoric can be traced back to this basic concern: that those who have had trouble getting heard *be* heard. Her work in recording the songs of Chinese women struggling to preserve and transmit the Bible story exemplifies this in the highest degree.

Perhaps key to this basic concern is what she told her 1996 audience. "I am the middle one of three sisters. In spite of what our society teaches about individuation as the way to maturity, and in spite of all our parents did to assure we could each do our own thing, at rock bottom I am one of three sisters." Mary Howland, Anne's older sister, recalls the year Anne "peaked": "she was a beautiful eleven-year-old. Of course she had always been a beautiful child, but neither she nor I—a year older—had seemed to know it. We made ourselves up, and imagined afresh each day who we would pretend to be and what the situation was. We were rarely ourselves when left alone to play, but in the collaboration we were most ourselves." In her collaboration with unvoiced women in Corinth, Palestine/Israel, or China, Antoinette Clark Wire is "most herself."

Women and Christian Origins

"What She Has Done Will Be Told . . .": Reflections on Writing Feminist History

Elisabeth Schüssler Fiorenza

ॐ

In celebrating the birthday of Antoinette Clark Wire we also celebrate "what she has done." Birthdays of feminists are milestones not only in the life of the wo/man[1] whose birthday we celebrate, but also for the feminist[2] movement to which she is committed. This is very important because, as the Australian feminist Dale Spender has shown, in the past four hundred years feminist ideas have been trivialized, silenced, and forgotten.[3] Consequently, the next feminist generation cannot learn from the thought of their predecessors, but are compelled to reinvent the intellectual wheel again and again.

Moreover, the historian Barbara Caine has shown that it is not just the dominant kyriarchal society and academy that foster the forgetting of feminist knowledge. Such forgetting frequently occurs with each new generation of feminists who find it hard to recognize the work of their forerunners and therefore feel

---

[1] I have adopted this way of writing wo/men in order to stand andro-kyriocentric language that claims to be generic language on its face. Hence I use the term inclusively, because in English the term wo/men includes men, she includes he, and female includes male. I also want to indicate that the feminists' debates around this term have shown that woman/women is an unstable term since it hides the differences between and within wo/men. Finally, I use this way of signification in order to include subordinated men among those wo/men struggling for liberation. For the problematic meaning of the term woman/women see Denise Riley, *"Am I That Name?" Feminism and the Category of Women in History* (Minneapolis: University of Minnesota Press, 1988), and Judith Butler, *Gender Trouble: Feminism and the Subversion of Identity* (New York: Routledge, 1990).

[2] Like Alice Walker I use "feminist" as a political umbrella term, fully aware of the variegated expressions of feminism as womanist, mujerista, Africana, critical, postmodern, or global feminisms. I myself have sought to develop feminist theology, history, and interpretation as a critical radical democratic discourse of emancipation and liberation.

[3] Dale Spender, *Women of Ideas (And What Men Have Done to Them)* (Boston: ARK Paperbacks, 1983).

compelled to distance themselves from the ideas of their predecessors in order to prove the novelty and creativity of their own ideas:

> At the same time historians have to recognize that the frequent rejection of the term "feminism"—and of any sense of connection with earlier feminists—by women who have embraced the notion of female emancipation indicates that women find it hard to establish trans-generational links or to set themselves up as legitimating or authoritative figures for each other or for future generations.[4]

For that reason such celebratory undertakings as *Festschrifts* also serve the function of recognizing and acknowledging the historical significance of feminist work by creating a feminist intellectual tradition. They are a small gesture to ensure that "what she has done will be told . . . ."

Anne is such an authoritative figure among feminist biblical scholars and historians. Her landmark work *The Corinthian Women Prophets*[5] has made the historical agency and struggles of the Corinthian wo/men prophets intellectually visible. She has given historical presence and voice to them by reading the rhetoric of Paul against its kyriocentric (Emperor, Lord, Slave-master, Father, Elite Male-centered) grain. She has not only developed a distinct historical-rhetorical method of reading, but also has convincingly shown how the different social locations of Paul and of the wo/men prophets engender different theological arguments. Since Anne's major work develops a rhetorical-historical approach in order to tell the story of the Corinthian wo/men prophets, it seems appropriate to explore the ensuing debate on the feminist writing of wo/men's history in early Christianity. Rhetorical-historical feminist reconstruction of wo/men's agency and leadership has recently come under fire not only from malestream,[6] but also from feminist scholars. Some argue that to search for emancipatory origins and roots is to create a "myth of origins," whereby "myth" is not understood in a positive sense as a sacred story that illuminates our understanding of the world, but in a negative sense as ideological legitimization of feminist Christian hegemony. Recognizing the linguisticality of our sources and the rhetoricity of historical reconstruction, other scholars reject the reconstruction of early Christian origins completely.

---

[4] Barbara Caine, "Women's Studies, Feminist Traditions and the Problem of History," in Barbara Caine and Rosemary Pringle, eds., *Transitions: New Australian Feminisms* (Sydney: Allen & Unwin, 1995) 3.

[5] Antoinette Clark Wire, *The Corinthian Women Prophets: A Reconstruction through Paul's Rhetoric* (Minneapolis: Fortress, 1990).

[6] I use the expression "malestream," which to my knowledge was coined by the feminist sociologist Dorothy Smith, not as a negative label but as a descriptive term, since scholarship and Christian tradition have been articulated by elite educated men.

MYTH OF ORIGINS

A feminist historical-rhetorical construction that is interested in the origins of Christianity on feminist methodological grounds and has expressed theological interests is accused of producing a "feminist myth" of origins by stressing wo/men's equality and leadership. The "entire focus on origins within feminist discourse on theology and biblical interpretation" allegedly participates in the production of this myth of Christian origins.[7] Moreover, it is argued, the contemporary "impulse to equality" stands on its own and does not need to be projected into the first century or to appeal to biblical writings and authority.

Burton Mack and his students[8] have taken up Foucault's critique of origins and forcefully questioned not only the myth of pristine Christian origins but also the search for Christian origins as such. The "myth of Christian origins," as they rightly point out, is related to the Protestant reconstructive historical model of decline and its attendant anti-Judaism. Like its Catholic counterpart, the developmental "myth of seed and growth," it functions to maintain culturally ecclesiastical relations of domination. Because of this necessary connection between religious origins and discourses of power and domination, I argue that scholars of "Christian origins" must abandon both the Roman Catholic and the Protestant Reformation form of the historiographic myth of origins. This myth imagines an originary pristine moment of Christianity that *a priori* was declared to be unique, *sui generis,* original, and by definition incomparable, but that in the Protestant version early on suffered fatal corruptions.[9] It has plainly served to inculcate Christian hegemony, ideas of Jewish decadence, notions of religious superiority, and exclusivist identity.

While this criticism of exclusivist and supremacist early Christian historiography is justified, it does not give an adequate account of why the search for origins is so pernicious. Is it the search for roots or other ideological frameworks and historical interests such as anti-Judaism, clericalism, or Christian hegemony that make it so? Furthermore, does the search for origins perform the same function for marginalized groups and people who have been excluded from the historical record? Is the search for historical origins not also a contemporary search for identity, memory, and a guiding vision? In other

[7] Kathleen E. Corley, *Women and the Historical Jesus: Feminist Myths of Christian Origins* (Santa Rosa: Polebridge, 2002) 147 n. 7, with reference to Elizabeth Castelli.

[8] See his *Festschrift, Reimagining Christian Origins,* edited by Elizabeth Castelli and Hal Taussig (Valley Forge: Trinity Press International, 1996).

[9] Jonathan Z. Smith, *Drudgery Divine: On the Comparison of Early Christianities and the Religions of Late Antiquity* (Chicago: University of Chicago Press, 1990) 143.

words, what may at first appear to be a quest for origins may in fact be the tracing of alternative genealogies connecting the lived experiences of marginalized communities to Christian narratives. If that is the case, the social location of those engaged in this search and of contemporary identity interests needs to be investigated. One must ask whether the critique of the myths of Christian origins does justice to the critical feminist search for wo/men as historical agents in early Christian origins and the attempts to trace their struggles in the beginnings of Christianity. It is not the search for early Christian origins, agency, memory, and history, I would maintain, but the rhetoric of exclusivist Christian uniqueness, negative boundary drawing, and claims to *sui generis* status that feminists must reject.

Early Christian feminist historians have argued that the story of Christian origins must be rewritten not just as the story of elite Western men but also as the story of wo/men from all walks of life who have made history.[10] In order to accomplish this project, much of feminist historical work has first focused on texts about wo/men and the reconstruction of wo/men's history. My own work elaborated early on that a feminist reconstruction of Christian origins must critically investigate androcentric (or more precisely, kyriocentric) language and theological hermeneutics as well as the positivist assumptions of historical, sociological, and theological biblical scholarship contained within their scientific models of reconstruction.

Analyzing kyriocentric language and rhetoric within a critical feminist reconstruction of Christian origins does not simply focus on texts about wo/men but places both the rhetoricity of the text and wo/men as historical agents at the center of its hermeneutical attention.[11] It does not engage in an "add wo/men and stir" approach to historiography,[12] but rather seeks a radical re-vision of all of history in the interest of emancipation. It does not look to a mythical pristine origin in order to find the promise of the "golden age" or the buried "stone of truth" —instead, it seeks to both identify and establish connection to certain potential roots of historical struggles for emancipation. It challenges malestream historical scholarship to recognize that its scientific historiography is a reconstructive and not a positivist descriptive practice that produces discourses of power by constructing knowledges and ideologies that sustain domination.

[10] See, for example, Sarah B. Pomeroy, ed., *Women's History and Ancient History* (Chapel Hill: University of North Carolina Press, 1991).

[11] See, for instance, Ross Shepard Kraemer and Mary Rose D'Angelo, eds., *Women and Christian Origins* (New York: Oxford University Press, 1999) for reworking a feminist approach into a wo/men's studies approach.

[12] See, e.g., the dissertation of Helga Melzer Keller, *Jesus und die Frauen: Eine Verhältnisbestimmung nach den synoptischen Evangelien* (Freiburg: Herder, 1997) 440–41: "Auch sonst

In addition, feminist scholars have elaborated on how the definition and practice of history have been shaped by gender and the interest in nationalist domination. Malestream historical scholarship has prioritized men's history over wo/men's, white history over the history of people of color, the political history of Western domination over the history of struggles against it.[13] And this prioritization has resulted in the production of scientific historical "facts" which malestream historiography is then able to wield in the continuing interests of sociopolitical and academic domination.

Finally, whereas in malestream biblical scholarship the past and its people are construed as the totally antiquarian "Other," feminist and critical emancipatory historiography have reconceptualized history as memory and stressed continuity with the past. As Deborah McDowell has put it, "what we call the past is merely the function and production of a continuous present and its discourses."[14] History as cultural memory of the past is firmly set in the present and looks toward the future. It emerges:

> out of a complex dynamic between past and present, individual and collective, public and private, recall and forgetting, power and powerlessness, history and

---

nahm Jesus in seinen Reden die patriarchale Gesellschaftsordnung als das Normale hin . . . . Die traditionellen Verhaltensmuster und Schablonen wurden von ihm in keiner Weise hinterfragt oder gar aufgesprengt. Für wen Jesus sich vor allem einsetzte, waren die Notleidenden, die religiös Marginalisierten und die sozial Benachteiligten—auch wenn er kein Reformprogramm oder sozialrevolutionäre Aktionen verfolgte . . . . Wir müssen vielmehr das Fazit ziehen, dass er überhaupt kein Problembewusstsein hinsichtlich der in einem patriarchalen Gesellschaftssystem ungleichen Verteilung von Rechten und Möglichkeiten zwischen den Geschlechtern hatte, kein Gespür für eine sowohl rechtliche als auch lebenspraktische Benachteiligung von Frauen, kein Interesse an einer diesbezüglichen Veränderung des Status quo." (Otherwise, as well, Jesus, in his discourse, accepted the patriarchal social order as normal. . . . The traditional patterns of behavior and stereotypes were not questioned by him in any way, certainly not exploded. Those on whose behalf Jesus engaged were above all the needy, the religiously marginalized, and the socially disadvantaged—even though he pursued no reform program or social-revolutionary actions. . . . We must instead draw the conclusion that he was in no way conscious of any problem as regards the unequal distribution of rights and opportunities between the sexes in a patriarchal social system, no sense of a legal and practical disadvantaging of women, no interest in any alteration of the status quo in that regard.)

[13] For a feminist account of the development of scientific history as a discipline see Bonnie G. Smith, *The Gender of History: Men, Women and Historical Practice* (Cambridge: Harvard University Press, 1998); Uta C. Schmidt, *Vom Rand zur Mitte: Aspekte einer feministischen Perspektive in der Geschichtswissenschaft* (Zürich and Dortmund: eFeF-Verlag, 1994). For antiquity see the excellent collection by Nancy Sorkin Rabinowitz and Amy Richlin, eds., *Feminist Theory and the Classics (Thinking Gender)* (New York: Routledge, 1993).

[14] Deborah McDowell, "Negotiating between Tenses: Witnessing Slavery after Freedom—Dessa Rose," in Deborah E. McDowell and Arnold Rampersad, eds., *Slavery and the Literary Imagination* (Baltimore: Johns Hopkins University Press, 1989) 147.

myth, trauma and nostalgia, conscious and unconscious fears and desires. Always mediated, cultural memory is the product of fragmentary personal and collective experiences . . . . Acts of memory are thus acts of performance, representation, and interpretation. They require agents and specific contexts . . . . Moreover, gender is an inescapable dimension of differential power relations and cultural memory is always about the distribution of and contested claims to power. What a culture remembers and what it chooses to forget are intricately bound up with issues of power and hegemony, and thus with gender. Finally, the tropes and codes through which a culture represents its past are also marked by gender, race and class.[15]

If emancipatory historical knowledge has the task of fostering the self-recognition and self-determination of subaltern wo/men, then feminist scholars cannot just engage in the play of unending deconstruction but must also participate in reconstructing and re-envisioning "historical origins" as an alternative discourse to that of domination. They must remain aware that they do so in a global context not only of colonialism,[16] market commodification, and positivist science, but also in one of variegated movements for emancipation. They do so not only within a religious fundamentalist context of exclusion and marginalization, but also within that of emancipatory movements in religion that seek to change institutionalized religions.[17]

I argue that feminist "Christian Origins" discourses that seek to position themselves not in the spaces of domination but in the critical alternative spaces of emancipation need to shift their theoretical focus away from Jesus or Paul

[15] See the editors' introduction, "Feminism and Cultural Memory," by Sandra Harding and Kathryn Norberg, to the issue of *Signs* 28:1 (2002) 1–19, on "Gender and Cultural Memory" (5–6).

[16] See Kwok Pui-Lan, "Jesus/the Native: Biblical Studies from a Postcolonial Perspective," in Fernando Segovia and Mary Ann Tolbert, eds., *Teaching the Bible: The Discourses and Politics of Biblical Pedagogy* (Maryknoll: Orbis, 1998) 76.

[17] For an excellent critical analysis of the involvement of religion in these global struggles see especially the work of the late Penny Lernoux, *Cry of the People* (New York: Penguin, 1982); eadem, *In Banks We Trust* (New York: Penguin, 1986); and her last book before her untimely death, *People of God: The Struggle for World Catholicism* (New York: Penguin, 1989); Robert B. Reich, *The Work of Nations* (New York: Vintage, 1992); Joan Smith, "The Creation of the World We Know: The World-Economy and the Re-Creation of Gendered Identities," in Valentine M. Moghadam, ed., *Identity Politics and Women: Cultural Reassertions and Feminisms in International Perspective* (Boulder: Westview, 1994) 27–41; see also Diana L. Eck, *Encountering God: A Spiritual Journey from Bozeman to Banaras* (Boston: Beacon, 1993) 176. Eck writes: "A new wave of exclusivism is cresting around the world today. Expressed in social and political life, exclusivism becomes ethnic or religious chauvinism, described in South Asia as communalism. . . . As we have observed, identity-based politics is on the rise because it is found to be a successful way of arousing political energy."

as creators of pristine Christian origins. On this point I concur with Burton Mack. They can, however, avoid reproducing the myth of pristine origins only if they shift their research to the disciplinary practices and ideological interests of scholarship on early Christian origins, the rhetoric of our source texts, and the reconstruction of wo/men's agency in early Christianity. Only after a critical deconstruction of the kyriocentric scientific practices of the discipline are scholars able to engage in a critical analysis of the sites on which the "facts" of early Christian origins have been constructed.

As theorist Michel de Certeau has pointed out: "Every 'historical fact' results from *praxis* . . . . It results from procedures which have allowed a mode of comprehension to be articulated as a discourse of facts."[18] Therefore, a favored metaphor for history writing by feminists is not that of archaeology as valorized by Foucault and Mack, but that of quilt-making. Quilt-making is a metaphor that understands historiography as "history making," as integrating the surviving and interpreted scraps of source-information like pieces of cloth into a new and distinct design whose colors project a different hue in a transformed hermeneutical light.

Since my book *In Memory of Her* is mostly indicted as an exemplar of a feminist myth of Christian origins, I will use it here as an example of a different feminist *"history making."* When I set out to develop the reconstructive model shaping the book's narrative I did not start with the goal of producing a factual description of what "actually happened" in early Christian beginnings. Nor did I want to prove that Jesus himself was totally egalitarian and without bias. Rather, I wanted to show that the historiography of early Christian beginnings participates in the theoretical-historical discourses of domination that have been produced by contemporary scholarship. Consequently, I did not set out to prove that malestream early Christian historiography was factually wrong, but rather that it was wrong-headed and incomplete because of its kyriocentric frameworks and positivist empiricist rhetoric.

Compelled by the feminist critique of androcentric language and historiography, I set out to show that the early Christian story could be told—and must be told—*otherwise.* My question was not "Did it actually happen?" or just "What do we factually know about wo/men in antiquity?" but whether we still find traces of egalitarian emancipatory tendencies and movements in the kyriocentric sources of the Greco-Roman world. "Do we still have sufficient information and source texts to tell the story of the movements carrying Jesus' name *otherwise?*"—envisioning them as egalitarian, a concept I defined in *In Memory of Her* with reference to the feminist sociologist Elise Boulding as

[18] Michel de Certeau, *The Writing of History* (New York: Columbia University Press, 1988) 15.

"serial reciprocity," a relationship that is the most obvious alternative to domi-nance-submission relationships.[19] My search was not for unique and unblem-ished Christian origins, but for the possibility of telling the early Christian story from a new perspective. The task, I argued, involves not so much dis-covering new sources as recognizing the rhetoricity of our available sources and rereading them in a different key.[20]

Not only was there plenty of material that could be read in an egalitarian frame of interpretation, I maintained, but such an egalitarian reading could also do more justice to our sources[21] that speak about wo/men's leadership in ways that malestream scholarship felt compelled to explain away, overlook, or interpret in terms of cultural femininity. The interpretation of Phoebe in Ro-mans 16, for instance, is notorious for depicting her as a servant at Paul's meetings, or interpreters focus on Mary of Magdala and the other wo/men sup-porting Jesus and his itinerant male disciples as doing the necessary "house-work" and helping the men out financially.

In Memory of Her and its reconstruction of Christian beginnings is often misread in terms of the liberal Protestant historiographical myth of "pristine egalitarian origins and rapid decline into patriarchy."[22] Thus the book's femi-nist historical dialectical model of struggle[23] between egalitarian vision and its

---

[19] Elisabeth Schüssler Fiorenza, *In Memory of Her: A Feminist Reconstruction of Christian Origins* (New York: Crossroad, 1983) 87.

[20] Ibid. xx.

[21] I thereby anticipated in a somewhat different form the criterion for the adjudication of His-torical-Jesus research that Larry Hurtado has formulated in analogy to that used in textual criti-cism: "where the aim in weighing 'internal evidence' is to reconstruct the reading that best explains all the variants" (Larry W. Hurtado, "A Taxonomy of Recent Historical-Jesus Work," in William Arnal and Michael Desjardins, eds., *Whose Historical Jesus?* [Waterloo, Ont.: Wilfrid Laurier University Press, 1997] 294).

[22] See Schüssler Fiorenza, *In Memory of Her,* 92: "The sociological-theological model for the reconstruction of the early Christian movement suggested here should, therefore, not be misread as that of a search for true, pristine, orthodox beginnings which have been corrupted either by early Catholicism or by 'heresy,' nor should it be seen as an argument for an institutional patriar-chalization absolutely necessary for the historical survival of Christianity. The model used here is that of social interaction and religious transformation, of Christian 'vision' and historical realiza-tion, of struggle for equality and against patriarchal domination."

[23] See, e.g., Mark A. Powell, *Jesus as a Figure in History: How Modern Historians View the Man from Galilee* (Louisville: Westminster John Knox, 1998) 2, who not only mistakes my hermeneutics of suspicion as "reading between the lines" but also misapprehends my reconstruc-tive model of ongoing struggle. He claims I argue that "by the second century the Christian church had become an extremely patriarchal institution, dominated by an all-male clergy." Although he perceives the paradigm shift I advocate ("Nevertheless she has been extremely successful in sen-sitizing modern scholars to an awareness of the social and political contexts in which the Gospels

realizations, on the one hand, and kyriarchal reality and its dehumanizing effects, on the other hand, is misperceived. To read early Christian history in terms of the reconstructive model of rapid decline from the heights of radical equality to the valleys of patriarchal institution is to overlook the continuing struggles in antiquity as well as throughout Christian history between those who understand Christian identity as radically inclusive and egalitarian and those who advocate kyriarchal domination and submission. In short, while conceptualizing *In Memory of Her* I endeavored to write not only a different, but a feminist history of Christian beginnings in Palestine and in the Greco-Roman cities by placing wo/men at the center of attention.

To avoid reproducing the myth of Christian origins as a golden age it is necessary to undertake an investigation of contemporary scholarly reconstructions as well as explore the values and visions that shaped emancipatory social movements that have and continue to carry Jesus as the Christ's name. In other words, it does not suffice to critically explore the kyriocentric rhetorical location of the gospel. Rather, it is necessary to shift attention to the social practices and contexts of the historical agents active at this location. The scholarly search for origins cannot simply focus on texts, but must pay attention to the people who have produced these texts. Such a shift in the focus of research requires that studies of "Christian beginnings" articulate an alternative ethos of biblical inquiry that can transform the discourses of "pristine origins" rather than uncritically incorporate them. It calls for a redefinition of historical science and research in the interest of emancipation.

The feminist sociologist Patricia Hill Collins has outlined three epistemological criteria for developing a critical self-reflexivity that could sustain emancipatory oppositional scholarly practices.[24] To adapt these criteria to the study of Christian origins one would need to ask the following:

1. Does a particular reconstruction of origins "speak truth to people about the reality of their lives" and the lives of wo/men in the first century? Who are the experts, what are the standards they used, and what counts as knowledge? Who decides, and why do we accept or reject what the experts say?

2. What is the "stance toward freedom" and equality in a particular source text as well as in a particular rendition of Christian origins? What are its visions of emancipation and the strategies of change suggested? Does it encourage people to resist relations of domination, and can it engender social and religious change?

---

were produced and to consideration of ways in which this might have influenced the stories they relate"), he then does not explore this paradigm shift further.

[24] Patricia Hill Collins, *Fighting Words: Black Women and the Search for Justice* (Minneapolis: University of Minnesota Press, 1998) 398–99.

3. Does a particular reconstruction of origins move people to struggle, or does it advocate the status quo? Does it provide an ethical foundation and framework grounded in notions of justice and authority for struggle? How effectively does it provide moral authority for the struggles for self-determination?

WRITING FEMINIST HISTORY

I am often asked whether it would matter to my reconstructive paradigm if it could be shown that in fact wo/men did not participate in the early Christian movements or that there was no impulse whatever in antiquity to radical equality. "Does it matter," my interlocuters inquire, "whether or not history provides us with any examples of emancipation, equality, and justice?" In reply one could ask, "Does it matter to feminists to have a written history?" Since history shapes identity and our view of the world, it matters in my view whether wo/men and other subjugated peoples have a history not just of violence and exploitation but also a history of liberation, agency, and equality—a history that is not just utopian, but has already been partially realized. As long as history is written by the winners, the marginalized and subjugated cannot afford not to have a written history.

To cease to write history in a different key would mean to concede the power of interpretation to the historical winners. To give an example from my own church context: Vatican pronouncements have insisted that wo/men cannot be ordained. First the fathers in the Vatican did so by relying on the myth that Jewish wo/men had the status of chattel. Now, because of the influence of feminist scholarship, they argue that wo/men cannot be ordained because Jesus and the apostles did not ordain them although they could have, since wo/men belonged to and had leadership in the early Christian movements. However, such an argument still neglects to mention the critical consensus of historical scholarship that Jesus did not ordain anyone.

It is obvious that historical argument serves here to maintain the second-class citizenship of wo/men. Moreover, it has been shown that those churches that ordain wo/men dropped their biblical-historical arguments against wo/men's ordination as soon as they admitted wo/men to holy office. It is obvious that the Vatican's historical argument is shaped in the context of a politics of non-ordination as a politics of power.[25] Hence it is critically important for Christian feminists to shape a historical counterargument that allows one to resist such discourses of domination. Rather than abandoning historical recon-

---

[25] See the *Concilium* issue, *The Non-Ordination of Women and the Politics of Power,* ed. Elisabeth Schüssler Fiorenza and Hermann Häring (London: S.C.M., 1999).

structive work, we have to tell the story of Christian origins differently! In order to do so we must de-legitimate not only the kyriarchal "myth of Christian origins," but also its producers.

Since feminists are not concerned with conserving the world "as it is" but changing it to fit their own experience of being as wo/men in the world, we are less interested in an apologetic defense of Christian origins than in the historical agents and subjects (predominantly Jewish wo/men) who have shaped the socio-religious Jewish movements named after Jesus, movements that, I have argued, are best understood as emancipatory *basileia*-movements.[26] It is obvious that one is able to imagine the beginnings of early Christianity differently as emancipatory movements if one is committed to contemporary social justice movements.

If one shifts from a kyriarchal frame of reference to a radical democratic or egalitarian one, then one can no longer argue that wo/men were not members of the communities that produced early Christian traditions and writings. If one cannot prove that wo/men did not participate in shaping the earliest traditions, one needs to give the benefit of doubt to the textual traces suggesting that they did. Rather than taking the andro/kyriocentric text at face value, one must unravel its politics of meaning.

The objection that this is a circular argument applies to all hermeneutical and historiographical practices.[27] For instance, social-scientific studies that posit dualistic oppositionals such as "honor and shame" as given "facts" of Mediterranean cultures will read early Christian texts "about women" within this theoretically "constructed" kyriocentric frame of reference and thereby reproduce the cultural "common sense" that wo/men are marginal people. So-called social scientific narratives appear, however, to be more "realistic" and "objective" than feminist ones because kyriocentric discourses function as ideologies that "naturalize" the structures of domination as "what is." That is, they make invisible the "constructedness" of their account of historical reality in terms of their own allegedly scientific understanding and experience of reality. Therefore malestream narratives of "how the Mediterranean world of Jesus or Paul 'really was'" are easily accepted as "common sense," objective, scientific-historical accounts despite the fact that they are as much a "construction" as feminist ones.

If one is intent on misreading feminist reconstructions of Christian origins in terms of the Protestant model of "decline" from pristine egalitarian beginnings

[26] See Elisabeth Schüssler Fiorenza, *Jesus: Miriam's Child, Sophia's Prophet* (New York: Continuum, 1994).

[27] See the forthcoming book of Francis Schüssler Fiorenza, *Beyond Hermeneutics: Theology as Discourse,* for a critique of the method of correlation.

to kyriarchal institutionalization, one does not grasp a feminist model of on-going debates and struggles between those advocating an egalitarian ethos and those espousing a kyriarchal one. These struggles, however, can only be traced by acknowledging the contemporary struggles of global wo/men's movements for radical equality and the rhetoric surrounding them. They can only be traced by reading the early Christian sources as rhetorical texts that advocate either the discourse of domination and submission or a radical democratic ethos of equal citizenship.

Egalitarian social movements striving to change unjust relations of domi-nation—which this reconstructive model assumes—are not just a product of modernity, but are found throughout history. Ancient social movements and emancipatory struggles against kyriarchal relations of exploitation do not begin with early Christian movements. Rather, they have a long history in Greek, Roman, Asian, African, and Jewish cultures. The emancipatory struggles of early Christian wo/men must be seen within this wider context of cultural-political-religious struggles. Such a historical model of emancipatory struggles sees the early Christian movements that kept Jesus' memory alive not over and against Judaism but over and against kyriarchal structures of domination in antiquity and today. The history of these struggles in antiquity and throughout western history, however, can only be written if and when the facticity and plausibility of criteria employed by malestream scholarship for judging historical source information are questioned.

To argue for their own preferred version of reconstruction, scholars have de-veloped the criterion of *plausibility,* which judges source materials on the grounds of whether their content can be made historically plausible by fitting into what we "know" about the time and culture of the early Christian movements.[28] Yet this criterion of plausibility overlooks the fact that what is regarded as "com-mon sense" or "plausible" in a culture depends on the hegemonic ideological understandings of the status quo, of "how the world really is." For instance, the assumption that wo/men were marginal or second-class citizens in all forms of first-century Judaism is steeped in present day kyriocentric assumptions and perceptions of Jewish culture and religion. Such presumptions often make it

---

[28] This hermeneutical circle between a pre-constructed image of Jesus and evaluations of in-dividual texts is recognized by Gerd Theissen and Dagmar Winter, *Die Kriterienfrage in der Je-susforschung: Vom Differenzkriterium zum Plausibilitätskriterium* (Göttingen: Vandenhoeck & Ruprecht, 1997) 206: "Ein zutreffendes historisches Gesamtbild ist eine Idealvorstellung, ein Grenzwert, dem wir uns immer nur in Form von Plausibilität Annähern können." (An accurate overall historical picture is an ideal concept, a boundary value we can never approach except in the form of plausibility.) However, they do not critically question the plausibility criterion on the basis of this insight.

impossible to assert plausibly that wo/men were equal members in the movements claiming Jesus' name if one understands them as Jewish movements.

The inability of even feminist scholars to assume the possibility of understanding the ethos of the early Christian movements as egalitarian and variegated, struggling against kyriarchal domination and believing in the basic equality of all the children of G*d, bespeaks antifeminist tendencies. It indicates a lack of feminist self-affirmation on the part of wo/men scholars who have been socialized into kyriarchal academic disciplines.[29] We know that everyone has internalized the prejudices, self-deprecation, and misogynism of the dominant culture to varying degrees. As Judith Plaskow so forcefully states: "To take seriously the notion that religious history is the history of women and men imposes an enormous responsibility on women: It forces us to take on the intellectual task of rewriting all of history . . . . It reminds us that we are part of a long line of women who were simultaneously victims of the tradition and historical agents struggling within and against it."[30]

If critical self-affirmation of wo/men is the *sine qua non* of writing history *otherwise and in a feminist key,* then it is not surprising that biblical Women's Studies has not always been able to resist the lure of "common sense" malestream reconstructions of early Christian origins in which wo/men are second-class citizens. Hence I suggest that the "common sense" criterion of "plausibility" that justifies a kyriarchal world must be replaced with the criterion of *possibility.*

What is "thinkable" or "possible" and even "probable" historically must be adjudicated in terms of an emancipatory reconstructive model of early Christian beginnings as well as in terms of how scholars utilize their source-information and materials. Instead of asking, "Is it likely or plausible that wo/men shaped the Jesus-traditions?" or that "the wo/men prophets in Corinth had a different theological self-understanding from Paul" one must ask, "Is it historically possible and thinkable that they did so?" This shift requires scholars to prove that such a possibility did not exist at the time. Such an argument would presuppose that scholars have studied not only hegemonic historical formations but also the emancipatory elements in Greco-Roman and Jewish societies. In using the criterion of possibility one must, however, be careful not to turn

---

[29] See my forthcoming articles, "Disciplinary Matters," in the proceedings of the 2002 Heidelberg Conference on Rhetoric, and "Rethinking the Educational Practices of Biblical Doctoral Studies," in *Teaching Theology and Religion* 6/2 (2003) 65–75.

[30] Judith Plaskow, "Critique and Transformation: A Jewish Feminist History," in Debra Orenstein and Jane Rachel Litman, eds., *Lifecycles.* Vol. 2: *Jewish Women on Biblical Themes in Contemporary Life* (Woodstock: Jewish Lights, 1997) 99.

around and answer it again with reference to what are deemed "plausible" and "common sense" truisms.[31]

Such a change of theoretical framework from one that uncritically re-inscribes "what is" to one that asks "what was possible" makes it easier to understand Christian origins as shaped by the agency and leadership of Jewish, Greco-Roman, Asian, African, free and enslaved, rich and poor, elite and marginal wo/men. Those who hold the opposite view, for instance, that slave wo/men or Jewish wo/men were not active shapers of life in antiquity, would have to argue their point. A feminist reconstructive historical model of egalitarian possibility is able to place the beginnings of early Christian movements "like the tip of an iceberg" within a broader cultural-religious historical frame of reference that allows one to trace the tensions and struggles between emancipatory understandings and movements inspired by the radical democratic logic of equality on the one hand and the dominant kyriarchal structures of society and religion in antiquity on the other.

To argue for a possible and probable rhetorical reconstruction of early Christian beginnings as egalitarian does not mean that the extant early Christian sources would not also allow for a hegemonic kyriarchal reconstruction of the early Christian movements. The opposite is the case, since our sources are all written in grammatically androcentric/kyriocentric language that functions as generic rhetorical language. It only means that one needs to show that a feminist egalitarian reconstruction not only is *possible,* in terms of a critical reading of the extant sources in terms of a hermeneutics of suspicion, but also *preferable* in terms of the constructions of Christian identity it engenders. In other words, scholars no longer can justify their reconstructive models in a positivist scientistic fashion, but need to stand accountable for them and their political functions in light of the values and visions they promote for today.

Such attacks against an egalitarian feminist model of reconstruction usually come from antifeminist scholars and churchmen who are concerned with maintaining the status quo. They are bent on debunking the possibility of an egalitarian ethos in the first century because they cannot imagine that early Judaism or early Christianity could have been egalitarian. Most importantly, they cannot assert an equal standing or even decisive leadership for wo/men in antiquity lest that serve as precedent and legitimation for contemporary feminist scholars who assert such equality. Finally, a reconstruction of Christian origins as egalitarian does not mean to assert that early Christian movements were

---

[31] This is the primary mode of arguing employed by Ekkehard and Wolfgang Stegemann (*The Jesus Movement: A Social History of Its First Century* [Minneapolis: Fortress, 1999] 361–409) when discussing wo/men's leadership in the Jesus movement.

"new" and incomparable or that they were the only movements at the time that were egalitarian. One wonders what is so threatening in the idea of an egalitarian movement at the root of Christianity (and in my view also of Judaism, albeit in a different socio-theological form) that provokes such misreadings.

In sum, I have argued here that feminist theoretical work and critical historiography that takes emancipatory praxis as its touchstone and theo-ethical vision as its goal provides a theoretical framework also for studies of Christian origin. Critical historical origins scholarship cannot but strive for the contemporary significance of its theoretical and historical work. Such significance must not only be negotiated historically but also theologically if it is to displace the hegemonic academic and ecclesiastical myths of Christian origins.

Whereas a Foucaultian approach to the quest for identity and the search for origins is primarily deconstructive, a critical feminist approach insists that historiography must also be constructive and create histories that aim toward a more just future. In 1971 Adrienne Rich was already reflecting on the importance of the newly emerging wo/men's liberation movement for historical consciousness. Hence I will quote her article "When the Dead Awaken: Writing as Re-Vision" to conclude my birthday reflections for Anne.

> The sleepwalkers are coming awake, and for the first time the awakening has a collective reality; it is no longer such a lonely thing to open one's eyes.
> Re-vision—the act of looking back, of seeing with fresh eyes, of entering an old text from a new critical direction—is for women more than a chapter in cultural history: it is an act of survival. Until we can understand the assumptions in which we are drenched we cannot know ourselves. And this drive to self-knowledge, for women, is more than a search for identity: it is part of our refusal of the self-destructiveness of male-dominated society. A radical critique of literature, feminist in its impulse, would take the work first of all as a clue to how we live, how we have been living, how we have been led to imagine ourselves, how our language has trapped as well as liberated us, how the very act of naming has been until now a male prerogative, and how we can begin to see and name—and therefore live—afresh. . . . We need to know the writing of the past, and know it differently than we have ever known it; not to pass on a tradition but to break its hold over us.[32]

The feminist debate about the "myth of Christian origins" seems to be engendered by the fact that different feminist authors have a different relation to tradition. Those who want to break the hold of Christian tradition over wo/men

---

[32] Reprinted in Barbara Charlesworth Gelpi, ed., *Adrienne Rich's Collected Writings* (New York: W. W. Norton, 1993) 167–68.

assert their academic location and use their scientific abilities to do so. Those of us who understand that both the academic and the Christian traditions have been permeated by discourses of domination seek to valorize wo/men's historical agency and emancipatory struggles in order to break the hold of religious, academic, and political *status quo* traditions over us. By claiming, as Anne did, the intellectual power of "listening into speech" (Nelle Morton) those who have been silenced, of making the lost voices of early Christian wo/men (who for the most part were Jewish wo/men) audible again, of sharing in feminist emancipatory struggles, "we can begin to see and name—and therefore live—afresh . . . ."

Phoebe, a Minister
in the Early Christian Church[1]

Sojung Yoon

꙰

Historical reconstruction of women's leadership in the early Church faces significant obstacles. First, we lack documentary sources for the historical situation of the early church, and the literary sources we do have minimize the contributions of women leaders and their role in establishing churches. Second, the androcentric point of view that readers bring to these documents often renders the women in them silent and invisible. In some instances attempts have even been made to suppress evidence of women's leadership in the early church. A good example of this is the case of Junia in Rom 16:7. Because she is identified as an apostle, Junia is assumed by many to be a man. Although several scholars have challenged this view, noting the lack of textual evidence to support rendering the proper name Junia as masculine, many interpreters continue to reject the possibility of a female apostle.[2]

Another example, and a more controversial one, is found in Rom 16:1-2. Here Paul introduces Phoebe to the Christian community at Rome. I suspect that what has happened to Junia—the diminishing of her role in Christian ministry—also has happened to Phoebe, a woman who was a leader in the church at Cenchreae and whose devotion to Christianity was acknowledged by Paul. Employing a hermeneutics of suspicion, the first step in feminist exegesis according to Elisabeth Schüssler Fiorenza, I will undertake a close examination

---

[1] This is a revision of a paper delivered to the Society of Biblical Literature in 1998.

[2] For more detailed arguments on this subject see Bernadette Brooten, "'Junia . . . Outstanding among the Apostles' (Romans 16:7)," in Leonard Swidler and Arlene Swidler, eds., *Women Priests: A Catholic Commentary on the Vatican Declaration* (New York: Paulist, 1977) 141–44; and John Thorley, "Junia, a Woman Apostle," *NovT* 38 (1996) 18–29.

of Rom 16:1-2 with the intention of restoring Phoebe to her place in the text and the early church.[3]

A HERMENEUTICS OF SUSPICION

I begin with a comparison of different modern translations. Paul calls Phoebe διάκονος in 16:1. This word is translated as "servant" in the King James Version, American Standard Version, and as "deaconess" in the Revised Standard Version. Διάκονος appears a total of nineteen times in the Pauline and Deutero-Pauline letters. Sixteen times the KJV and ASV translate it as "minister," while in Phil 1:1 and 1 Tim 3:8, 12 they translate it as "deacon," and in Rom 16:1 as "servant." Therefore one can say that the KJV and ASV imply that διάκονος refers to an official position within the church, since normally they translate it as "minister." Only in Rom 16:1 do they translate διάκονος as "servant," thus implying that Phoebe was not a leader in the church but a devoted lay person.[4] The RSV translates διάκονος as "deaconess," also differentiating Phoebe's leadership from other male διάκονοι by making the masculine noun διάκονος feminine, a distinction not found in the Greek. Finally, the New Revised Standard Version translates διάκονος as "deacon," with a footnote suggesting the alternative translation "minister."

Are these accurate translations for Phoebe's title, διάκονος? What could be the true implication of the title when applied to her? What aspect of Phoebe's identity as a first-century Christian woman can we draw from Rom 16:1-2?

APPLICATION OF NARRATIVE CRITICISM TO ROMANS 16:1-2

In reconstructing Phoebe's role in the first-century church I will employ the narrative criticism used by Norman R. Petersen in *Rediscovering Paul*. Petersen identifies two significant features in the literary character of letters. First, he notes that letter-writers do not distinguish the "narrative world" (the world within the letter) from the real world (the world to which a letter refers, or "the referential world"). The "real world" is, consequently, embedded in the narrative world of the letter. According to Petersen the events described in the letter to Philemon are Paul's description of the "real world," but they represent a "selective sequence" by means of which Paul creates his own narrative.[5]

---

[3] Elisabeth Schüssler Fiorenza, *Bread Not Stone: The Challenge of Feminist Biblical Interpretation* (Boston: Beacon, 1984) xii, 15–18.

[4] Kazimierz Romaniuk discusses the role of Phoebe in the same vein in "Was Phoebe in Romans 16,1 a Deaconess?" *ZNW* 81 (1990) 132–34.

[5] Norman R. Petersen, *Rediscovering Paul* (Philadelphia: Fortress, 1985) 8.

Second, Petersen indicates that, just as the form of a story dominates the form of discourse in narrative, so the form of discourse dominates the form of story in letters. In other words, "in narratives, the message is in the story. In letters, the story is in the message."[6] On the basis of these observations Petersen draws the convincing conclusion that "letters have stories, and it is from these stories that we construct the narrative worlds of both the letters and their stories."[7]

In order to establish the narrative world in Rom 16:1-2, I will follow the method outlined by Petersen. He suggests, as a first step, identifying the actions referred to or implied in the letter and then enumerating them in their *chronological sequence.* The sequence of the events as they appear in the text is defined as the *poetical sequence,* while its re-enumeration in the chronological order is described as the *referential sequence.*[8] The two sequences can be identical, but more often than not the writer changes the order, employing her/his literary creativity for the sake of rhetorical effect. By examining the differences between two sequences one can discern how the writer selected the events, the order in which she/he arranged them, and the rhetorical effect the writer created by this arrangement.

Let us consider the *referential sequence* in Romans 16:[9]

1. The greetings in 16:3-23 reveal that Paul knew some of his addressees. Thus Paul had become acquainted with at least some of the presumed recipients of the letter before writing. Since Paul had never been in Rome, it is likely that he knew them in other places.[10]
2. Paul must have met and known Phoebe in Cenchreae. Although their precise relationship is not clear from this letter, Paul describes her as his προστάτις (benefactor, NRSV translation).[11]
3. Phoebe plans a trip to Rome.[12]

[6] Ibid. 9.

[7] Ibid. 43.

[8] Ibid. 47–48.

[9] I assume that Romans 16 is part of the original letter to the Romans, agreeing with the point of view expressed by Karl P. Donfried in his article, "A Short Note on Romans 16," in idem, ed., *The Romans Debate: Revised and Expanded Edition* (Peabody, Mass.: Hendrickson, 1991) 44–52.

[10] I am here employing Peter Lampe's thesis in "The Roman Christians of Romans 16," in Donfried, ed., *The Romans Debate,* 216–30. Lampe points out that there were a number of Christians who immigrated from the east to Rome. Some of them, such as Aquila and Prisca (Acts 18:2; Rom 16:3), were expelled from Rome because of the edict of Claudius, and returned after the emperor's death (ibid. 219).

[11] The order between 1 and 2 can be reversed. That is to say, it is also possible that 2 may have happened before 1.

[12] Phoebe's purpose in her visit to Rome is not clear. If it was personal, it is questionable why Paul includes this section in Romans. Could it be possible that her visit is related to some mission

4. Phoebe asks Paul to write a letter of commendation on her behalf, or Paul volunteers to write one. Since Phoebe is προστάτις of Paul, Paul would feel a need to write the letter in order to repay her favor toward him.

5. Paul writes this letter, asking the Christians at Rome to help Phoebe.

6. Phoebe arrives at Rome.

7. The Christians at Rome receive Paul's letter.[13]

8. Presumably Phoebe is welcomed and supported by the Christians at Rome and she stays there for some time.

Let us now establish the *poetic sequence* as it appears in the letter. The actions—implied but not explicitly described in the letter—will be marked by parentheses. Numberings follow the *referential sequence:*

(3) Phoebe plans to go to Rome.

4. Paul commends Phoebe (v. 1).

5. Paul informs the Christians at Rome that Phoebe is coming to Rome and asks them to help her (v. 2a).

2. Phoebe was a προστάτις of many, including Paul (v. 2b).

1. Paul made acquaintance with some people among the Christians at Rome (vv. 3-23).[14]

(6) Phoebe arrives at Rome.

(7) The Christians at Rome receive Paul's letter of commendation on behalf of Phoebe.

(8) Phoebe is welcomed and supported by Christians in Rome.

Let us make a diagram to compare the *referential sequence* and the *poetic sequence:*

Referential Sequence	1	2	3	4	5	6	7	8
Poetic Sequence	(3)	4	5	2	1	(6)	(7)	(8)

In the *poetic sequence* 2 and 1 (Phoebe as προστάτις; Paul's acquaintance with those in Rome) follow after 4 and 5 (Paul commends Phoebe; Paul asks the Romans to help Phoebe): that is, Paul clarifies his relationship with the church at

---

of her own in Rome? If this is so, Paul's request for παραστῆτε (Rom 16:2) can be understood as "assisting her mission."

[13] Whether Phoebe delivered the letter to Rome or not is a subject of debate. According to Robert Jewett, scholars who assume that ch. 16 is part of the original letter to the Romans tend to agree that Phoebe was the bearer of the letter (Robert Jewett, "Paul, Phoebe and the Spanish Mission," in Jacob Neusner et al, eds., *The Social World of Formative Christianity* [Philadelphia: Fortress, 1988] 161 n. 84).

Rome (no. 1: vv. 3-23) after he introduces Phoebe (nos. 4, 5, 2). Paul also specifies his relationship with Phoebe (no. 2), stating that she was his προστάτις
only after he introduces Phoebe and asks that the Christians at Rome support
her (nos. 4, 5, 2).

This relocation of the actions in the *poetic sequence* raises two questions.
First, what relationship did Paul have in the past with the Christians he names
in 16:3-23? When we look at the greetings in Rom 1:1-7, no specific relationship between Paul and his addressees is revealed, in contrast to the introductory
sections in the other Pauline letters. It is only at the end of the letter (16:3-23)
that Paul mentions his relationship with the addressees and then only after rec-
ommending Phoebe to them.

A letter of commendation (or introduction) is based on a relationship between the addresser and the addressees. The essential features of the letter of
commendation are summarized by Stanley K. Stowers as follows:

1. The writer and the recipient share some positive relationship or reciprocity and are most often social peers in some respect (e.g., friends,
   family, government officials).
2. The writer intercedes on behalf of a third party in order to perform a
   favor for or through the third party and to establish a positive social relationship between the recipient and the third party.[15]

In his letters of commendation Paul's usual rhetorical strategy is to state first his
close association with the addressees, to whom Paul stands in a superior position, and then to go into a commendation or exhortation. His emphasis on the relationship is intended to motivate the addressees to show hospitality to the one
being commended. For example, in Philemon, Paul emphasizes that Philemon
owes a debt to Paul when he commands Philemon to show generosity to Onesimus the slave (vv. 18-19). Before Paul commends Timothy to the Corinthian
congregation (1 Cor 16:10-11) he establishes himself throughout the letter as a
person who has the authority to make the commendation: For example, he states
that he proclaimed the gospel to them (1 Cor 1:17), founded their church and became their father through the gospel (1 Cor 3:6; 4:15). In Phil 4:3 Paul expresses
his confidence in his relationship with an addressee through the vocative γνήσιε
σύζυγε (loyal companion). Strangely, the designation of such intimacy is absent
in Paul's commendation of Phoebe. In his greetings in 16:3-16 Paul names nine

---

[14] Although vv. 3-23 do not belong to the commendation, they are crucial for the rhetorical effect of the commendation since they illustrate the connection between Paul and his addressees.

[15] Stanley K. Stowers, *Letter Writing in Greco-Roman Antiquity.* Library of Early Christianity
5 (Philadelphia: Westminster, 1986) 155.

women and seventeen men among the Christians at Rome, yet he does not imply any obligation on their part such as would be necessary for a letter of commendation. It is not obvious that Paul taught or helped their church. Rather it seems that certain people among the congregation were equal, or superior, to Paul in their position as apostles (v. 7: Andronicus and Junia) or because they had helped Paul (v. 4: Prisca and Aquila). One could argue that Paul was not able to indicate any intimate relationship with the addressees since he had never been in Rome before. However, if no connection existed there would be no one to whom Paul could address his letter of commendation. To propose an alternative view, it is possible that Paul intentionally downplays his relationship with the addressees for rhetorical purposes. By naming his relationship with the addressees *after* the letter of commendation (*referential sequence* no. 1 relocated to the fifth place in the *poetic sequence*) and giving no indication of their obligation to listen to his request Paul subtly implies that he was not enthusiastic about emphasizing rhetorically the reasons why the Christians at Rome should welcome Phoebe.

The second question raised by relocation in the *poetic sequence (referential sequence* no. 2 relocated to fourth place in the *poetic sequence)* concerns Paul's description of Phoebe as a person who deserves assistance from the church at Rome. In his examination of forms of commendation in Paul's letters Chan-Hie Kim identifies three parts: (a) an "introduction" that includes a petition and discloses the identity of the person(s) recommended; (b) the "credential," where Paul praises or commends the person by describing the person's relationship to himself; (c) the "desired action," where Paul states what he wants the recipient to do.[16] Kim notes that Rom 16:1-2 does not conform to this pattern, but repeats the "credential," first in v. 1b and then in v. 2b, following the statement of the "desired action"—a variation that is unique to Romans. It appears as follows:[17]

(a) "Introduction": Συνίστημι δὲ ὑμῖν Φοίβην (Now, I commend to you Phoebe).

(b) "Credential": τὴν ἀδελφὴν ἡμῶν, οὖσαν καὶ διάκονον τῆς ἐκκλησίας τῆς ἐν Κεγχρεαῖς (our sister, who is [even] a deacon of the church at Cenchreae).

(c) "Desired action": ἵνα αὐτὴν προσδέξησθε ἐν κυρίῳ ἀξίως τῶν ἁγίων, καὶ παραστῆτε αὐτῇ ἐν ᾧ ἂν ὑμῶν χρῄζῃ πράγματι (so that you may receive her in the Lord in a manner proper to the saints, and provide her with whatever she may desire from you).

---

[16] Chan-Hie Kim, *The Familiar Letter of Recommendation.* SBLDS 4 (Missoula: Scholars, 1972) 120–35.

[17] Ibid. 132. The translation here is taken from the NRSV.

(b') "Credential": καὶ γὰρ αὐτὴ προστάτις πολλῶν ἐγενήθη καὶ ἐμοῦ αὐτοῦ (for she has been a benefactor of many and of myself as well).

This repetition of the "credential" does not appear in any other letter of
commendation by Paul. In the "credential," according to Kim, "the writer usually identifies the recommended in terms of family relationship or by degree of
intimacy, in the hope that the recipient would accept him as if the writer himself were being recommended."[18]

Accordingly Paul's clarification of his relationship with Phoebe is crucial
in order to motivate the addressees to help her. It is, consequently, necessary
to question what Paul's rhetorical intention is in placing a second credential (v.
2b: Phoebe's being his προστάτις) at the end. What effect does this have on
the addressees? It is likely that by mentioning Phoebe's role as a προστάτις at
the end Paul downplays the significance of this relationship. The addition of
ἐμοῦ αὐτοῦ (of myself as well) at the very end suggests that, rhetorically, this
is intended as a kind of passing remark. This observation suggests that Paul
does not want to emphasize Phoebe's role as a προστάτις for him.

This *poetic sequence* stands in contrast to that in Philemon. Petersen observes that in the letter to Philemon negative information about Onesimus is
presented by Paul only after he has provided all the positive information about
Onesimus he could give. Petersen explains that one of the chief effects of this
relocation is the letter's rhetorical power to encourage Philemon to receive
Onesimus favorably.[19] Kim's examination of the structure of another letter of
commendation (1 Cor 16:15-16) will further clarify Paul's subversion of rhetorical strategy for recommendation in Rom 16:1-2.[20]

   (a) "Introduction": Παρακαλῶ δὲ ὑμᾶς, ἀδελφοί· οἴδατε τὴν οἰκίαν Στε-
       φανᾶ (Now I urge you, brothers and sisters, you know that members of
       the household of Stephanas)
   (b) "Credential": ὅτι ἐστὶν ἀπαρχὴ τῆς Ἀχαΐας καὶ εἰς διακονίαν τοῖς
       ἁγίοις ἔταξαν ἑαυτούς (who are the first converts in Achaia, and have
       devoted themselves to the service of the saints)
   (c) "Desired action": ἵνα καὶ ὑμεῖς ὑποτάσσησθε τοῖς τοιούτοις καὶ
       παντὶ τῷ συνεργοῦντι καὶ κοπιῶντι (that you also obey those people
       and everyone who cooperates and toils with them).

In this letter, just as in Philemon, Paul gives all the positive information
about those he is commending before urging his addressees to offer favor to

---

[18] Ibid. 127.
[19] Petersen, *Rediscovering Paul*, 73.
[20] Kim, *The Familiar Letter of Recommendation*, 130. I alter the NRSV translation here.

them. One can also find the same pattern in Phlm 10-17 and 1 Thess 5:12-13a. However, in Rom 16:1-2 Paul breaks his rule of rhetoric. Even though he does not relate negative information about Phoebe, neither does he present the crucial credential regarding his relationship with her at the beginning of the recommendation—the strategy that would have produced the most favorable impression. He describes Phoebe as his προστάτις at the end of the paragraph as if it were an insignificant, secondary thought.

We have noticed two features in Paul's narrative. First, Paul undercuts the rhetorical impact of mentioning his relationship with the Christians at Rome whom he knows by naming them after of the letter of commendation without any indication of their obligation, thus making his letter of commendation less effective. Second, Paul's description of Phoebe as his προστάτις is made as if it is a passing remark and in an odd place. In other words, he does not highlight this positive information about her. But before we draw a conclusion from these observations it will be helpful to create a sociological map of the relationship between Paul and Phoebe.

THE SIGNIFICANCE OF PHOEBE'S TITLES

Who was Phoebe? What historical information does Paul provide about her? Given the Greek origin of her name, Phoebe is probably a Gentile.[21] Phoebe is called τὴν ἀδελφὴν ἡμῶν (our sister) and διάκονος (minister), with no mention of her father or husband, which is rare in the first century C.E. Elisabeth Schüssler Fiorenza thus concludes that "Phoebe is not defined by her gender role and patriarchal status but by her ecclesial functions."[22]

Phoebe's title, διάκονος, is often found in Paul's letters. He uses this word twice in reference to Jesus (Rom 15:8; Gal 2:17), once in reference to people who are not involved with the Christian mission (Rom 13:4), and once in reference to his own opponents in ministry (2 Cor 11:15). At other times Paul uses διάκονος when speaking of those in positions of leadership in God's ministry (1 Cor 3:5; 2 Cor 3:6, 6:4, 11:23; Phil 1:1). Looking at the people Paul labels διάκονος, such as Apollos (1 Cor 3:5), Paul himself (1 Cor 3:5; Phil 1:1), and Timothy (Phil 1:1), it is appropriate to assume that Phoebe, also called διάκονος, is a Christian leader. Although it is not clear when this word came to indicate an official Christian title, Paul greets διάκονοι along with ἐπίσκοποι (bishops) in Phil 1:1, which implies official standing of some sort within a

---

[21] For a more detailed discussion about the name see Joseph A. Fitzmyer, *Romans: A New Translation with Introduction and Commentary.* AB 33 (New York: Doubleday, 1993) 729.

[22] Elisabeth Schüssler Fiorenza, "Missionaries, Apostles, Coworkers: Romans 16 and the Reconstruction of Women's Early Christian History," *WW* 6/4 (1986) 424.

church.[23] Further, Phoebe is not simply a διάκονος, but διάκονον τῆς ἐκκλη-σίας τῆς ἐν Κεγχρεαῖς (a deacon of the church at Cenchreae). The use of δι-άκονος in association with a particular church suggests that Phoebe is a leader within that congregation. This would be consistent with Paul's use of the same word in reference to other members of the Christian community. Thus several scholars propose that Phoebe was "a local leader," who taught and preached in her Christian community.[24] It is also possible that Phoebe was more highly ap-preciated in her congregation than Paul was, since she would have been a resi-dential pillar of the church while Paul was a traveling minister who was accustomed to stay at the church for only a short period.

Another controversial word that is used to describe the relationship be-tween Paul and Phoebe is προστάτις. Romans 16:2 is the only place where προστάτις appears in the New Testament. Thus it signifies the unique charac-ter of Phoebe's position. It is translated as "a helper of" (RSV), "a good friend of" (NEB), "a great help to" (NIV), "come to the help of" (NJB). The verb form of προστάτις is προΐστημι, which means primarily "to be leader or ruler of."[25] It is frequently used in Greek literature to refer to political leadership (e.g., Plato, *Laches* 197d; Herodotus, *History* 1.123; 4.80, Plato, *Republic* 565c.). This verb appears eight times in the New Testament. It implies leader-ship in ministry (Rom 12:8; 1 Thess 5:12; 1 Tim 5:17) or management of a household (1 Tim 3:4, 5, 12).[26]

The masculine noun form of προΐστημι, προστάτης, generally refers to a ruler (e.g. Herodotus, *History* 1.127, 5.23; Plato, *Gorgias* 519b). It is often used in association with the word δῆμος (citizen), indicating a leader in a democracy.[27] Aristotle enumerates the names of the people who were in the position of προστάτης τοῦ δήμου, such as Pericles, Solon, Peisistratus, etc. (Aristotle, *Athenian Constitution* 2.2, 23.1-2). In the Roman period it began to take on the meaning of patronage. Plutarch explains προστάτης as follows:

---

[23] Hermann W. Beyer, διάκονος, *TDNT* (2d ed. Grand Rapids: Eerdmans, 1964) 2:89.

[24] Jewett, "Paul, Phoebe, and the Spanish Mission," 149. Also see Schüssler Fiorenza, "Mis-sionaries, Apostles, Coworkers," 426; and Beverly Roberts Gaventa, "Romans," in Carol A. New-som and Sharon H. Ringe, eds., *The Women's Bible Commentary* (Louisville: Westminster John Knox, 1992) 320.

[25] Henry George Liddell and Robert Scott, *A Greek-English Lexicon.* 9th, rev. ed. by Sir Henry Stuart Jones and Roderick McKenzie (Oxford: Clarendon Press, 1940) 1482.

[26] It appears twice in the middle voice (Titus 3:8, 14), meaning "devote oneself."

[27] Liddell and Scott, *A Greek-English Lexicon,* 1526; Plato, *The Republic,* trans. Paul Shorey. LCL (Cambridge: Harvard University Press, 1935) 318 note d. Also see Thucydides, *War* 3.75, 4.46, 66.

For down to the present time foreign peoples call the members of their senate "chief men," but the Romans themselves call them "conscript fathers," . . . by this . . . title Romulus distinguished the senate from the commonalty, and in other ways, too, he separated the nobles [δυνατούς] from the multitude, calling the ones "patrons [πάτρωνας]," that is to say, protectors [προστάτας], and the others "clients [κλίεντας]," that is to say, dependents [πελάτας].[28]

Obviously the word προστάτης is connected with political leadership. It is not surprising that the feminine word προστάτις appears fewer times than the masculine προστάτης in antiquity, given the scarcity of women in leadership roles. One good example that helps us understand the significance of the feminine προστάτις is found in Lucian's *Charidemus*. Lucian writes: "In the wide range of all other customary pursuits, each goddess is a patroness (προστάτις) of one particular thing and never quarrels with another over her sphere of power . . ." (*Charidemus* 10). Therefore it seems feasible to say that προστάτις implies a leader who has power to control certain areas.

Considering all the evidence, προστάτις must have signified a position of leadership, involving governance or management. Therefore the translations "helper" (RSV), "a good friend of" (NEB), "a great help to" (NIV), "come to the help of" (NJB) in Rom 16:2 have little validity. The second edition of the *Greek-English Lexicon of the New Testament and Other Early Christian Literature* defines προστάτις as "protectress, patroness, helper,"[29] while the third edition offers the definition "a woman in a supportive role, patron, benefactor."[30] There seems to be no clear reason why the second edition adopts the meaning "helper" while the revised version replaces it with "a woman in a supportive role." It may be helpful to note that the Western Texts F and G offer the variant reading παραστάτις, which means "one who stands alongside" or "helper." Ray R. Schulz explains this change as follows: "This variant reading points to the discomfort some copyists felt with the implication of [προστάτις]; hence the change."[31] Is it possible that modern scholars also feel the same discomfort about the implication of προστάτις?

---

[28] Plutarch, *Romulus* 13.4-5; cf. Plutarch, *Caius Marius* 5.4.

[29] Walter Bauer, *A Greek-English Lexicon of the New Testament and Other Early Christian Literature*. 2d ed. trans. and rev. by W. F. Arndt, F. W. Gingrich, and F. W. Danker (Chicago: University of Chicago Press, 1979) 726. Ray R. Schulz notices that "helper" was not in Bauer's *Wörterbuch* (p. 1425) but was later added by Arndt and Gingrich (p. 726) (Schulz, "A Case for 'President' Phoebe in Romans 16:2," *Lutheran Theological Journal* 24 [1990] 124).

[30] Walter Bauer, *A Greek-English Lexicon of the New Testament and Other Early Christian Literature*. 3d ed. trans. and rev. by F. W. Danker (Chicago: University of Chicago Press, 2000) 885.

[31] Schulz, "A Case for 'President' Phoebe in Romans 16:2," 125.

Recognizing that the translation of προστάτις as "helper" is inappropriate, some scholars have chosen instead the translation "patron."[32] This translation evokes the patron-client system which, as Matthew Collins has shown, underlay the connection between wealth and public leadership roles in the Greco-Roman world. Public officials were expected to function as patrons of the town or city they governed. As a result, to hold public office required a certain financial status on the part of the officeholders. They, in turn, received a payoff in terms of social status, being the recipients of public honor and prestige. A similar relationship existed between the patron and the private association. The patron provided the association with funds, protection, and political influence. In return, the association would have been expected to furnish the patron with honor and praise.[33]

However, the translation of προστάτις as "patron" is not without problems: (1) If one focuses only on the financial role of patrons, the dimension of leadership in προστάτις is overlooked and thus Phoebe tends to be understood simply as a financial supporter of Paul; (2) The evidence is ambiguous with regard to whether προστάτις is the usual word to indicate a patron or benefactor in terms of financial support.[34] Therefore a more proper and literal translation for προστάτις is "leader, supervisor," and thus possibly "minister," with focus on a leadership position in a church. As Meeks explains, "the term was used in that official sense in some Hellenistic cities, in the place of the more usual *prytaneis* ('executive officers'), and as a title, or in the general sense of 'leader,' of officers of clubs or guilds."[35] Yet immediately following this explanation he adds: "that meaning, however, is rendered impossible by the context, for it is difficult to imagine what Paul could have meant by describing Phoebe as 'also presiding over me.'"[36] There is room to question whether Meeks is projecting an androcentric presumption that a woman would not have been an overseer of Paul's activity.

Not a few scholars have attested Phoebe's high social standing and wealth as a προστάτις. Thus they consider it probable that "Paul considered her his

---

[32] Wayne A. Meeks, *The First Urban Christians* (New Haven: Yale University Press, 1983) 60.

[33] Matthew S. Collins, "Money, Sex, and Power: An Examination of the Role of Women as Patrons of the Ancient Synagogue," in Peter J. Haas, ed., *Rediscovering the Role of Women: Power and Authority in Rabbinic Jewish Society* (Atlanta: Scholars, 1992) 13–14.

[34] Frederick Danker relates "benefactor" to εὐεργέτης ("Benefactor," *ABD* 1:669–71). See also Edwin A. Judge, "Cultural Conformity and Innovation in Paul: Some Clues from a Contemporary Document," *TynBul* 35 (1984) 17–18.

[35] Meeks, *The First Urban Christians,* 60.

[36] Ibid.

social superior."[37] However, it is unclear, as Caroline F. Whelan suggests, whether church leadership on the basis of spirituality is explicitly separated from social power on the basis of financial resources in antiquity. If Phoebe was devoted to her church to the degree that she is called διάκονος, and had social and financial power in addition, it is more than likely that she had a certain authority over her Christian community. Furthermore, as a local resident she served the congregation on a consistent basis, in contrast to Paul who would stay with the congregation only on occasion and for a limited time. Therefore, even if Paul was the founder of Phoebe's church, Phoebe must have maintained the stronger connection with her community and thus possibly become a more influential leader within the congregation than Paul.

This reconstruction of the complicated relationship between Paul and Phoebe may, perhaps, answer the question raised about Paul's deviation from his standard rhetorical structure in his letter of commendation for Phoebe. It is obvious that Paul and Phoebe are formally in an agreeable relationship, given the fact that Paul introduces her to the Romans. Paul may have felt a political need to support Phoebe since she had helped him in Cenchreae and would help him again in the future, if necessary. Phoebe, in turn, was dependent upon Paul's commendation in Rome. Phoebe was a διάκονος of the church at Cenchreae. While she had a strong connection with a limited number of local Christians, Paul was a traveling missionary who "moved from missionary center to missionary center using the hospitality of local churches."[38] Thus she was dependent upon Paul because of his broad connections among the churches in many different areas.

Yet Phoebe was also a προστάτις, a woman not only of social and financial standing in her community but, in addition, a woman who appears to have had authority within and over certain areas in the life of her congregation. It is in this capacity that she may also have had authority over Paul. It is possible that it was only through Phoebe that Paul was able to carry out his ministry among the Christians at Cenchreae. Considering the fact that Paul never identifies any other Christian leader as superior to him or having authority over him, including James, Cephas, and John (Gal 2:6, 9), Phoebe's status in the church at Cenchreae must have been considerable. This may also be the reason why Paul downplays her role as προστάτις "even of me." Paul wants the Christians at Rome to welcome Phoebe as a διάκονος, a leader in a local congregation—not

---

[37] Caroline F. Whelan, *"Amica Pauli:* The Role of Phoebe in the Early Church," *JST* 49 (1993) 83. Also see Jewett, "Paul, Phoebe, and the Spanish Mission," 149–50, and Judge, "Cultural Conformity and Innovation in Paul," 21.

[38] Schüssler Fiorenza, "Missionaries, Apostles, Coworkers," 431.

as a προστάτις, a woman with the financial, social, and political standing sufficient to become προστάτις not only of the Christians at Cenchreae, not only of Paul, but perhaps even of the Christians in Rome.

The geographical proximity of Cenchreae to Corinth may also be worth taking into account. Corinth posed a serious problem for Paul, in part because the Christians there followed other leaders in addition to Paul (1 Cor 1:10) and accommodated gospels different from the one proclaimed by Paul (2 Cor 11:4; see also 2 Cor 11:1-13). In addition, women appear to have played a significant role in the Corinthian churches.[39] Therefore Phoebe's leadership and influence within the church at Cenchreae may have led Paul to fear her capacity as a potential competitor for influence and allegiance in Rome.

CONCLUSION

From this limited literary source I have tried to sketch out the figure of Phoebe. She has generally been understood as a mere helper and financial supporter of Paul. But a feminist reading, inspired by a hermeneutics of suspicion, revives her as a powerful leader who governed her own area of ministry and was not subject to Paul's authority in her Christian mission, but may in fact have supervised Paul. Surely Phoebe must have been a woman of excellence because she is described as διάκονος and προστάτις, titles rarely given to women. Yet her leadership and devotion to her church have been hidden and ignored in the shadow of the history of biblical exegesis dominated by the androcentric perspective.

---

[39] For a consideration of the role of women in the Corinthian churches see Antoinette Clark Wire, *The Corinthian Women Prophets* (Minneapolis: Fortress, 1990) 73.

Listen to the Voices of the Women

Holly E. Hearon and Linda M. Maloney

During the past twenty-five years feminist scholars have made significant strides in bringing women in the Second Testament to visibility by calling attention to their presence in the texts and, through careful analyses of these texts, identifying ways in which women were engaged in the life of the early church. Among efforts to raise women to visibility, the more difficult task has been to identify the voices of the women: what they are saying and why. This is a task to which Anne Wire has dedicated much of her scholarship, particularly in her two studies *The Corinthian Women Prophets* and *Holy Lives, Holy Deaths: A Close Hearing of Early Jewish Storytellers.* It also is a task Anne recognizes as an ongoing challenge for the lives of church and academy, a challenge she has taken up through her support of female students and colleagues. Holly, as a former student, and Linda, as a former colleague, offer this study in gratitude and appreciation.

In this essay we will explore ways in which women's voices may have given shape to traditions that emerged within the early church. The "traditions" we refer to include sayings, remembrances, parables, miracles, legends, liturgical formulas or actions, confessions of faith, prophetic utterances, technical language or expressions, and other literary materials or verbal reminiscences of ecclesial practices that are represented in our texts as belonging to teachings of the church or as material that is known and held in common or performed in common by believers.[1] In some instances this may include material that is held in common by some believers but is disputed or even rejected

---

[1] As Richard Horsley notes, the term "tradition" is problematic because it is both overworked and vague (*Whoever Hears You Hears Me: Prophets, Performance, and Tradition in Q,* with Jonathan Draper [Harrisburg: Trinity Press International, 1999] 10). The definition offered in this paper is illustrative. The challenge resides not only in terminology but also in our capacity, or lack thereof, to adequately identify form, content, and process.

by others.[2] While a part of our concern is to identify traditions that were transmitted by women, our primary focus is the question of how women's voices made an imprint on the traditioning process.

There is by no means agreement among scholars about how the traditioning process took place. While some argue in favor of a "formal controlled" process in which traditions were handed on by authorized teachers (generally identified with the apostles—the "Twelve," the "inner circle" of James, John, and Peter, or a larger group)[3]—others see a less controlled process at work, driven in part by the effects of rumor and performance.[4] Evidence can be claimed for both in the biblical text: For example, some interpretations of Acts suggest that it describes a formal process controlled by the apostles (see especially Acts 15; also 1 Cor 11:23; 15:3), while references in the gospels such as "a report went out" or "[someone] had heard" (e.g., Mark 1:45; 5:16; Matt 9:26; 14:1; Luke 1:58; 4:37) point to an informal, uncontrolled process of transmission.[5] How one pieces together the evidence is, to a large degree, driven by how one envisions the life and organization of the early church. All attempts at describing the traditioning process are, in any event, heuristic, based on lim-

---

[2] We recognize that which portions of a text constitute a "tradition" and which represent the invention of an author is, in many instances, a subject of debate. However, space does not allow us to engage this debate in reference to specific passages.

[3] Birger Gerhardsson, *The Origins of the Gospel Traditions* (Philadelphia: Fortress, 1979); idem, *The Reliability of the Gospel Tradition* (Peabody, Mass.: Hendrickson, 2001). See also Bruce Chilton, *Profiles of a Rabbi: Synoptic Opportunities in Reading about Jesus* (Atlanta: Scholars, 1989) 160–67; Rainer Riesner, "Jesus as Preacher and Teacher," in Henry Wansbrough, ed., *Jesus and the Oral Gospel Tradition* (Sheffield: Sheffield Academic Press, 1991) 185–210. E. Earle Ellis assumes that the traditioning process occurs in apostolic and prophetic circles (*The Making of the New Testament Documents* [Leiden: Brill, 1999] 36–47, 328).

[4] Pieter Botha, "The Social Dynamics of the Early Transmission of the Jesus Tradition," *Neotestamentica* 27/2 (1993) 205–31; Werner Kelber, *The Oral and the Written Gospel* (Philadelphia: Fortress, 1983; Bloomington: Indiana University Press, 1997) 1–43; Richard A. Horsley, *Whoever Hears You Hears Me,* 7–8; Ahn Byung-mu, "The Transmitters of the Jesus-Event," *CTC Bulletin* (Dec. 1984–April 1985) 26–39.

[5] The account in Acts has great appeal to some because it appears to outline a distinct process by which the early church gave rise to tradition in the midst of conflict. This assumes that Acts represents a historical record at this point, which may be questioned when Acts is read alongside Galatians 2. Yet even if one believes that Acts describes one process by which the early church developed and passed on traditions, there is no reason to assume that this was the only way in which such development took place. One of the authors of this study has described a very different and more diffuse process for recognizing the emergence of traditions identified with the divine will in Acts itself: Linda M. Maloney, *"All That God Had Done With Them." The Narration of the Works of God in the Early Christian Community as Described in the Acts of the Apostles* (New York: Peter Lang, 1991).

ited evidence. The authors of the biblical texts were more concerned with passing on traditions than with describing for us how traditions arose and were transmitted. Notably absent from nearly all constructions is consideration of ways in which the voices of women may have participated in the process.

In this study we assume that the traditioning process was complex (i.e., traditions arose out of conflict as well as consensus and competing traditions could coexist), and that it was at one and the same time controlled and uncontrolled: controlled to the degree that traditions went through some process of adoption that required the assent of certain individuals or groups and those traditions were self-consciously passed on;[6] uncontrolled to the degree that some traditions arose as rumors, while many took shape in performance contexts in which certain elements in the tradition might be modified or omitted and the tradition itself framed in ways that gave a specific focus to its interpretation.[7] In order to gain access to women's voices in this process we have adopted a twofold approach: to identify material that appears to be encoded with women's voices, and to describe ways in which women's voices were heard in early Christian communities although those voices may not be recorded in the text. Within the confines of this essay we can do no more than suggest the outlines of a much larger conversation. Nonetheless, it is our hope that this essay will prompt further exploration of the role of women, and most especially the presence of their voices in the formation of traditions by the early church.

HOW SHALL WE LISTEN?

The voices of women in the Second Testament are difficult to hear, in part because the texts of the Second Testament are androcentric—i.e., male centered: driven by and written from the perspectives of men. In these texts the voices of women are obscured, buried, and sometimes erased. The voices of women are also difficult to hear because we do not expect to hear them. The exclusion of women from the "Twelve," coupled with texts such as 1 Cor 14:33-35 and 1 Tim 2:12-15, has conditioned us to believe that women, at least "good" women, were silent, guided by the voices of men. Yet the voices are there, waiting for the ears that are ready to hear them. In a few rare instances they are present to us in direct speech. More often they are filtered through the voices of others who quote (or misquote) them or respond to them, requiring us to reconstruct the voices of the women from counterarguments and allusions. As a means of

---

[6] We do not assume that a "controlled" process was necessarily a formalized process.

[7] Ahn Byung-Mu, "The Transmitters of the Jesus-event," 26–39; Kenneth Bailey, "Informal Controlled Oral Tradition and the Synoptic Gospels," *AJT* 5 (1991) 34–54.

entrance to our exploration of the role of women in the traditioning process we turn to references to women as teachers within early Christian communities.

WOMEN AS TEACHERS

Numerous texts in the Second Testament attest to the presence and activity of teachers in early Christian communities (e.g., 1 Cor 12:28; Eph 4:11; 1 Tim 5:17; 2 Tim 4:2; Heb 5:12; Jas 3:1; Matt 28:20; Acts 13:12). These references highlight not only the role of teachers in transmitting "traditions" of the church (e.g., Rom 6:17; Acts 2:42; 1 Tim 4:6; Titus 1:9; 2:1; 2 John 9), but also the complex nature of the traditions themselves: they were not uniform. For every teacher mentioned in our texts there is some other teacher to whose teachings the authors of these texts strongly object (e.g., Rom 16:17; 1 Tim 1:10; 6:2-3; 2 Tim 4:3; Heb 13:9; 2 John 10; Rev 2:24). The vehemence with which our authors speak against these teachers suggests that they are enjoying at least some success.

In the midst of these various references, three texts point explicitly to women who are engaged in teaching. Acts 18:26 speaks of Priscilla (along with Aquila) taking Apollos aside and "explaining" the word of God to him more accurately.[8] Anne Wire notes that since this report serves no dramatic or theological purpose in Acts, it is unlikely to be an invention of the author.[9] Prisca (so named in Paul's letters; Acts uses the diminutive Priscilla) first appears at Acts 18:2, in Corinth. Paul is said to have "found" Aquila and Priscilla there on his arrival; the couple had recently come from Italy "because Claudius had ordered all Jews to leave Rome." Many scholars believe that this is an echo of the expulsion of Jews from Rome occasioned by riots supposed to have been stirred up by "Chrestos." Chrestos or Chrestus was a common slave name that to Roman ears would have sounded very much like "Christos," or "Christus," and the supposition is that the disturbances in the Jewish quarter were brought on by disputes between followers of Jesus and other Jews who were not of "the Way."[10] That Luke, at least, understood the dynamics of Jewish life in Rome in that way is evident from his description of Paul's reception there in Acts 28.

---

[8] The word translated "explain" is ἐκτίθεμαι, which occurs only in Acts. It is used of Peter when he "explains" to those in Judea why he has been eating with Gentiles (11:4), and of Paul when he testifies about Jesus and the kingdom of God to the Jews in Rome (28:23).

[9] Antoinette C. Wire, *The Corinthian Women Prophets* (Minneapolis: Fortress, 1990) 50.

[10] Peter Lampe, *Die stadtrömischen Christen in der ersten beiden Jahrhunderten.* WUNT 2d ser. 18 (Tübingen: J.C.B. Mohr [Paul Siebeck], 1987) 4–8, 137–39, and for Prisca and Aquila especially 156–64.

If we see Prisca and Aquila in this scenario, we may conclude that they were probably, like Andronicus and Junia (Rom 16:7), "in Christ" before Paul. Rome had a vibrant Jewish community with regular links to Palestine. There is every reason to believe that Jewish followers of Jesus reached the capital city very quickly, perhaps even before Paul's own conversion, and one school of thought sees the Gospel of Mark as having been written at Rome within a few years after the death of Paul—an accomplishment that would have required a significant community to support and receive the written testimony. The presence of "apostles" like Andronicus and Junia at Rome indicates that people had been "sent," just as Paul was sent, either from Jerusalem or from Antioch or another major early center, to advance the gospel in Rome, and this even before Paul was "in Christ."[11] In turn we may regard Prisca and Aquila as "apostles" of the Roman church to Corinth, once again in place before Paul arrived. Fortunately for Paul, they were hospitable to him and supportive of his mission. According to Acts they subsequently accompanied him to Ephesus to strengthen the mission there, and their instruction of Apollos at Ephesus is further evidence that they were trained evangelists, well instructed and sent by their communities to teach.

We are never allowed to hear Prisca's voice. However, her consistent association with the Pauline mission and the close relationship Paul apparently enjoys with her suggest that the gospel proclaimed by Paul may be similar in content to that taught by Prisca. Yet similarity does not presume uniformity. Wire proposes:

> As Paul's coworkers, Priscilla and Aquila probably shared the early baptismal tradition, "You who were baptized into Christ have put on Christ . . . there is no male and female," with its programmatic rejection of sexual and other social discrimination. When Paul dissociates himself from baptizing (1 Cor 1:13-17), he may be reacting to some understanding of this new identity by Priscilla and Aquila or by Apollos.[12]

It is possible that Prisca and Paul proclaim the same baptismal tradition, yet the ways in which they teach others to live out that tradition may differ. For example, Prisca may proclaim the abrogation of certain social boundaries that restrict women's life choices while Paul maintains them, at least with respect to the situation in Corinth. In this regard it is striking that only in 1 Cor 16:19 is Prisca named after Aquila (cf. Acts 18:18, 26; Rom 16:3; 2 Tim 4:19). This subordination of Prisca to Aquila is consistent with Paul's attempts at several points in the letter to restrict the activity of women (7:36-38; 11:2-16; 14:34-35). By

[11] Ibid., especially 1–9 and, for Junia, 53, 138, 147–48.
[12] *The Corinthian Women Prophets,* 50.

listing Prisca after Aquila, Paul may be co-opting her name for the purposes of his rhetoric. In order for this strategy to have the desired effect Paul must assume that his audience would both recognize the names of Prisca and Aquila and expect to hear Prisca's name listed first. By placing her name second he undercuts Prisca's voice and reinforces the social construction he wants the Corinthians to adopt (1 Cor 11:3; 14:34-35).[13]

Although we cannot be certain of the exact nature of Prisca's teachings, her association with Corinth is striking because of the prominence of women's voices in that community. From the letter we learn that women are active as prophets and that at least some have forsaken marital relations in order to dedicate themselves in service to the Lord as "virgins."

Virgins and Prophets

It has become a truism of church history that the ascetic practice of virginity arose late, as a substitute for martyrdom. However, there is evidence in the Second Testament itself and in apocryphal writings that a deliberate choice of the unmarried state was possible, and even lauded, in earliest Christianity, both Jewish and Gentile.[14] It was an element of the "alternative lifestyle" or "counterculture" of Christianity, in a society in which marriage was mandated by law and in which both survival in old age and the continuation of one's memory after death were seen to be dependent on having children (sons, in particular).

In earliest Christianity there was a special link between virginity and prophecy, for both men and women. We will have something to say below about this in connection with the Pastoral Letters, but here let us simply point to an intriguing passage in Acts 21:9. The tradition Luke is using here reports that Philip "the evangelist, one of the seven," i.e., Philip the deacon, "had four daughters, virgins, who had the gift of prophecy." Although he mentions some women prophets in his Gospel Prologue, and even quotes them, Luke never gives us the words of the women prophets in Acts. The women who are either called prophets (Anna) or who speak prophetically (Elizabeth, Mary) in the Lukan Prologue are married (though Mary is a virgin), and their prophecy is reminiscent of the words of First Testament women prophets, who were also married. Why are the virgin prophets of the Christian movement mute in Acts? Can it be that their prophecy called the church in a direction different from what Luke desired or wished to portray?

---

[13] For a discussion of the issues related to the question of whether 1 Cor 14:33-35 belongs to the original text see Wire, *Corinthian Women Prophets*, 149–52, 229–32.

[14] The definitions of "virgins" and "widows" appear to have been somewhat loose, and sometimes overlapping; see the discussion below.

Anne Wire has done a close analysis of the women prophets in Corinth, discovering that indeed their prophesying did not always (or often?) accord with the direction aimed for by Paul. At several points in his first letter to the Corinthians, Paul appears to be quoting or paraphrasing teachings that may reflect traditions circulating within the Corinthian community.[15] In some instances it is probable that the "tradition" has arisen in Corinth. Wire observes, for example, with regard to 1 Cor 7:4, where Paul denies the statement that "the woman has authority over her own body" that ". . . any slogan in Corinth claiming authority over one's own body must have come from women because it would be redundant in that society for a man to claim such authority over himself."[16] In other instances the "tradition" appears to be one that is shared by Paul and the Corinthians, or at least reflects a theological perspective on which they agree (e.g., "Christ, of God the power and of God the wisdom").[17] However, the way Paul employs these shared traditions in the structure of his argument reveals that there are significant differences between how he and the Corinthian women interpret and consequently implement the traditions.

According to Wire's reconstruction, the differences arise from how the Corinthians understand and experience baptism. In baptism, she proposes, the Corinthian women experience a transformation when they "put on Christ" and are "remade in the image and glory of God,"[18] "who is not male and female."[19] The results of this transformation are several. The women find themselves filled with God's spirit, which "is given without reserve or limitation."[20] They experience this spirit as wisdom, present in their own "hearing and speaking"[21] and manifested in their prayer and prophecy.[22] Through the power of this spirit they know themselves to be raised up in Christ, experiencing resurrection as a "present and communal experience of . . . coming to life in Christ."[23] No longer defined by their gender status, the women are freed to embrace "new sexual choices and responsibilities,"[24] with the result that both unmarried and no-longer-married women consecrate themselves in body and spirit to serve God.[25]

---

[15] *The Corinthian Women Prophets,* 51, 94, 111, 184.

[16] Ibid. 82–83.

[17] Ibid. 51.

[18] Ibid. 131.

[19] Ibid. 134.

[20] Ibid. 187, 137, 174.

[21] Ibid. 53. See also Elisabeth Schüssler Fiorenza, *Jesus: Miriam's Child, Sophia's Prophet* (New York: Continuum, 1995) 149.

[22] Wire, *The Corinthian Women Prophets,* 175.

[23] Ibid. 105, 175.

[24] Ibid. 96–97. See also Schüssler Fiorenza, *Jesus,* 150.

[25] Wire, *The Corinthian Women Prophets,* 88, 90.

Wire proposes that what leads to these striking differences in interpretation of shared traditions between Paul and the Corinthians is social location. For Paul, who has experienced a loss of social status as a result of his call to proclaim Christ,[26] the confession "Christ is raised from the dead" witnesses to a past event and signals a future event for believers—i.e., it corresponds to the rise in status Paul anticipates for himself in recompense for the loss in status he currently experiences.[27] For the Corinthian women, who have gained status in almost every way as a result of their call,[28] this same confession signals that they now have access to the power of the resurrected Christ through the spirit of God—i.e., it corresponds to their present experience as a result of their call to "put on Christ."[29] These differences demonstrate that even traditions that are shared across communities cannot be understood apart from context, and that the "performance," or transmission of a tradition in any given context may lead to different or even competing interpretations of that tradition. Thus while Paul and the Corinthians share certain traditions, the differences between them in status and experience lead them to interpret the traditions differently.

What Wire's reconstruction provides is evidence of teachings and traditions that are being transmitted by the Corinthian community. Some of those who are transmitting the traditions are evidently women, serving in their capacity as prophets and virgins. While some of the traditions they teach may be shared with Paul, the interpretation they offer sets them at odds with Paul, although not with others in the church at Corinth. This is signaled by the lengths to which Paul goes in his efforts to persuade the Corinthians to alter their perspective. In addition, it is very probable that women prophets are the source of some of the traditions quoted by Paul, but which he opposes. The acceptance of these traditions by others in Corinth demonstrates that the community has undergone some process by which the traditions have gained standing. The description of worship in Corinth (1 Corinthians 14) may offer evidence of this process at work: e.g., a word of a prophet is offered to the congregation, then interpreted, and subjected to the assent or dissent of those gathered.[30] What is clear is that Paul is not the only source of the traditions circulating in the Corinthian community. It is possible that some traditions were transmitted to the community

[26] Ibid. 67.

[27] Ibid. 185.

[28] Ibid. 65, 68.

[29] Ibid. 184, 185.

[30] See the description of a similar process in various early Christian communities in the Acts of the Apostles. The literary schema with which Luke describes the process, and its possible relation to recollected events, is examined in Linda M. Maloney, *"All That God Had Done With Them"* (see n. 5 above).

by Prisca. It is certain that the voices of women in Corinth played a significant role in the traditioning process by offering up prophetic utterances for the community to claim or reject, by actively transmitting the traditions claimed by the community, and in teaching others the implications of these traditions for faith and practice.

Philippians may offer another example of a situation in which conflict has arisen between Paul and women as a result of differing interpretations of a shared tradition. Cynthia Kittredge proposes that the Christ hymn in Phil 2:5-11 represents a tradition known to both Paul and the Philippians that Paul employs in order to exploit "the positive associations that the audience has with the piece toward his rhetorical purposes in the letter."[31] She demonstrates that the primary emphasis of the hymn, as an independent narrative, is on the universal reign of Christ as Lord, who vanquishes all earthly and heavenly powers.[32] When Paul integrates the hymn into the rhetorical structure of his argument he shifts the focus from Christ's lordship to his obedience, an attitude the Philippians are exhorted to adopt in relation to Paul—not only in his presence, but even more during his absence (2:15).[33] This "obedience" is to be demonstrated by "being of the same mind" with one another, but most especially with Paul (3:15).[34] According to Kittredge's reconstruction of the historical situation, the primary objects of this exhortation are Euodia and Syntyche.[35] While many scholars have assumed that the two women are in conflict with one another, Kittredge (following Mary Rose D'Angelo) proposes that the conflict is, instead, between the two women and Paul.[36] One possible source of the conflict is differing interpretations of the shared tradition represented by the Christ hymn. For the women, the hymn may reflect a rise in status when they "put on Christ" and share in his exaltation; for Paul, the hymn may reflect Christ's willingness to assume the lowest status—that of a slave—reflecting his own loss of status when he accepted the call to proclaim Christ.[37]

What is of interest here in relation to the traditioning process is the description of Euodia and Syntyche as "co-contenders in the gospel" with Paul. The active role of these two women in the Philippian community suggests that

---

[31] Cynthia B. Kittredge, *Community and Authority: The Rhetoric of Obedience in the Pauline Tradition* (Harriburg: Trinity Press International, 1998) 76–77.

[32] Ibid. 77–83.

[33] Ibid. 83–86.

[34] Ibid. 105–06.

[35] Ibid.

[36] Ibid. 105. See also Mary Rose D'Angelo, "Women Partners in the New Testament," *JFSR* 6 (1990) 65–86, at 76.

[37] Kittredge, *Community and Authority,* 99, 106.

they may also have played a significant role in bearing, transmitting, and teaching traditions of the early church, just as the prophets and virgins did in Corinth. The evidence for women missionaries in the earliest period of the church is, in fact, striking. Paul's complaint that he has the right (which he does not exercise) to be accompanied on his missionary travels by "a sister as wife" (1 Cor 9:5), as are Cephas (Peter) and the other "apostles," shows that it was expected that women would travel as missionaries, either with their husbands, or in cases like that of Euodia and Syntyche, in pairs or groups of women. In the list in Romans 16 we find another such pair, Tryphaena and Tryphosa, as well as "the beloved Persis, who has worked hard in the Lord"—doing what? If she is known to Paul, who has not yet visited Rome, it is likely that her work was missionary in nature. The same is probably true of most of the people in the list. Finally, we return to the reference in Acts 21 to Philip "the evangelist" and his daughters. Since Philip is called "evangelist"—and indeed, he has appeared earlier in Acts in that role (cf. Acts 8:5-8, 26-40)—can we doubt that his virgin daughters are also schooled in the arts of preaching and teaching, as well as prophesying?

The final two references to women teaching are found in the Pastoral Letters. The first comes in the form of a negative command ("I permit no woman to teach or to have authority over a man; she is to keep silent" [1 Tim 2:12]), while the second is a positive command (older women should be "teachers of what is good" [καλοδιδασκάλους], teaching [σωφρονίζωσιν] young women to "love their husbands, love their children, to be temperate, pure, good household managers, and obedient to their husbands" [Titus 2:3-5]). Both references are polemical. The need to prohibit women from teaching indicates that women are, in fact, teaching—not only women, but also men. The instructions concerning what older women should teach younger women are clearly an attempt to regulate not only whom women teach, but what they teach. In this regard it is striking that there are no parallel instructions to men in Titus. Although bishops must have a "firm hold of the word" (Titus 1:9), it is only in the instructions to older women that the content of their teaching is specified. This suggests that what the women are, in fact, teaching is viewed by the author as counter to "sound teaching" and sufficiently influential to pose a threat. From a positive point of view this indicates that the women are transmitting traditions that are accepted by some as authoritative and viewed as generative of sound faith and practice.

Widows

It is probable that among those who are teaching are members of the order of widows, described in 1 Tim 5:3-16. Widows are a strikingly omnipresent group in the New Testament texts, especially given their social insignificance.[38] Individual widows appear in the gospels of Mark and Luke and several times in Acts. Widows as a group are addressed by Paul in 1 Corinthians and by the author of 1 Timothy.[39] There is evidence also to suggest that the term "widows" covered a larger category than women whose spouses were deceased. Probably women who had been abandoned by living husbands, especially if the cause of the breach was the woman's embrace of Christianity, were classed with the widows. We have reason to think that unmarried women could also join the "widows' order," or at least that the categories of virgin and widow somehow overlapped, for Ignatius of Antioch, writing to the Smyrnaeans at a time not far removed from the period when the Pastorals were composed, refers to "the virgins who are called widows."[40]

The emergence of a solidary group of women within the churches who recognized a common calling to celibacy *and* to speaking/preaching/teaching would have presented a formidable challenge to those who hoped to see the church become an orderly part of society. This was no small consideration: the fledgling movement could have been crushed by social ostracism and overt persecution if it appeared too threatening to good order.[41] Consequently, commentators on the Pastorals and other Second Testament books that include so-called "household codes" (e.g., Colossians, Ephesians, 1 Peter) have regularly argued that the authors were concerned to restrain heretical or upstart teaching and practice within their communities that would have undermined good order and made the churches look bad in the eyes of the neighbors.[42]

---

[38] For a thorough summary of and commentary on the role of widows in the Bible and the early church see Bonnie Bowman Thurston, *The Widows: A Women's Ministry in the Early Church* (Minneapolis: Fortress, 1989).

[39] This is independent of parabolic or generic usage in Matthew, James, and Revelation.

[40] Ign. *Smyrn.* 13.1: τὰς παρθένους τὰς λεγομένας χήρας.

[41] See only the concerns expressed in 1 Pet 2:12-13; 1 Tim 2:1-2.

[42] Random examples from the bookshelves: the very good and balanced treatment by Robert A. Wild in *The New Jerome Biblical Commentary* (Englewood Cliffs, N.J.: Prentice Hall, 1990) on 1 Tim 2:2, ". . . out of a desire that such authorities might allow the Christians to live in peace . . . and out of an (implied) hope that these authorities might come to 'a clear knowledge of the truth' (vv. 3-4)," and on 1 Tim 5:13, *"saying what they must not:* In Titus 1:11 almost the same words are applied to the false teachers, *going from house to house:* This almost certainly (cf. Titus 1:11) involved not simple gossip but the spreading of teachings abhorrent to the author of the Pastorals . . . ." We would not disagree. But in Jürgen Roloff's major commentary the matter appears a good deal more sinister (*Der Erste Brief an Timotheus.* EKK XV [Neukirchen-Vluyn: Neukirchener Verlag, 1988] 298; the reference is to 1 Tim 5:13): "That with the things the widows are saying in the houses the author is thinking not merely of gossip and chatter, but of something much more dangerous, is indicated by the closing formula: 'saying what they should not say (τὰ μὴ δέοντα).' These 'things they should not say' are, as appears from the almost identical statement about the false teachers in Titus 1:11 ('teaching . . . what it is not right to teach'), false

One of us has proposed elsewhere[43] that we consider a different scenario for the Pastorals: rather than the "Pastor" being the reigning authority in the community, trying to suppress novelties and strange teachings, what if he is, instead, an angry out-of-power elder, enraged that control of his communities has passed to people (including women) whose leadership he rejects? (A similar situation may be reflected in Rev 2:18-28.) It is difficult to reconstruct what the women are teaching, since the author is careful to give no voice to their words. Nonetheless, the content of the letters points to three possibilities. First, the description of the widows' order intimates that their teaching encourages women to adopt a celibate lifestyle. This evidence is underscored by the author's opposition to those who "forbid marriage" (1 Tim 4:3) combined with the dire warning that women are "saved through childbearing" (1 Tim 2:15).[44] The command in Titus that older women teach younger women domestic virtues also seems intended to counteract women who are encouraging women (and men) to refrain from marriage. The similarities to Corinth are striking. Whether the women referenced in the Pastoral Letters are passing on traditions such as those found in Corinth (e.g., "consecrated in body and spirit") is unknown, but it is evident that one result of this teaching is that women are freed to undertake itinerant teaching and preaching (characterized by the author of the Pastorals as "going about from house to house") while enjoying the support of the community of faith.[45] Thus what is professed in faith has a direct correlation, not to say benefit, in practice.[46]

A second possibility is described by Dennis R. MacDonald in his study *The Legend and the Apostle,* where he offers persuasive evidence that one of

---

teachings. At least potentially the institution of the widows is, accordingly, regarded by the author as an open door to gnostic heresy. It remains questionable whether he had a concrete basis for his suspicion." Roloff remarks in a footnote that we must distinguish between the real situation in the communities and the viewpoint of the author. Our essay here in hearing the voices of the voiceless instead of attending merely to the speaking voice of the author is an attempt, indeed, to "overhear" a different perspective on the situation, granting that neither corresponds exactly to any putative "objective" situation.

[43] Linda M. Maloney, "The Pastoral Epistles," in Elisabeth Schüssler Fiorenza, ed., *Searching the Scriptures: A Feminist Commentary* (New York: Crossroad, 1994) 361–80.

[44] Joanna Dewey, "1 Timothy," in Carol A. Newsom and Sharon H. Ringe, eds., *The Women's Bible Commentary* (Louisville: Westminster John Knox, 1992) 447–48. See also Maloney, "Pastoral Epistles," 372–73.

[45] Ibid. 374.

[46] The benefit may be almost entirely to the women; for men there is the loss of a sexual partner (for women, sexual relations always involve the potential of pregnancy, and pregnancy the potential for loss of life) and household manager. Women lose the support and protection of a spouse, but this is, presumably, made up for in part by the support of the community.

the "old wives' tales" (1 Tim 4:7) told by the women is the oral ancestor of the *Acts of Thecla*.[47] The *Acts of Thecla* tells the story of a young woman who forsakes marriage in order to follow Paul, yet Paul plays only a minor role in the story. After luring her away from her family he, in effect, abandons Thecla, leaving her to fend for herself. She is rejected by her family, placed under arrest, tried, and condemned to death. As she waits for her sentence to be carried out she is taken into the care of a widow who adopts her as her own daughter. During her ordeal she is defended by the women of the city (as well as by a lioness) and, at the very last minute, baptizes herself. When the authorities see that she is protected by God, Thecla is released. After proclaiming the word to many others, she dies at a good age. As MacDonald observes, the largely positive portrayal of women in the story, combined with Thecla's agency on her own behalf (which, ultimately, is rewarded), points toward women as the tellers of this story.[48] The focus on a celibate life, women's agency on their own behalf, the mutual support among women, the care by widows of younger women, and the proclamation of Christ all find parallels in the activity of the widows described in 1 Timothy. It seems likely, then, that stories such as the *Acts of Thecla* were among those taught by the women.[49]

A third dimension of the women's teaching is suggested by 2 Tim 2:17b-18a: "Among whom are Hymenaeus and Philetus who, concerning the truth, have missed the way, saying that the resurrection has already happened." In the *Acts of Thecla* characters named Demas (mentioned in 2 Tim 4:10a as having deserted Paul) and Hermogenes (named in 2 Tim 1:15 as turning away from Paul) are said to proclaim that the resurrection has already taken place.[50] The reference

---

[47] Dennis R. MacDonald, *The Legend and the Apostle: The Battle for Paul in Story and Canon* (Philadelphia: Westminster, 1983). MacDonald notes a number of connections between the Pastoral Letters and the *Acts of Paul* that suggest the author of the Pastorals was writing, in part, to counteract the portrayal of Paul in the *Acts:* 2 Tim 3:6 warns against those "who make their way into households and capture weak women," as "Paul" does in the *Acts of Thecla;* 1 Tim 4:7 objects to those who "forbid marriage" as "Paul" does in the *Acts of Thecla;* Titus 1:10-15 demonstrates concern for the welfare of the household, which "Paul," in the *Acts of Thecla,* disrupts [57]. There are references to Onesiphorus (2 Tim 1:15-18) and his association with Asia Minor, and to Hermogenes, who is twinned with a companion and deserts Paul in Asia Minor [60]; both refer to Demas' desertion of Paul (2 Tim 4:10) [60].

[48] MacDonald, *The Legend and the Apostle,* 35.

[49] Tertullian, *De praescriptione haereticorum* 41.5 (CCL 1.221.12-15). Tertullian elsewhere confirms, by condemning, the practice of enrolling virgins among the widows. In *De virginibus velandis* 33 he writes: "I know plainly, that in a certain place a virgin of less than twenty years of age has been placed in the order of widows!" See Thurston, *The Widows,* 81, 135.

[50] MacDonald argues that the author of the Pastorals and the author of the *Acts of Paul* are drawing on the same oral tradition (*The Legend and the Apostle,* 65–66).

to this teaching in both the Pastoral Letters and the *Acts of Thecla* suggests that it may characterize an aspect of the women's teaching. It represents, in addition, "a shared conviction with those in Corinth."[51] In each case the independence enjoyed by women who have forsaken the constrictions of marital relationships apparently reflects their experience of being raised in Christ. There is, in consequence, congruence between what they profess ("Christ is raised from the dead") and what they practice. The vehemence with which the author of the Pastorals opposes these teachings indicates the degree to which they have taken hold and are valued by members of some communities. The "sound teaching" the author of the Pastorals encourages his audience to adopt is represented by the author as "the" tradition when it is, apparently, one of several traditions circulating within early Christian communities where traditions are weighed, in part, by their capacity to transform women's lives in life-giving ways.

The Pastorals are a parade example of the way in which attention and concern came to concentrate on teaching as the church settled into a second century of existence. The focus is on "sound teaching," ὑγιαίνουσα διδασκαλία, and the word field of teaching, instruction, telling, and talk is intensively represented. Thus we have here a better-than-average opportunity to overhear women's voices.

Storytellers

The "old wives' tales" attributed to the women in the Pastoral Letters point to still another way in which traditions were transmitted by women as well as men: i.e., through storytelling. The texts of the Second Testament give little evidence of how stories gained status as traditions and were circulated. In Acts, for example, Peter's account of the conversion of Cornelius is repeated three times, pointing to its importance within the text and, perhaps, its importance as a definitional story in the memory of the community, but it is depicted as a "report" rather than a tradition.[52] In the gospels, when the texts describe someone telling a story about Jesus it is almost always a personal account of their encounter with Jesus.[53] Yet it is the evidence of the gospels themselves, which are composed almost entirely of such stories, that highlights the importance of stories for the lives of early Christian communities and points to their status as traditions within those communities. An examination of storytelling in the world of antiquity reveals that both men and women were active as story-

---

[51] Maloney, "Pastoral Epistles," 372–73.

[52] The story is originally given as narrative in Acts 10:1-48. It is then recounted as a "report" in 11:4-17, and finally offered as testimony at the Council of Jerusalem (15:7-11).

[53] E.g., Mark 1:45; John 4:49; 5:10-15; 9:1-34.

tellers.[54] The stories these women and men told were distinguished not by content but by the manner in which the story was told, what was stressed, and what point of view was presented.[55] This provides an entryway for hearing women's voices among those giving shape to the stories recorded in the gospels.

While women appear in numerous stories within the gospels, it cannot be assumed that all stories in which women appear reflect the voices of women. Joanna Dewey observes that in the manuscript tradition stories about women are minimized, not only in terms of number and length, but also in terms of the voice and action ascribed to the women.[56] Nonetheless, she finds that two stories in the Gospel of Mark exhibit evidence of being shaped by women's voices: the Syrophoenician woman (Mark 7:24-30) and the woman with the flow of blood (Mark 5:25-34).[57] In the former the woman's request is fulfilled because of her words, making the woman the central character in the story. In the latter the story, which is narrated from the perspective of the woman, reveals her internal thoughts. The prominence given to the woman in each story suggests to Dewey that the stories "might well have been told and retold by and among women before they were textualized in Mark."[58] Both stories feature women who continue to press their need until it is met.[59] Notably, neither woman is described in relation to a man. Like Thecla, each must demonstrate agency on her own behalf (or on behalf of her children). The result in each case is that the woman is rewarded.

The story of the healing of Peter's mother-in-law recorded in Matthew (8:14-15) also may offer evidence of being shaped by women's voices. Although the story is rendered as a healing narrative within the context of Matthew's gospel (see 8:16-17), there are indications that it is structured as a call narrative with a healing motif. Elaine Wainwright detects in this narrative the following elements (found also in Matt 4:1; 9:9): an introduction (in which the caller approaches and sees the one to be called), an exposition (in which a description of the one called is given), a middle (the call, given in a word or action),

[54] For a reconstruction of storytelling in the world of antiquity see ch. 2 in Holly Hearon, *The Mary Magdalene Tradition: Witness and Counter-Witness in Early Christian Communities* (Collegeville: Liturgical Press, 2004).

[55] Linda Dégh, *Narratives in Society: A Performer-Centered Study of Narration* (Helsinki: Suomalainen Tiedeakatemia, 1995) 69.

[56] Joanna Dewey, "From Storytelling to Written Text: The Loss of Early Christian Women's Voices" *BTB* 26 (1996) 76.

[57] Joanna Dewey, "Women in the Synoptic Gospels: Seen but not Heard?" *BTB* 27 (1997) 56.

[58] Joanna Dewey, "Jesus' Healings of Women: Conformity and Non-Conformity to Dominant Cultural Values as Clues for Historical Reconstruction," *BTB* 24 (1994) 122–31.

[59] Antoinette C. Wire, *Holy Lives, Holy Deaths: A Close Hearing of Early Jewish Storytellers* (Atlanta: Society of Biblical Literature, 2002) 386.

and a conclusion (a response to the call).[60] Several scholars have noted that the healing of Peter's mother-in-law stands apart from other healing narratives in Matthew because it is Jesus who takes the initiative for the healing rather than the supplicant.[61] The response by Peter's mother-in-law, in which she "serves" (διακονέω) Jesus is also reminiscent of call narratives rather than healing stories. The possibility that Matt 8:14-15 reflects a remembered call narrative is strengthened when it is considered alongside the story of the Samaritan woman (John 4:1-42), which, similarly, appears to function as a call narrative.[62] Such stories can be expected to have been told by and among women.

The Magdalene stories also may be encoded with the voices of women. Attempts to hear the stories about Mary Magdalene apart from their written texts have led to proposals that these stories were told to legitimate the visionary and prophetic activity of women in post-resurrection communities,[63] and may reflect a movement that might be termed "Magdalene Christianity," in which Mary is depicted as a successor to Jesus much in the way Elisha succeeded Elijah.[64] The Magdalene stories are of particular interest because they appear in all four of the canonical gospels and perhaps represent a cycle of stories in which Mary follows Jesus from Galilee, is present at the crucifixion, seeks out the tomb, and encounters the risen Jesus.[65] This suggests that stories about Mary circulated in much the same way as stories about Peter, or James, or Thomas. Like stories about these figures, the stories about Mary were understood to describe a historical person who was a close follower of Jesus. Although she is never called an apostle in the canonical texts, the actions attributed to Mary clearly describe apostolic activity and were recognized as such by later interpreters, earning for her the title of "apostle to the apostles."[66] Such a narrative would have been valued as an important tradition among women who proclaimed Christ and engaged

---

[60] Elaine Wainwright, *Towards a Feminist Critical Reading of Matthew* (Berlin: de Gruyter, 1991) 91, 181.

[61] Francis Beare, *The Gospel According to Matthew* (San Francisco: Harper & Row, 1981) 210; Robert Gundry, *Matthew* (Grand Rapids: Eerdmans, 1982) 148; Eduard Schweitzer, *The Good News According to Matthew* (Atlanta: John Knox, 1975) 217; Elaine Wainwright, *Towards a Feminist Critical Reading of Matthew*, 84; Antoinette C. Wire, "Gender Roles in a Scribal Community," in David Balch, ed., *Social History of the Matthean Community: Cross Disciplinary Approaches* (Minneapolis: Fortress, 1991) 104.

[62] Wainwright, *Towards a Feminist Critical Reading of Matthew*, 179, 181.

[63] Hearon, *The Mary Magdalene Tradition*, Chapter 4.

[64] Jane Schaberg, *The Resurrection of Mary Magdalene: Legends, Apocrypha, and the Christian Testament* (New York: Continuum, 2002) 300–44.

[65] Another cycle of stories may be represented by Mary and Martha.

[66] Elisabeth Schüssler Fiorenza, "Mary Magdalene: Apostle to the Apostles," *UTS Journal* (April 1975) 22–24.

in prophetic activity. The survival of the Magdalene stories in the androcentric texts of Matthew and John underscores the importance of these narratives in the memory of early Christian communities.[67]

PROMINENT AMONG THE APOSTLES

Although Mary is not called an apostle in the canonical texts, one woman is: Junia, "prominent among the apostles" (Rom 16:7). These are Paul's words, and for centuries Paul was taken at his word, astonishing though it appeared even then. John Chrysostom, no particular friend to women, applauded Junia as one who must have been very great indeed for Paul to have accorded her such honor.[68] Only one voice dissented before the end of the Middle Ages.[69] In the sixteenth century, however, with renewed interest in the Greek text and a revised view of the roles of women in the first centuries (the Reformation was not an unadulterated plus for women), a way was discovered to topple Junia from her exalted rank. Depending on where one placed the accent mark, the Greek dative could be read to refer either to a woman named Junia or to a man named Junias. Undeterred by the absence of any such masculine name in contemporary documents,[70] divines seized instantly on this "solution" to the "problem" of Junia, and the first modern vernacular Bibles—as well as all their successors before the late twentieth century—read "Junias." Successive published versions of the Greek text, now furnished with diacriticals, locked Junias in place for scholars as well. Junias persists in some modern vernacular versions, and rates a footnote as an alternative reading even in the NRSV.

Another scholarly move that accidentally—not deliberately—shifted Junia (as well as Phoebe, Prisca, Mary, Tryphaena, Tryphosa, Persis, Julia, the mother of Rufus, and the sister of Nereus, all named in this chapter) from the center of the action was the proposal that Romans 16 does not belong to that letter, but instead was a fragment of a letter to the Christians in Ephesus (where Acts 18 locates Prisca and Aquila; and see the reference to Epaenetus as "the first convert in Asia"). This proposal is currently less favored,[71] but it is worth noting that

---

[67] See Hearon, *The Mary Magdalene Tradition,* Chapters 6 and 7, for descriptions of how the Magdalene narratives may have functioned in the memory of the communities represented by the gospels of Matthew and John.

[68] See Bernadette J. Brooten, "Junia . . . Outstanding Among the Apostles (Romans 16:7)," in Leonard S. Swidler and Arlene Swidler, eds., *Women Priests* (New York: Paulist, 1977) 141–44.

[69] Aegidius of Rome (13th c.).

[70] See the discussion in Brooten, "Junia," and in Ulrich Wilckens, *Der Brief an die Römer (Röm 12–16).* EKK VI/3 (Neukirchen-Vluyn: Neukirchener Verlag, 1982) 135 n. 647.

[71] See Brendan Byrne, *Romans.* SP 6 (Collegeville: The Liturgical Press, 1996) 29; see also the thorough discussion of the problem in Lampe, *Die stadtrömischen Christen,* 124–35.

there can be unconscious agendas in reading, and the effect, if not the intent, of detaching Romans 16 from the body of the letter is to remove from its audience the ears of the largest collection of women addressees in the Second Testament.[72] This fundamentally alters the rhetorical character of the letter because it eliminates the closing greetings, thereby making Romans a letter addressed to no concrete persons, but rather spoken, as it were, into empty air. In *The Corinthian Women Prophets,* Anne Wire has convincingly demonstrated the vital importance of identifying the audience of any rhetorical composition. To strip Romans of the clues to its hearers is to change its character altogether, and to deprive it of its collection of women respondents is to silence half the echo.

While the reference in Rom 16:7 does not allow us direct access to Junia's voice, the power of her voice can be inferred from the inclusion of her name among those to be greeted. It is probable Paul hopes that, in response to his greeting, Junia will speak a good word on his behalf, commending him to the church at Rome, and that he assumes her word will carry weight in that context. Further, by describing Junia as "prominent" among the apostles Paul signals to his audience that her reputation ranges far beyond the church at Rome. Her voice is known and respected among those called apostle.[73] We also may deduce that Junia proclaims a gospel to which Paul subscribes, unlike that proclaimed by the "super apostles" in Corinth (see 2 Corinthians 10–12), since he is co-opting her to his cause.

Despite the fact that Junia's voice is forever mediated for us by the voice of Paul, this fleeting reference in Romans challenges us to listen for her voice whenever we read of apostles teaching, engaging in polemics, or preaching the gospel. In this respect one other comment made by Paul in reference to Junia may be significant: he says that she was "in Christ" before him. Paul is adamant that he received his gospel from no one (Gal 2:12), yet in two places he refers to traditions that were handed on to him (1 Cor 11:23; 15:3). From whom Paul received these traditions remains a mystery. However, he undoubtedly received them from one who was "in Christ" before him, perhaps even Junia.

---

[72] Byrne mentions (*Romans,* 29) that the influential papyrus $\mathfrak{P}^{46}$ "places the doxology comprising 16:25-27 at the close of chapter 15, thus providing some evidence for the existence of a fifteen-chapter edition to which chapter 16 would have been added at a later time." There may be no connection, but it is at least interesting to note that the same $\mathfrak{P}^{46}$ reads the relative clause in Rom 16:7 in the singular (ὅς rather than οἵτινές), as though the title "apostle" belonged only to Andronicus, and not to Junia! (Wilckens, *Römer,* 3:135 n. 648).

[73] See Wilckens, *Römer,* 3:136.

HEARING WOMEN'S VOICES INTO SPEECH[74]

Listening to the voices of the women, we become alert to the variety of ways in which women contributed to the traditioning process. In some instances women appear to be the source of traditions, perhaps through prophetic utterances as in Corinth. In others women bear and transmit traditions through storytelling, interjecting the voice of their own experiences and perspectives into the narrative. In yet other instances the formal roles embraced by women in the early church—virgins, widows, prophets, deacons, teachers, missionaries, apostles—grant them authority to teach and transmit traditions in local communities and across communities. Here the distinctive accent of women's voices is often heard in how they interpret shared traditions. This interpretive task required reflection on how faith impacted the social behaviors and boundaries that defined women's lives. The voices of women recovered above, although not uniform, reflect this shared vision: autonomous actions by women on their own behalf are rewarded, either through healing or deliverance or by the transformation of their lives in ways that transgress social boundaries. While such a vision need not be limited to the lives of women, it is, in context, a vision that is clearly responding to a particular social construction of gender and the lived experiences of women.

This reminds us that, in the words of Anne Wire, ". . . the integral relation of social experience and theological confession shows that neither should be studied in isolation from the other."[75] The study of early Christian traditions, their transmission, acceptance or rejection, and interpretation, cannot be wholly understood apart from an understanding of the role and status of women in early Christian communities. Further, the participation of women's voices in the traditioning process signals the active role women played in shaping the faith of the early church and interpreting that faith for praxis. Any study of Christian origins produced in the twenty-first century that does not take into consideration this role of women must be considered simply incomplete.

The relationship between social experience and theological confession points toward another issue raised by this brief introduction to the role of women in the traditioning process: i.e., who controls the process. Dewey observes, "As long as Christianity remained orally based, women both had their own oral traditions and also were important contributors to the common or 'great' tradition to which both male and female community members had

---

[74] The expression is Nelle Morton's (cf. *The Journey Is Home* [Boston: Beacon, 1985]).

[75] Wire, *The Corinthian Women Prophets*, 68. Similarly Kittredge, *Community and Authority*, 178.

access."[76] This observation corresponds to the evidence provided by the women's voices, which suggests that, very early in the life of the church, local communities, including communities of women, played a significant role in determining which traditions were accepted or rejected by the community. However, Dewey goes on to observe that as "manuscripts proliferated and gained authority . . . the role of women was minimized and distorted as oral traditions were written down by the few relatively high-status men."[77] The result was the nearly wholesale exclusion of women's voices from the written text. The opposition by canonical authors to the teachings and traditions represented by the women's voices further marginalized and undermined the authority and role of women in the traditioning process. This marginalization is perpetuated when we read the dominant voices in the canonical text as if they are immune to the relationship between social experience and theological confession. Attentiveness to the voices of the women challenges such a reading and invites us to read the text, instead, as testimony to the struggle among early Christians to understand how theological confession might be experienced as "good news" in relation to particular social experiences.

The voices represented here are not inclusive of all women in the early church. Chloe, for example, may well concur with Paul's critique of the Corinthian women prophets.[78] Yet these are the voices that are most accessible to us precisely because they stand in tension with the dominant voice of the text. This tension is a reminder that the New Testament canon not only transmits traditions of the early church but is itself a witness to competing voices in the traditioning process. In many instances the competition revolves around interpretations of shared traditions, serving as an important reminder that "tradition" alone is no guarantor of uniformity. In other instances we see traditions being worked out in relation to one another: a teaching that has been adopted as tradition by one community is opposed by another, leading to the development of a countertradition. Unquestionably, the canon does not value these voices equally, but their very presence should challenge us to examine more closely the dynamics that are driving the traditioning process: specifically, who benefits from the received tradition and who does not, and the degree to which power and access play a role in determining which tradition prevails. In every instance the traditions must be measured in relation to their capacity to transform women's lives in life-giving ways.

[76] Joanna Dewey, "From Storytelling to Written Text," 74.

[77] Ibid. See also Ross S. Kraemer, *Her Share of the Blessings* (New York: Oxford University Press, 1992) 144–45.

[78] Wire, *The Corinthian Women Prophets,* 41.

Despite all the changes that have occurred in two millennia of history, even today, and especially in the churches, the voices of women are hard to hear. Androcentrism still shapes both our texts and our hearing. The following incident illustrates this in a physical form that can serve as a metaphor for the larger reality.

In April 2003 one of us (Linda) was ordained to the Episcopal priesthood. The ordination was held, by the kind hospitality of the Benedictine monks, in the Abbey Church at Collegeville, Minnesota. A woman in the congregation remarked afterward that when the male ordinand spoke, his voice sounded out loud and clear; by contrast, the voices of the two female ordinands sounded muffled. This can, in fact, be verified from the videotape of the service. All three ordinands spoke with full voice. Of course, men's voices are naturally louder than women's, but there was another factor. The sound system in the Abbey Church is adjusted to amplify men's voices, because on every ordinary day it is men alone who speak there. Women's vocal tones are off the spectrum and are not amplified in the same way.

The techniques and media of scholarship are very much like auditory systems. They must be adjusted to different kinds of sound, different pitches of voice. Heretofore they have been attuned to the voices of men; women have been not so much heard as overheard, distantly or as mediated. In our attempt to listen to the voices of women directly we are not making any radical changes to the texts themselves. All we are doing is adjusting the mikes.

Placing Women
at the Hermeneutical Center

Why Did Sarah Laugh?

Gina Hens-Piazza

❧

As liberated as we like to think we are, not many women I know would ever consider, much less welcome a gathering of women colleagues and graduate students into their home during the disruption of a kitchen renovation. But there we were—making dinner again in Anne Wire's torn up kitchen, too many of us to count. Our numbers filled this space under renovation where we often gathered and spread beyond into the adjacent living room area. This was just another of countless occasions when Anne had graciously made her home a haven for women of the Graduate Theological Union. She has hosted our serious discussions, our resolutions of disputes, our building up of women's community, and the grounding of our friendships. Her own rejoicing in others' accomplishments, her delight in her own work as teacher and scholar, and her gracious hospitality have occasioned much joy, merriment, and laughter among the many women who cherish her. In that spirit, this essay fixes upon Sarah's laughter as one small expression of gladness and gratitude for Anne and her countless gifts.

Beginning in Genesis 12, the Abraham-Sarah traditions introduce Israel's salvation history with rich and variegated story units. Dominant among the central ideas crafting this first ancestral saga across these chapters (Genesis 12–25) is the theme of Sarah's barrenness. Even before God calls Abraham and tells him to take his family and leave Mesopotamia for the land he will be shown, we learn that the matriarch is barren. At the very first mention of her name, unprecedented as it is in that patriarchal genealogy (11:30), Sarah is introduced to us as childless. Just a few verses later, the record of Abraham's age at 75 and Sarah's age at 65 (12:4) suggests that this childlessness has had a long history. Moreover, this barrenness is not just a passing bit of sidebar information that, in tandem with the very few other details we are afforded, rounds out the character of Sarah. Rather, her barrenness introduces a crisis warranting the plot that unfolds in the subsequent chapters. For alongside this introduction to these first ancestors, and in conjunction with the alert to their infertility problem, comes a divine pledge. God promises Abraham that he will have descendants. The first pronouncement of the promise comes soon after the problem of infertility is established (12:7). Next, the promise is reiterated in 15:4. Finally, it receives its fullest and most graphic exposition in 15:5 when Abraham is not only promised descendants, but "descendants as numerous as the stars." Now we do have a problem, as well as a plot with a good bit of narrative tension. With all this taken together—the couple's ages at 65 and 75, the matter of Sarah's barrenness, and a divine promise of descendants as numerous as the stars to Abraham—the plot thickens. It pulsates with a heightened sense of urgency as well as crafting a narrative with a bit of comic relief.

In response to the crisis and the implicit crunch that old age imposes regarding urgency in conceiving offspring, Sarah, as we know, takes matters into her own hands. In accordance with accepted practices of surrogacy in the ancient world, she offers Hagar, her maidservant, to Abraham (Gen 16:1-4). And though this action proves immediately successful, it is apparently not acceptable to the divine one making the promise. Hence we are hurled deeper into the growing complexity of the storyline, skippered by the intensifying crisis of offspring for old Abraham and Sarah.

A glimmer of hope dawns in Gen 17:15-21 and again in Gen 18:1-15. We encounter not one, but two birth announcements from God addressed to these desperate wannabe parents. With the formality of the twice employed genre "birth announcement," first in ch. 17 followed by another in ch. 18, God promises that the divine scheme will overturn Sarah's barrenness and fulfill the promise of offspring to this couple. Such announcements often signaled not only the fulfillment of the promised birth but also some kind of upcoming supernatural unfolding on the part of the deity. Given the prospect of miraculous intervention, the problem seems headed for resolution. Abraham and Sarah will have a son.

That there are two birth announcements is especially encouraging. While the setting and circumstances of these proclamations differ, parallel features yoke them together, urging readers to hear them as real assurance. Abraham is featured in the first, and Sarah eventually assumes center stage in the second. Both accounts carry the explicit announcement that Abraham and Sarah will have a son. In both accounts each parent-to-be laughs, on hearing the news, in the presence of the Lord. As each laughs, they both express the reason for their incredulity. Abraham replies: "Can a child be born to a man who is a hundred years old? Can Sarah, who is ninety years old, bear a son?" (17:17).[1] And Sarah re-

---

[1] All translations are from the NRSV unless otherwise indicated.

sponds, "After I have grown old, and my husband is old, shall I have pleasure?" (18:12). Additionally, they both keep their skeptical responses to themselves. Moreover, both responses serve as anticipation and affirmation regarding the child's name, Isaac, which in Hebrew *(ytzok)* means "to laugh." Later, when the child is named, Sarah expresses the significance of the name for herself even further. She exclaims, "God has brought laughter for me; everyone who hears will laugh with me" (Gen 21:6). Nevertheless, despite the parallels at the level of the text and at the level of interpretive impact, the kinship between these two vignettes breaks down over the matter of divine response. When the incredulity expresses itself in both instances, Abraham's laughter is not questioned but Sarah's laughter is. God asks, "Why did Sarah laugh?" (18:13).

The history of interpretation has addressed this breach in congruity across the two accounts in a fairly exhaustive manner. On the one hand, proposals emerge from years of historical-critical excavations and history-of-composition studies. Many of these wrestle the matter of compositional origin and settle the question indirectly by assigning the two birth announcements to separate sources.[2] Genesis 17:15-21 is most often argued as the product of the Priestly writer (P), with Gen 18:1-15 originating from the Yahwist source (J). At the other end of the vast interpretive spectrum, contemporary feminist studies argue the difference in the divine response as evidence of a textual remnant from matriarchal society.[3] God's concern over Sarah's laughter and not Abraham's is indicative of a context where women's response before the deity carried far more weight than that of men. Between these two extremes come myriad proposals and argumentative explanations for the differences in divine response.

Given the history of research addressing the matter of Sarah's laughter and God's follow-up inquiry, this study risks redundancy. I, too, intend to study this matter and weigh in on the question, "Why did Sarah laugh?" However, I am not concerned with explaining the difference between God's response to Sarah's laughter and the lack thereof to Abraham's chuckle. Instead, I am interested in a New Historicist reading of this story in relation to the question God asks—both at the level of the text and at the level of interpretation.

[2] See, for example, Ephraim A. Speiser's discussion in *Genesis*. AB 1 (Garden City, N.Y.: Doubleday, 1983) 124–31.

[3] Savina J. Teubal, *Sarah the Priestess: The First Matriarch of Genesis* (Athens, Ohio: Swallow, 1984).

Excursus

New Historicism marks a turn away from pursuit of rhetorical integrity or literary unity.[4] Rather, it attends to the cracks, to fleeting comments, to the underside of a story, and to signs of disarray latent in a work. Convinced that "whole readings" are but a self-satisfying illusion, New Historicism opts for more fragmentary kinds of considerations. Resisting the tendency to integrate dominant images, dialogues, and characters into a single master discourse, it hosts the playfulness in texts. It attends to fleeting references (e.g., a laugh), incongruities (God's response to Abraham in ch. 17 versus God's response to Sarah in ch. 18), or unanswered questions (why did Sarah laugh?) resident at the borders of the text.

Attention to these matters at the margins of a story discloses a complicated past that resists the coherence of reigning historical reconstructions or readings founded on literary coherence at the level of both text and constructed context. Attention to these unaddressed questions and to these cracks lurking in the margins disrupts the integrity of unified readings. In lieu of producing an outcome that conforms to the monological tendencies of traditional historical or even literary interpretation, New Historicism uncovers other versions of the past and other interpretations of ignored elements in stories. In this study I explore the question concerning Sarah's laughter as a discursive force in the narrative that disrupts the course of the story line and discloses "a past of competing voices, values, and centers of power . . . ."[5] In the process, wrestling with this unanswered question in the narrative may prove fruitful in forging further understandings of both the story and the question it poses, "Why did Sarah laugh?"

THE TEXT

Genesis 18:1-16 is considered to be originally a self-contained unit consisting of two easily identifiable parts: first, the visit of the three men to Abraham (vv. 1-8), and second, the promise of a son (vv. 9-16a). In part one, Abraham is sitting outside his tent pitched near the great trees of Mamre in the heat of the midday sun. While he is sitting there, three visitors approach. Though the nar-

---

[4] For an introduction to New Historicism in literary studies see Catherine Gallagher and Stephen Greenblatt, *Practicing New Historicism* (Chicago: University of Chicago Press, 2000), and Jeremy Hawthorn, *Cunning Passages: New Historicism, Cultural Materialism and Marxism in the Contemporary Literary Debate* (London: Arnold, 1996). For discussion of New Historicism in biblical studies see the New Historicism issue, ed. Stephen Moore, *BibInt* 5 (Leiden: Brill, 1997), and Gina Hens-Piazza, *The New Historicism.* Guides to Biblical Scholarship (Minneapolis: Fortress, 2002).

[5] Brian Rosenberg, "Historicizing the New Historicism: Understanding the Past in Criticism and Fiction," *Modern Language Quarterly* 50 (1989) 376.

rator informs the reader that this is a divine visit, Abraham only knows them to be "three men standing near him" (v. 2). This quiet opening (vv. 1-2a) abruptly shifts to a story narrated in haste (v. 2b). With no formal introductions or exchanges of identity, Abraham runs to greet the three, bows down before them, and urges them to stay. He offers them water, food, and a place for resting, to which they are receptive (vv. 3-5). Despite the heat of the day, Abraham moves about hurriedly and hurries others about in order to prepare a rather sumptuous refreshment for these three strangers. He runs to the tent and orders Sarah to make cakes (v. 6). He races to the cattle and secures a nice tender calf (v. 7a). He gives it to his servant who prepares the meat "in haste" (something our visitors might have been leery of had they known) (v. 7b). Then he takes milk and curds, which he prepares along with the calf. He sets all the food before the visitors, who then feast on homemade bread, "veal, milk, and curd" (v. 8). In the meantime Abraham positions himself nearby, ready to wait on them and respond to their every need. To us this hospitality appears extreme. We might even be suspicious that some strings are attached to such unsolicited kindness. Some even interpret this as a gift offering for the promise of the child that is to follow. However, nothing in the story indicates that Abraham knew who these visitors were or the reason why they came. A more likely interpretation is founded on social scientific studies' investigation of such activities in the context of the Ancient Near East. Findings disclose that such gestures of hospitality were characteristic of sedentary peoples in these early contexts.[6]

The second half of the story opens when the visitors ask Abraham a question. "Where is Sarah, your wife?" (v. 9). With no segue and at this juncture in the story, the question is peculiar. How do they know about Sarah, and how do they know that she is his wife? Since Abraham has been hurrying about and hosting this whole event himself, why are they even asking about her? Or given the patriarchal context, perhaps it is precisely because he has been doing all the preparing and serving that they want to know where in the world his wife is. Whatever the reason behind their question, Abraham seems unfazed by the inquiry. He answers straightaway, "There in the tent" (v. 9). At this point one of the visitors makes the birth announcement: "I will surely return to you in due season and Sarah will have a son" (v. 10).

Next, the scene shifts to inside the tent; only the reader is allowed to enter and see what is going on in this domestic enclosure. Sarah is listening at the entrance to the tent, which is behind the one who was speaking (v. 10). She laughs! Then she muses about her physical status being all used up, about sexual pleasure, and about her husband's age.

[6] Gordon Wenham, *Genesis 16–50.* WBC 2 (Dallas, Tex.: Word Books, 1994) 46.

Then something quite unexpected happens. The messenger, identified only to the reader as the LORD (v. 13), turns to Abraham and asks, "Why did Sarah laugh and say 'shall I indeed bear a child now that I am old?' Is anything too wonderful for the LORD?" (vv. 13-14a). This is quite strange, because Sarah was in the tent when she laughed and the Hebrew description, *biqirbah,* qualifies her laughter as laughing "inside herself." In the tent, out of sight, out of earshot of Abraham, and by herself, Sarah laughs inside herself. How is Abraham supposed to know that she laughed, much less *why* she laughed? The LORD speaks again to Abraham and reiterates the promise made just before this little incident regarding Sarah's private laughter. "At the set time, I will return to you in due season and Sarah shall have a son" (v. 14).

Now Sarah, who evidently suspects the identity of the stranger, is afraid and quickly tries to correct the situation: "I did not laugh" (v. 15). That she was afraid discloses further her hunch about God's identity. As the story draws to a close it creates a further complexity. Someone responds to Sarah: "And he said 'O yes, you did laugh'" (v. 15). However, it leaves unspecified whether the reference to the final speaker as "he" refers to God or to Abraham. Most translations and interpreters assume it to be God, since Abraham had no knowledge of her laughter. Finally, the account concludes as starkly and abruptly as it began. It closes with, "Then the men set out from there" (v. 16a).

Our close look at this story discloses some glaring peculiarities. In the first half of the tale Abraham is the protagonist. He is in charge of the action. He issues commands and initiates the dialogue. However, the second half unfolds quite differently. While Abraham continues to be addressed, he has no idea what is going on. He does not know who the messengers are. He does not know about Sarah's laughter. Thus he surely does not know why she laughed. And he must be incredibly perplexed when, in response to Sarah's denial, the visitor retorts, "O yes, you did laugh" (v. 15), suggesting that the visitor has a knowledge about his wife, Sarah, that Abraham himself does not even possess. Read closely, this story line and its literary arrangement are more than peculiar; the story, with its cracks and gaps, approaches being downright funny. Hence, as Sarah's laughter rings across the history and tradition of interpretation, we are invited to hear it as an expression of amusement at much more than the incomprehensible announcement that she and old Abraham are about to conceive a child. The multidimensional nature of this laughter and its interrogation embrace much more.

SARAH'S LAUGHTER AS DISCURSIVE FORCE

From a literary standpoint the organization and balance of the story are odd enough to be noteworthy. The whole first half of the story is introduction (vv.

1-8). It is so detailed (greeting, time of day, food preparation, menu, etc.) as to be determinative of the story's identity. Numerous commentaries refer to this tale in 18:1-16a with such titles as "Abraham Entertaining the Three Messengers from Heaven," or "Abraham and the Three Messengers," or "Abraham and the Visitors at Mamre."[7] Such headings are already interpretations and have a determinative influence on this text's reception. As a result, readers experience this first introductory half of the tale as integral or essential to the heart of the story, even though without it the account of the annunciation of Isaac's birth in vv. 9 -16a could stand on its own.

While these opening verses relate the encounter between Abraham and the three visitors, they do not govern and constrain the story line. Rather, they function only as introduction. And as introduction, we might note how nonessential this first part is. What could have been introduced in one sentence, "And three men came to visit Abraham and Sarah," would then have been a more appropriately paralleled component to the conclusion, "The men set out from there" (v. 16a). Instead, the lengthy introduction with its elaborate detail (vv. 1-8) creates a most uneven envelope structure. The detailing of food preparations bears no relationship to the story at hand. In fact, in another story where a divine messenger delivers a birth announcement to Minoah, Samson's father, the divine emissary declines food offered by Minoah (Judg 13:15-16). At best, the exceedingly long introduction of our tale (vv. 1-8) appears to create its own story but with no real plot line—visitors, food gathering, food preparation, serving, eating, resting—not much of a story. At worst, this long, unrelated description delays the commencement of the real plot, the birth announcement that Sarah will have a son, but it hardly builds suspense. Moreover, these opening eight verses overshadow the story that unfolds in the second part, but without poetic purpose. Part one (vv. 1-8) fixes upon the character of Abraham even though the plot line will ultimately feature Sarah. Hence the introduction actually competes with the plot, overshadowing it and rendering it secondary. This is a most awkward literary arrangement. Such an imbalance struggles to rewrite this story of the birth announcement to Sarah as another birth announcement to Abraham. However, at work across these verses are some discursive forces that oppose and resist the dominance of this long introduction as well as the centrality of Abraham's character. The first of these elements is the mention of the "tent." There are five references to the tent in this story, with most of them occurring in the first half of the tale. The first time Sarah is mentioned, we hear she is in

[7] For example, see Speiser, *Genesis,* 128; Gerhard von Rad, *Genesis* (Philadelphia: Westminster, 1972) 203; and Claus Westermann, *Genesis 12–36: A Commentary,* trans. John Scullion, s.j. (Minneapolis: Augsburg, 1985) 272.

the tent (v. 6). In fact, this particular reference constitutes the centerpiece around which the other references to the tent occur making the first mention of Sarah the chiastic center of these iterations. Following this first identifying citation, she is named thereafter every time the tent is mentioned.

18:1	He was sitting at the opening of his **tent**.
18:2	He ran from his **tent**.
18:6	Abraham hurries to *Sarah* in the **tent**.
18:9	Sarah is in the **tent**.
18:10b	Sarah is listening in the **tent**.

In the midst of Abraham rushing around greeting visitors, fixing food, serving, and being something of a distraction to the real story at hand, the narrative references to "tent" persist in soliciting the reader's curiosity and fixing it upon this site in the story. It is reminiscent of a good suspense movie where the camera keeps cycling back to an ashtray with a tiny stub of a cigarette resting on its edge while everyone in the scene is involved in an animated discussion about how that dreaded cigarette-smoking intruder could never break into this apartment. Moreover, the pattern fashioned by the iteration of "the tent" transgresses the outer limits of the introduction (vv. 1-8) and navigates our attention to the story following in part two (vv. 9, 10b). And when that story finally begins, focalization on Sarah replaces the spotlighting of the tent where she has been concealed. The question: "Where is Sarah, your wife?" opens this section. Following, we hear, "Sarah was listening," "Sarah laughed," "Why did Sarah laugh?" "Sarah is to have a son," "Sarah feared," "Sarah denied." The narrative is riveted on Sarah. This is her story, and the birth announcement is intended for her.

Another element that works to raise questions and shift our attention away from Abraham and this introduction is the matter of genre. The genre here, "birth announcement," is a familiar occurrence in the biblical stories. For his part, Abraham has already received a visitation from God in the preceding chapter, with a birth announcement attached. Given the recurrence of this literary form across the biblical traditions, we could expect Sarah to be visited and told the same news. This format of an announcement to one parent, then to the other has its counterpart in the book of Judges. Like Sarah, Samson's mother, who was barren, receives a messenger from God promising her a child. Soon after, the messenger returns to confirm this same news to her husband, Minoah (Judg 13:17). More characteristically, however, women are the recipients of these visitations and announcements. Hannah receives assurances from Eli and is granted a son (1 Sam 1:12-18). The childless Shunnamite woman is the recipient of the same promise at the word of Elisha the prophet

(2 Kgs 4:13-17). The recurrence of this genre continues on into the New Testament. Mary, though not barren, receives a proclamation that a child will be born to her. Well documented across biblical narratives as well as other Ancient Near Eastern traditions, this genre, "birth announcement," characteristically features an announcement or revelation to the mother-to-be.

In our story, when the birth announcement finally occurs, the shift in language also indicates this was to be a birth announcement for Sarah. When God spoke to Abraham in ch. 17 the patriarch was promised "I will give *you* a son by her (Sarah)" (17:16). A few verses later the rhetoric emphasizes Abraham again: "No, but your wife Sarah shall bear *you* a son and *you* shall name him Isaac" (17:19). Here the emphasis on "give you" and "bear you" designates the intended addressee of the announcement. Abraham is the recipient of this promise. However, in our story the messenger's language changes. After trying to establish the whereabouts of Sarah, the messenger delivers to Abraham what is formulated to be her announcement. ". . . *Sarah* shall have a son" (18:10). Parallel to the birth announcement to Abraham, it is reiterated again in v. 14: "Your wife *Sarah* shall have a son." The rhetoric, "your wife Sarah shall bear you a son" in the preceding ch. 17, in contrast to "and Sarah shall have a son" in our story, encourages us to hear the earlier announcement to Abraham and this one to Sarah.

Additionally, a more integral element works against the dominance of the introduction as the heart of the story. It is the matter of plot development. Typically plot entails the exposition of a conflict/problem, climax, and resolution. However, in our text this does not occur until the second half of the story. The conflict/problem is introduced with the question "Where is Sarah?" focusing upon the tent where she is located and will soon be laughing in response to the promise of a son for her. The climax occurs when the LORD asks: "Why did Sarah laugh?" and the resolution takes places when God manifests divine omniscience and counters Sarah's denial with "O yes, you did laugh." The visitors' departure paralleling their arrival are the bookends—introduction and conclusion to the little story within.

So now let us turn our attention to this climax and consider in detail: "Why did Sarah laugh?" First we might note, at least from the contemporary reader's vantage point, the resident reflection here of an all-too-familiar scene in our own legislative bodies of government. It is a bit comical as well as unsettling, watching and listening in on a group of men sitting around a meal discussing matters of conception, especially in regard to women. However, when we focus on the text there is something surprising and humorous that takes place here as well. In conjunction with Sarah's laughter, she says, "After I have grown old and my husband is old, shall I have pleasure?" (v. 12). However, the

Hebrew here is more graphic and blunt. What makes Sarah laugh finds expression in her words. The verb *belah,* "to be worn out" (used of old clothes in Josh 9:13 and of bones dried up in Ps 32:3), along with *ednah,* referring to "sexual pleasure," communicates Sarah's private amusement.[8] Her thoughts are first fixed upon the process leading up to conception, which at this stage is a bit of a hurdle. "Now that I am used up, shall I have sexual pleasure? And my husband is old." When the messenger repeats what Sarah said inside herself, he strips Sarah's musing of its bluntness. Recasting it as "Shall I indeed bear a child now that I am old?" he makes what was privately appropriate more palatable for public consumption. This need not be heard as a censure of Sarah. Actually, in a somewhat humorous vein it might best be heard as an illustration of just how differently men and women think about these matters.

The theological linchpin of this announcement is the messenger's follow-up query, "Is anything too wonderful for the LORD?" This is the first time God has been referenced in the conversation among the characters. Sarah's laughter here plays a pivotal role in unveiling the divine presence in this tale. Up to this point only the reader knows of God's presence. However, the detection of Sarah's laughter inside herself discloses divine omniscience on the part of the messenger who is speaking. Hence, Sarah's laughter unmasks God in the story. Veiled in the character of the messenger, God's presence at this meeting is disclosed. Sarah seems to get it. When the messenger accuses her of laughing, "fear" prompts her denial. Fear is one of the most frequently acknowledged responses on the part of those who encounter God. For example, when the midwives disobeyed Pharaoh in Exod 1:17 they did so because of their fear of the LORD. Hence Sarah's laughter and fear verify the divine backing of the promise in this story.

Finally, we return again to the question whose trajectories we have been chasing, "Why did Sarah laugh?" Out of sight, and out of earshot, this woman's silent little snicker catapults her to the center of the tale. When she laughs, she becomes present to the narrative. When she laughs, her confinement in the tent ends. When she laughs, her husband recedes to the sidelines. When she laughs, the divine presence in the episode is unveiled. Upon her laughter she finally assumes her rightful place in this tale. When a laughing Sarah enters as an essential player of this story she is no longer easily relegated to the margins of the story or absent altogether.

As testimony to the role laughter plays here, Sarah laughing in the story equals Sarah front and center in a story that otherwise tries to obscure her.

---

[8] Andrew A. McIntosh, following Pseudo-Jonathan, proposes the meaning "sexual pleasure or conception" in "A Third Root in Biblical Hebrew?" *VT* 24 (1974) 454–73.

Caught laughing, Sarah commands our attention and the attention of others in the scene.

In classical literature, comedy perennially takes up arms against the forces that stifle life, silence voices, or shut out the deserving. It ridicules the arrogant and boastful. It deflates the pretentious and pompous. And it does so with humor, all in the interest of celebrating life and its players. This little story of the birth announcement to Sarah hardly qualifies as comedy in the classic sense, but it does depend upon some of comedy's same dynamics. Stifling the forces that keep her out of sight and earshot in the tale, Sarah's laughter makes a case for her role as central rather than peripheral in this story. That should teach us something. And . . . if that is all we can say at the end of this text study, it at least serves as testimony to the transforming power of a good laugh!!

Metaphor and Ambiguity
in *Liber Antiquitatum Biblicarum:*
A Cognitive Linguistic Analysis

Mary Therese DesCamp

ॐ

INTRODUCTION

In Pseudo-Philo's *Liber Antiquitatum Biblicarum* characters regularly make speeches without counterpart in biblical or intertestamental literature. In ch. 31, for example, the biblical character Jael holds forth in a soliloquy that is notable for three contradictory variations on the biblical metaphor ISRAEL IS GOD'S FLOCK. This metaphoric conflict has been taken as evidence of errors in translation or the literary ineptitude of the author.

In this study, using the theories of conceptual blending and metaphor analysis from cognitive linguistics research, I argue that the seeming conflict in these three metaphors demonstrates the skillful characterization of a woman who is problematic within the text's moral schematic rather than blunders in transmission or compositional incompetence. These metaphors build related but conflicting conceptual spaces, underscoring the ambiguous standing of Jael, a foreign woman, vis-à-vis the Jewish community. This analysis uses the tools of cognitive blending to reduce or eliminate the tendency to "read in" aspects of narrative structure that are not present in the text, and to highlight those aspects of narrative structure that are present but may be obscured by preconceptions.

THE TEXT

Liber Antiquitatum Biblicarum[1] is a text written by an unknown Jewish author sometime in the first century C.E.[2] It is generally classified as "rewritten bible," that is, a document that

> . . . takes the biblical text itself as the focus of attention. . . . Using the framework of scripture, these documents include elements from the biblical narrative but freely omit words and whole incidents and add material without any foundation in the text.[3]

Pseudo-Philo retells the biblical narrative from creation through the rise of King David, with major emphasis on the book of Judges. New names, details, and dialogue appear; paraphrases of biblical text are mixed with direct quotes; the biblical narrative is drastically revised and large sections of Scripture are summarized peremptorily.

All extant manuscripts are in medieval Latin,[4] although Daniel J. Harrington has argued convincingly for a Hebrew *Vorlage* that was translated into Greek and then Latin.[5] These "third hand" texts have many obscurities, lacunae, and variants.

The *LAB* is replete with distrust of foreign women. They are to be avoided at all costs, as they provide a double occasion for sin: an invitation to fornication and an incitement to idolatry. In numerous passages Pseudo-Philo has penned additions that underscore the evil of consorting with these women. The tale of Balaam's curse is revised to read that Israel's downfall was effected by stationing naked Midianite women at the borders, waiting to seduce Jewish men into idolatry. Samson is said to have died as punishment for his sin of intermingling with foreign women. The medium of Endor, who in 1 Samuel 28 was a Hebrew, becomes a Midianite witch in Pseudo-Philo's retelling. And in ch. 44, when God details how the Israelites broke every commandment, the summary indictment is, "And they lusted after foreign women."

---

[1] This text will also be referred to as Pseudo-Philo, or *LAB*, throughout this document.

[2] Following the dating of Daniel J. Harrington in "Pseudo-Philo," *The Old Testament Pseudepigrapha*, ed. James H. Charlesworth (New York: Doubleday, 1985) 2:299.

[3] Daniel J. Harrington, "Adaptation of Narratives," in Robert Kraft and George Nickelsburg, eds., *Early Judaism and Its Modern Interpreters* (Philadelphia: Fortress, 1986) 240.

[4] The earliest extant manuscripts of Pseudo-Philo's *Liber Antiquitatum Biblicarum* are from the eleventh century. There are eighteen complete and three fragmentary texts of *LAB*, all in Latin, and all of German or Austrian origin.

[5] Daniel J. Harrington, "The Original Language of Pseudo-Philo's *Liber Antiquitatum Biblicarum*," *HTR* 63 (1970) 503–14. This theory of Hebrew as Pseudo-Philo's original language was advanced as early as the sixteenth century by Sisto da Siena, according to Howard Jacobson in *A Commentary on Pseudo-Philo's Liber Antiquitatum Biblicarum* (Leiden: Brill, 1996) 215.

Given the overall orientation of Pseudo-Philo toward foreign women, the character of Jael presents a difficulty. The biblical story clearly portrays her as a non-Israelite who acts as an instrument of salvation for the Israelites when she slays Sisera. Telling her story while reviling foreign women is a difficult path to walk.

COGNITIVE LINGUISTICS AND METAPHOR

In 1977, at a multi-disciplinary conference on metaphor, Michael Reddy presented a paper analyzing the metaphors humans use to speak about language and information exchange. This analysis laid the foundation for modern claims that metaphor is a matter of thinking, not just language, and that metaphor is imbedded in everyday thinking and speech.[6]

Contemporary metaphor theory, as elucidated by Lakoff, Johnson, Turner, Sweetser, and Grady,[7] holds that metaphorical capacity springs from embodied cognition; humans perceive the world through the senses in combination with cognitive capacities. While infants or young children, all humans appear to learn primary metaphors, which are grounded in primary scenes—"recurrent, basic event-types which involve a tight correlation between perceptual experience and subjective response"[8]—such as the relationship of vision and knowledge. Most infants experience salient and persistent coactivation of these two neural domains, since visual input is one of the most important sources of information on which human knowledge is based. Repeated coactivation results in permanent neural connections between portions of the brain dedicated to different experiences.[9]

---

[6] Michael Reddy, "The conduit metaphor: a case of frame conflict in our language about language," in Andrew Ortony, ed., *Metaphor and Thought* (2d ed. Cambridge: Cambridge University Press, 1998) 164–201.

[7] See, for instance, George Lakoff and Mark Johnson, *Metaphors We Live By* (Chicago: University of Chicago Press, 1980); Mark Johnson, *Philosophical Perspectives on Metaphor* (Minneapolis: University of Minnesota Press, 1981); George Lakoff, *Women, Fire, and Dangerous Things: What Categories Reveal about the Mind* (Chicago: University of Chicago Press, 1987); Mark Turner, *Death is the Mother of Beauty: Mind, Metaphor, Criticism* (Chicago: University of Chicago Press, 1987); George Lakoff and Mark Turner, *More Than Cool Reason: A Field Guide to Poetic Metaphor* (Chicago: University of Chicago Press, 1989); Eve E. Sweetser, *From Etymology to Pragmatics: The Mind-As-Body Metaphor in Semantic Structure and Semantic Change* (Cambridge: Cambridge University Press, 1990); and Joseph Grady, *Foundations of Meaning: Primary Metaphors and Primary Scenes* (Ph.D. diss., University of California at Berkeley, 1997).

[8] Grady, *Foundations of Meaning*, 2.

[9] George Lakoff and Mark Johnson, *Philosophy in the Flesh* (New York: Basic Books, 1999) 46, after Srini Narayanan, *Embodiment in Language Understanding: Sensory-Motor Representations*

This relationship motivates the common metaphor, KNOWING IS SEEING.[10] Research on child language has shown that, prior to the use of this metaphor, children conflate the two domains; the earliest uses of vision verbs refer not just to physical vision or just to cognition, but to visual experience as a source of new mental input.[11] *See the duckies!* or *Let's see what is in this box* are common examples of early uses both to and by young English-speaking children. In these instances knowledge actually co-occurs with and depends on vision. As the child grows and develops more complex understanding of both vision and knowledge the two domains develop more complex and separable mental representations. This differentiation between the domains of seeing and knowing does not, however, remove the neural links between them, and this connection motivates a metaphorical mapping between the source domain of vision and the target domain of knowledge, as exemplified by uses such as *I see what you mean,* where knowledge does not depend on actual sight but on "insight." [12]

Sweetser and Grady's research argues for cross-linguistic metaphorical similarity, holding that these correspondences are not arbitrary, but rooted in biology and human experience. Sweetser's research uncovers a widespread pattern in Indo-European languages where a word like "perspicacious," which originally signified vision, has lost its original sense and now denotes a mental rather than visual event.[13] Grady argues that these patterns of association between language and conceptual structure at the primary level may be universal.[14]

---

for Metaphoric Reasoning About Event Descriptions (Ph.D. diss., University of California at Berkeley, 1997).

[10] In cognitive metaphor research the standardized notation for a cognitive metaphor is "TARGET DOMAIN IS SOURCE DOMAIN." This convention will be used throughout the paper.

[11] Christopher Johnson, "Learnability in the acquisition of multiple senses: SOURCE reconsidered," *Proceedings of the 22nd Annual Meeting of the Berkeley Linguistics Society* (Berkeley: Berkeley Linguistics Society, 1996) 469–80.

[12] It is common for the source domains of primary metaphors to be perceptual experience, and for the target domains to be some area of subjective response (KNOWING IS SEEING, ACQUIESCENCE IS SWALLOWING, for example). Recent findings in metaphor theory have clarified some of the distinctions between source and target domains. For primary metaphors (though not necessarily all metaphors), target domains have less sensory content than source domains, but they are not necessarily abstract and difficult concepts. Rather, target domains are essential parts of everyday human experience. As Grady argues, primary metaphors ". . . map not from lower-level to higher-level concepts, but between very fundamental concepts of different sorts . . . [Primary m]etaphors link the basic 'backstage' operations of cognition with the kind of sensory images (in any modality) that we are most able to maintain and manipulate in our consciousness. In this sense, primary metaphors may be responsible for much of the substance of subjective mental experience" (Grady, *Foundations of Meaning,* 135–36).

[13] Sweetser, *From Etymology to Pragmatics,* ch. 2.

[14] Grady, *Foundations of Meaning,* 2. Grady samples ancient Greek, Japanese, Russian, Swahili,

Metaphor theory argues that these primary metaphors born of the relationship between perceptual experience and subjective response are building blocks for cognition; primary metaphors are the material of more complex metaphors with which humans conceptualize the world.

In their 2002 book *The Way We Think,* Gilles Fauconnier and Mark Turner situate primary metaphor within the framework of cognitive blending. Fauconnier and Turner hypothesize that the processing of cognitive material by the brain takes place instantaneously and unconsciously, and that human beings engage in cognitive blending—the ongoing, real-time process of thinking—by recruiting and combining meaning from well-established cognitive structures (e.g., local context and primary or culturally licensed metaphors) in order to build new meaning. According to Fauconnier and Turner, this conceptual blending is an active and virtually unconscious cognitive process that occurs even as one thinks, and it is capable of performing new conceptual work on structures that have been previously entrenched. The brain uses cognitive blending in order to make complex ideas accessible at a human level. Blending enables humans to manipulate and to learn complex concepts easily. Such processing involves linkages and compressions: linkages between concepts that correspond in some way, such as time, role, or identity; and compressions as when diffuse items are compressed into a single framework.[15] For instance, "George Bush" is a value for "President of the United States"—they are linked through the vital relation "role." And when one says *The president always wants to stack the Supreme Court,* we are compressing numerous individual people into a single person who has served since the inception of the country.

Cognitive blending, like metaphor, is both a biological action—taking place at the neural level of the brain—and a cultural action, as culturally approved/accepted/substantiated blends are appropriated into the cultural fabric. Whether one uses the language of cognitive blend or cognitive linguistics metaphor theory, the phenomenon under study is not confined to language use, but rather is a matter of thinking. Human beings use blends and metaphors in order to conceive of one mental domain in terms of another. This allows one to reason about one input in the language and frame of the other input, and like primary metaphors, culturally entrenched blends may form permanent neural pathways in the brain.

Conceptual blends range widely in their creativity and stability. On one end are simplex blends, where elements from one input (such as the names George

---

Arabic, and medieval Irish to establish that these speech communities all share the association between physical weight and emotional experience, regardless of differences in geography and era.

[15] Gilles Fauconnier and Mark Turner, *The Way We Think: Conceptual Blending and the Mind's Hidden Complexities* (New York: Basic Books, 2002).

and Leslie) are projected as values of another input that contains a frame with its projected roles (father, daughter). Slightly more dynamic are mirror networks, where both inputs share the same organizing frame: for instance, a graphic showing the times of all winners of the Big Sur marathon during the last ten years. While there may be clashes at levels more specific than the frame—weather conditions, date, opponents—the blend will resolve these clashes by linking and compressing them.

Single and double scope blends are increasingly complex. A single scope blend involves two input spaces with different organizing frames, where the inferential transfer is exclusively from one of the inputs to the blend. Blending theorists categorize these primary or conventional metaphors such as LIFE IS A JOURNEY as single scope blends.[16]

A metaphor, or single scope blend, involves a systematic pattern of mapping between the source domain, which provides language and images (the frame), and the target domain, which is the actual concept being considered. The relationships that hold in the source domain carry over into the blend produced; the language of the source becomes the language of the blend; the structure of the source becomes the structure of the blend. For instance, if the source domain is physical proximity and the target is emotional intimacy (EMOTIONAL INTIMACY IS PHYSICAL PROXIMITY), one speaks of an interpersonal relationship as close or distant. *We're tight like this* or *I'm sensing a great gulf between us* are conventional illustrations of how one speaks of the target in source domain language. This preservation of source relationships in the resulting blend also holds in more novel applications, and in more complex metaphors. The statement *You need warp drive to get next to her* would still be understood in terms of the source domain language of physical proximity.[17]

While the structure of the source is systematically highlighting features in the target, by definition other features will be suppressed. When reading the metaphorical statement *His job pushed them apart* (EMOTIONAL INTIMACY IS PHYSICAL PROXIMITY) readers know that two inanimate objects resting next to

---

[16] Fauconnier and Turner, *The Way We Think,* 126. See Joseph Grady, Todd Oakley, and Seana Coulson, "Blending and Metaphor," in Raymond Gibbs and Gerard Steen, eds., *Metaphor in Cognitive Linguistics: Selected Papers from the Fifth International Cognitive Linguistics Conference* (Amsterdam and Philadelphia: John Benjamins, 1999) 101–24, for a thorough examination of the relationship between metaphor theory and cognitive blending theory.

[17] George Lakoff has also argued that the preservation of source relationships has a corollary, in that the image-schema structure of a target domain must also maintain its integrity. Hence the mapping possibilities between source and target in metaphor are limited by the structure of both domains ("The contemporary theory of metaphor," in Ortony, ed., *Metaphor and Thought,* 215–16).

each other do not move unless some physical force is applied to one or both of them. But no physical force need be applied to decrease intimacy between two people. In this case knowledge of the target domain (emotional intimacy) is suppressed and overridden by the source domain structure (physical proximity).

Directionality is the observation that the relationship between source and target domains is not symmetrical. Inferences are transferred in one direction only, from the source to the target. In the previous example the language of physical proximity is used to describe emotional intimacy. But the language of emotional intimacy is not understood to describe physical proximity: *The lamp loves the door* does not mean that the lamp is physically close to the door.[18]

The fact that metaphors (and other cognitive blends) impose structure on our thinking and pick out salient features of a concept, allowing one to reason about the "target" in the language and concepts of the "source," does *not* imply that similarities are already present in our conceptual representations, and that the source domain merely allows one to pick them out.[19] Mapping takes place because the creative human mind can find some relationship, structure, or attribute shared by source or target, not because the salient characteristic of the target is actually similar to a perceived salient characteristic of the source.[20] Whether the composition works as a satisfying metaphor depends on the richness of the domains and the thinker's creativity, not on pre-existing similarity between the two domains. For instance, one can compress two people, as when one says, "She's a real Hitler." This metaphor may highlight the target's malignant behavior, but any actual identity between the individuals is purely fiction, the result of creative thinking.

At times a given metaphor will not exhibit the systematicity, suppression, or directionality outlined above, or two seemingly contradictory metaphors may be used side by side. These should be analyzed as a double rather than single scope blend.

Double scope blends, like single scope blends, involve inputs (e.g., context, conventional metaphor, etc.) with different organizing frames. The meanings from the inputs are projected into a separate mental space where they are blended together. Unlike metaphor, where the central inference comes from a

---

[18] Though there are some metaphors where the source and target are interchangeable (HUMANS ARE MACHINES, MACHINES ARE HUMAN), they represent two different metaphors, not a single metaphor that transfers inferences in both directions. Different inferences are mapped in the metaphorical concept HUMANS ARE MACHINES (e.g., *I pumped out six pages so far*) than in MACHINES ARE HUMANS (e.g., *That car is so fussy*). See Lakoff and Turner, *More Than Cool Reason*, 131–33.

[19] Turner, *Death is the Mother of Beauty*, 19.

[20] Perceived shared attribute differs from the idea of pre-existing similarity that motivates many literary theories of metaphor.

single domain (the source domain), in blends meaning is constructed from two or more input spaces. The resulting cognitive structure of the blend is not dictated by the source (as in metaphor), nor is it a consequence of the target, but rather the structure develops from the blended space, through elaboration, inference, and completion. The blend will have structure of its own, sometimes wildly original. *My ear is open like a greedy shark to catch the tunings of a voice divine* blends a ravenous shark with the ear's capacity for hearing: the open ear maps onto the shark's open jaws in a startling image.[21]

APPLICATION OF THE METHOD

A cognitive linguistic analysis of a text should identify the metaphors or blends that are central to its worldview. Blending theory provides the opportunity to examine such constructions in a systematic fashion.

Pseudo-Philo, like any other text, is replete with such primary metaphors as KNOWING IS SEEING and IMPURITY IS PHYSICAL CORRUPTION. Pseudo-Philo also abounds with culturally entrenched non-primary metaphors such as GOD IS FATHER and ISRAEL IS A COMPLEX INTERRELATED PHYSICAL OBJECT. While these metaphors for God and the divine-human relationship may not be physiologically instantiated as early in life as a primary metaphor, they are so culturally rooted that they function as if they were literal truth for the culture in question.[22]

Pseudo-Philo also uses metaphors for the God-human relationship that resemble the culturally entrenched biblical metaphors, but with small divergences. In this application three such metaphors will be analyzed individually and in concert, to explore the cognitive blends they create.

Jael's story opens when Sisera, fleeing from a losing battle against Israel, arrives at her tent. As in the biblical story, Jael invites Sisera in, extending refuge and food. Pseudo-Philo adds the offer of an escort home in the evening. When Sisera requests a drink, Jael instructs him to sleep while she milks her flock. His request serves as an excuse to leave the tent, and as she works, she prays to God to remember *(memor)* her. She then launches into a series of metaphors related to the culturally entrenched metaphor, ISRAEL IS GOD'S FLOCK *(Figure 1)*.

---

[21] My thanks to the incomparable Dorothy L. Sayers, who parades this outrageous construction by Keats in *Gaudy Night* (New York: Harper and Row, 1986) 284.

[22] This level of stability for a blend is not necessarily uncommon. One need only look at such concepts as names for distant relatives that require multiple blends; human language and culture have standardized these into handy cognitive packets, such as "my great-great-grandmother." These are remarkably stable cultural blends.

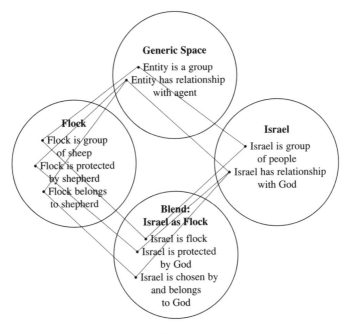

Figure 1

In this culturally licensed metaphor the relationship between God and the people Israel is given structure via the source domains of flock and attendant shepherd. A shepherd has the job of protecting the sheep in his flock; the sheep in turn belong to the shepherd. Israel is conceptualized through this metaphor as a group protected and claimed. In the traditional biblical metaphor the term "flock" designates Israel alone. No other nation or people is included in the term.

But the first of Jael's metaphors establishes a different blend, one where Israel is represented by a single animal from among the sheep rather than the whole flock.

Nonne	**elegisti**	**solum Israel**		**et**	**non**	**assimilasti**	**eum**
adv.	*choose–PF 2s*	*adj.*	*n.*	*conj.*	*neg.*	*liken–PF 2s*	*dem. adj.*
Did you not choose		alone Israel		and	did you not liken		him

animalibus	**nisi**	**velut arietem**	**precedentem**	**et**	**ducatorem gregis?**	
n.	*conj.*	*adv. n.*	*P PT*	*conj.*	*P PT*	*n.*
to no animal		except the ram	who goes before	and	leads the flock?	

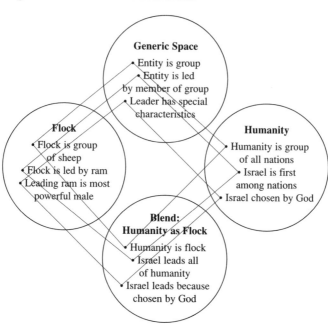

Figure 2

In Jael's opening metaphor the flock, *grex,* consists of all people rather than just Israel. While the initial evocation is of the traditional metaphor with all its attendant relationships, membership in the flock is quickly expanded. Viewed through the lens of this blend, Jael herself is a member of the "flock." All humanity should be following the lead of Israel, the chosen, the ram who leads and guides the other sheep *(Figure 2)*.

Jael's second metaphor again involves the use of "flock" as an input to the blend, but with a slightly different connotation *(Figure 3)*.

... **Sisara cogitavit**	**dicens:**	**Vadam**	**et**	**puniam**	**gregem Fortissimi**
n. *plan–PF 3s*	*PT*	*go–F 1s*	*conj.*	*punish–F 1s*	*d.o.* *adj.*
Sisera made a plan,	saying:	I will go	and	I will punish	the flock of the Most High.

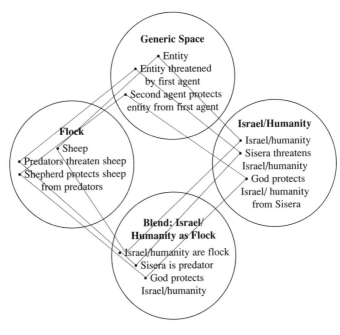

Figure 3

Flock, in this second metaphor, is used to refer to a group of people who belong to God. How do we understand this "flock," *grex,* placed immediately after the first metaphor that included the nations among the flock? The initial mention of flock in this sequence encompasses all humanity: should this second metaphor also evoke the nations, or just Israel as is customary in the existing culturally primary blend? Does one follow Jacobson when he says, *"LAB* appears to have unthinkingly reverted to the common metaphor of Israel as God's flock,"[23] or does the reader allow the possibility that Pseudo-Philo intended to carry the broader notion of flock-as-all-humanity from the immediately preceding metaphor? Could both meanings possibly be intended? Certainly one must argue that both meanings are cognitively active, because of the preceding metaphor.

One might argue that only Israel is threatened by Sisera. But earlier in the chapter Sisera plots secretly to carry Jael back to his home, which surely constitutes a threat to Jael.[24]

---

[23] Jacobson, *A Commentary on Pseudo-Philo's Liber Antiquitatum Biblicarum,* 852.
[24] See *LAB* 31:3.

Before attempting to answer these questions, let us examine the third and final flock metaphor of Jael's speech *(Figure 4)*.

Et	**ecce**	**ego**	**accipiam**	**de**	**lacte**	**pecorum**	**istorum,**
conj.	*imp.*	*p.p.*	*take–F 1s*	*prep.*	*n.*	*n.*	*dem.adj.*
And	behold,	I	will take	from the milk		of these sheep	

quibus	**assimilasti**	**populum**	**tuum . . .**
rel. p.	*liken–PF 2s*	*n.*	*p.p.*
which	you have likened	to your people . . .	

Again the text speaks of people and sheep. Now the emphasis is on the lactating ewes as this group of animals is compared to God's chosen ones. The reference to milking reminds the reader that females are not just productive members of the flock, but are productive specifically because they are female. The highlighting of these female reproductive qualities of the sheep echoes both the narrator's and Sisera's assessment of Jael's attributes earlier in the chapter.[25]

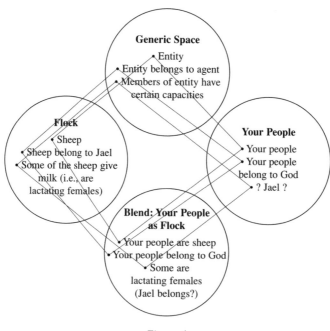

Figure 4

---

[25] Jael is very beautiful, *mulier autem erat bone speciei valde,* says the narrator in v. 3, and Sisera, observing her beauty and the roses she has scattered on her bed, tells himself that if he is saved Jael will be his wife.

For the third time one asks, are we to read this sheep metaphor as referring to Israel, which is its usual sense, or as carrying over the meaning of flock that was established at the beginning of the sequence? Is the evocation of female reproductive traits merely coincidence, or is it an attempt by the author to hint at Jael's inclusion within the protected sphere of God's people?

It is clear that one cannot read the three flock metaphors presented by Jael with identical understandings of "flock": in some instances the nations are included along with Israel in the flock, and sometimes Israel is represented by a (male) ram and at others by a (female) lactating ewe. One could assume, with Jacobson, that *"LAB'*s inconsistency is all too clear."[26] Or one could look at the way these three metaphors blend cognitively with the culturally entrenched metaphor of God and Israel to create Jael's multifaceted character.

CONCLUSION

I would argue that Pseudo-Philo has established, in these three metaphors, a complex conceptual blend, where the first metaphorical statement establishes a mental space that remains in cognitive interplay with the culturally traditional metaphor. Yes, Israel is conventionally the flock of God, and Sisera is clearly at war with the Hebrew people—no other participants are mentioned. However, the first metaphor has established a new understanding of "flock," one in which Jael is included, and that cognitive concept is still active as the next two blends are voiced. Those whom Sisera has threatened to destroy are the chosen of God, and Jael, using the first definition of a flock, is included among that number. Those whom God has selected, in the third blend, are (or include) lactating beasts, and Jael's reproductive capacity has already been noted. It is as if Jael slips in as a member of the flock "Israel" when she is really just a member of the flock "nations." A reader could almost choose to ignore the fact that she is not a Hebrew.

Further proof of Jael's inclusion, however tenuous, among those in relationship to God can be found later at 31:7. Here is another speech that projects ambiguity about God's chosen people.[27] Jael prays that God strengthen her arm—for God's sake, the sake of God's people, and for those who trust in God *(propter te et propter populum tuum et propter eos qui sperant in te)*. Here, as in the flock metaphors, one can see both distinction and inclusion between the chosen people Israel and others who might trust in God—namely, Jael herself. One would expect that the people of God, Israel, are those who trust in God.

---

[26] Jacobson, *A Commentary on Pseudo-Philo's Liber Antiquitatum Biblicarum*, 852.

[27] Commentators note that this speech begins with a quote from the book of Judith, but Pseudo-Philo's particular embellishments are the words under examination.

Or are there people who trust in God who are not among the chosen ones? Again, the language is ambiguous enough to include Jael with the insiders.[28]

In this study I have examined a series of metaphors within Pseudo-Philo's portrait of Jael in light of contemporary cognitive linguistics blending and metaphor theories. These metaphors establish three successive cognitive spaces; activated in quick succession, they highlight the possibility of Jael's inclusion among the chosen people. By "unpacking" these blends, examining the domains that contribute to them, and viewing the emergent structure resulting from the blends, I have shown that these metaphors need not be read as evidence of faulty translation or poor literary technique. Rather, they result from an attempt to come to grips with the historically positive interpretation of this foreign woman. Pseudo-Philo may want to portray all foreign women as negative, but Jael cannot be shoehorned into that category. So Pseudo-Philo rewrites her story and uses this series of seemingly contradictory metaphors to show both her difference and her inclusion. While Jael is not openly numbered among the chosen, the metaphors Pseudo-Philo places in her mouth indicate her desire to be closely aligned with God's elect and point to the ambiguous possibility that she is to be considered among God's chosen ones.

---

[28] And conversely, do some of the chosen not trust God? Here the stage is being set to show that Jael has more faith than some of the Israelites. Jael trusts *(spero)* in God: the people in ch. 33 trust in the fathers, which is decried as error.

Purity and Holiness of Women and Men in 1 Corinthians and the Consequences for Feminist Hermeneutics

Luise Schottroff

⤳

1. INTRODUCTION

First Corinthians begins with two weighty remarks about holiness. First, the people of the Corinthian community are sanctified by Jesus the Messiah. Second, they are holy because of God's calling (1:2). Holiness is fundamental to their belonging to God and to the body of Christ. According to Paul, to be holy means to be holy as part of the community. Holiness is not an individualistic concept, and it has no reference apart from life within a community. Another important point: holiness cannot be split into a cultic-magical aspect of life on the one hand and an ethical one on the other. Usually these two are seen in a dualistic way, in opposition to one another, but we should not separate what is meant to belong together, namely ethics and cultic experience. A third conceptual distinction is necessary: In the biblical tradition holiness is not identified with sexual purity, asceticism, or virginity—as even feminists have often supposed in discussions about 1 Corinthians in which the influence of traditional understandings of early Christianity has prevailed. On the contrary: In 1 Corinthians holiness includes all aspects of life—how to relate to people, what to eat, how to use possessions or cope with poverty. All aspects of life are part of one's relationship to God; that is what holiness is about. This understanding of holiness goes back to the First Testament. It takes shape through controversial discussions within the community. Paul's is just one voice in these discussions, neither a leading voice nor one vested with more authority than those of his so-called opponents.

From 1 Corinthians I am learning to look at holiness as a way of life that is helpful for us today when we hunger for God and justice. Concerning purity and impurity I am learning from the First Testament that we have to discern carefully between Jewish traditions and Christian assumptions about those traditions. The message that ritual impurity in Judaism means being dirty or polluted, and that this impurity separates people from God and other people is merely evidence of a Christian perspective, one that is wittingly or unwittingly anti-Jewish.

What separates people from God is sin, and sin includes what later Christian terminology calls "ritual" and "ethical" aspects. Sin—not ritual impurity, which is not considered sin[1]—endangers the holiness of Christ's body. So we have to be clear about Paul's terminology: Ritual purity/impurity in the sense of Leviticus 15 is not mentioned in 1 Corinthians. Holiness/purity and impurity/sin are understood as comprising "ritual" and "ethical" realities of life.

The work of Antoinette Clark Wire on 1 Corinthians provides my exegetical starting point. My work addresses and seeks to extend her insights. But before beginning the exegetical analysis I need to point out that two historical assumptions with which I begin are not part of scholarly consensus: First, I am assuming that 1 Corinthians is a Jewish document and, as such, a contribution to Jewish *halakhic* discussions, even though the role of 1 Corinthians in relation to these discussions is still debated.[2] Second, I assume that it is inappropriate to refer to Christians with a non-Jewish background in Paul's time as "law-free."[3] Law-free Christianity emerges only later, in the second century, when some Christians try to distance Christianity from Judaism in a hostile way. Therefore Paul is not the apostle of law-free Gentile Christianity; he is,

---

[1] Jonathan Klawans, *Impurity and Sin in Ancient Judaism* (Oxford: Oxford University Press, 2000), uses the terms "ritual impurity" and "moral impurity," but shows that these "terms do not appear in the texts and neither one is a category as such in biblical or post-biblical Jewish literature" (22). This book is very helpful for understanding sin as inclusive of so-called ritual and moral/ethical aspects and also for understanding ritual impurity according to Leviticus 15. In a Christian context I cannot use Klawans' terminology, because separating "moral" and "ritual" purity has a history of anti-Judaism and of confining sin to moral understanding in an individualistic sense. Michael Newton, *The Concept of Purity at Qumran and in the Letters of Paul* (Cambridge: Cambridge University Press, 1985) 92: "To point out the fact that the purity that Paul calls for stems from what the modern mind sees as moral questions (sexual immorality, greed, etc.) only clouds the issue. Such a division between the realm of the cult and that of morality was not apparent to the semitic mind."

[2] See n. 1 above, and especially Peter Tomson, *Paul and the Jewish Law. Halakha in the Letters of the Apostle to the Gentiles* (Assen/Maastricht: Van Gorcum; Minneapolis: Fortress, 1990).

[3] See Luise Schottroff, "Gesetzesfreies Heidenchristentum—und die Frauen?" in eadem and Marie-Theres Wacker, eds., *Von der Wurzel getragen. Christlich-feministische Exegese in Auseinandersetzung mit Antijudaismus* (Leiden: Brill, 1996) 227–45. English: "'Law-Free Gentile Christianity'—What About the Women?" forthcoming in Amy-Jill Levine, ed., *The Feminist Companion to the Authentic Paul* (Sheffield: Sheffield Academic Press).

rather, the apostle of Gentile Christianity devoted to the Torah of the Jewish people. When I refer to Paul's times and speak of "Christians," what I have in mind are Jewish proselytes or "God fearers" who understand themselves and are understood by Jews and Gentiles as part of the Jewish people. Moreover, at the time in question a Christian church did not yet exist.

2. FIRST CORINTHIANS 7:14: THE HOLINESS OF CHRISTIAN WOMEN'S CHILDREN BORN AS GENTILES

I have learned from Antoinette Wire that the rhetoric of equality in 1 Corinthians 7 addresses women first of all.[4] To be more precise, it addresses women who became Christians by devoting their lives to the Torah and Jesus as the Messiah of Israel. In 1 Corinthians we learn just how profound a change it was for these women to go from Roman-Hellenistic cults to the worship of Israel's God. Did they have to leave their homes, their partners, and even their children? These are the dramatic existential questions to which Paul tries to give an answer.

In 7:12-16 Paul attempts to convince the women to stay with their Gentile partners, though not at all costs (7:15). They should be free to leave marriage when they see no other way: for example, when the man does not want to continue the marriage. In 7:14, where Paul mentions children, the rhetoric of equality is misleading. According to patrilineal law the children of proselyte or "God-fearing" fathers would without question be Jews/Christians, but in regard to the children of proselyte or "God-fearing" mothers there were questions. Therefore we have to understand 7:14 as addressing the problem of the children of proselyte women. Do they remain Gentiles and, therefore, impure? Could living with them mean supporting Gentile sin, especially idolatry?[5] Paul

---

[4] Antoinette Clark Wire, *The Corinthian Women Prophets. A Reconstruction through Paul's Rhetoric* (Minneapolis: Fortress, 1990); see especially pp. 72–82. For 1 Cor 7:14, see p. 85: "The intensity of his argument from justice suggests that he is focused on women." See also eadem, "1 Corinthians," in Elisabeth Schüssler Fiorenza, ed., *Searching the Scriptures: A Feminist Commentary* (New York: Crossroad, 1992) 153–95, at 170: "Perhaps most of these single Christians were women, because Paul's reference to 'your children' suggests that mothers, whose children belonged by law to their fathers, had sought assurance about their children's status. There is also some external evidence that women were attracted to Christianity independently of their families . . . whereas male converts largely could expect their households to convert with them."

[5] The "impurity" of these children does not have a background in the ritual law of Leviticus 15 (see n. 1 above), but in the sins of Gentiles, especially idolatry, sexual sins, and bloodshed. What that meant for Jewish midwives and wet nurses is discussed in *m. ʿAbod. Zar.* II.1 and in the related Talmud texts. As midwives, Jewish women should not help Gentile babies to birth, and as wet nurses they should not feed them.

The statement about children in 1 Cor 7:14c is ordinarily seen, grammatically, as contrary to fact, even though that would be an unusual usage. As a result of this grammatical assumption the

declares these children holy. He decides that in this case they are holy just as the unbelieving partners of Christian women are. That does not mean that they are now believers (7:16), nor do they become Jewish. Their holiness means that Christian women will not become sinners by supporting Gentile sins, e.g., idolatry. Paul helps to free them from the fear that they are educating children for idolatry. The women are not forced to leave their children, because the impurity of their children is not what would separate them from the community of Christ and from the God of Israel. For us today it might be hard to understand that women would ever see a religious conversion as requiring them to leave their children, but we hear of it in the first century from other sources as well (Mark 10:28 *parr.;* Philo, *Spec. leg.* 1:52; Tacitus, *Hist.* 5.5).

There is another important aspect to Paul's decision: declaring the children of proselyte or God-fearing Jewish or Christian women to be holy can be seen as a first step toward matrilineal law in Judaism. Shaye Cohen has shown that matrilineal law in Judaism emerged during the second century C.E., at a time when non-Jewish women were converting to Judaism while their partners remained Gentiles.[6] It is the status of the mother and her devotion to Torah, not the status of the nonbelieving father, that defines the status of the children; that is, their status is determined in relation to the woman who is, from Paul's perspective, a Jewish person.

Traditional exegetes of 7:14 see holiness as a magical quality transferred by physical contact and are troubled—especially when the exegetes are Protestant—to discover that Paul, the Protestant hero, is thinking in that kind of magical way. I can console them on that point. The reason for the holiness of the children, as for the husbands, is that Rabbi Paul has decided that in this case there is no threat of impurity (that is, the sin of the Gentiles).

3. FIRST CORINTHIANS 7:34: THE HOLINESS OF THE BODIES AND LIVES OF WOMEN

In 7:34 we learn from Paul that there are women whose bodies and spirits are holy. They are not married, or not yet married; *parthenoi* here means

---

sentence is interpreted as stating an absurd consequence that no one would assume. Hence the sentence appears only as an argument supporting the thesis that the unbelieving partner is sanctified by the believing spouse. But the indicative should be taken seriously, and 1 Cor 7:14c should be translated: "Since your children are unclean, but now they are holy."

[6] Shaye J. D. Cohen, "The Origin of the Matrilineal Principle in Rabbinic Law," *Judaism* 34 (1985) 5–13; he understands 1 Cor 7:14c as showing that there was not *yet* a matrilineal principle, but he takes Paul's rhetoric as speaking equally of women and men. That this rhetoric points, instead, to women has been convincingly shown by Anne Wire (see n. 4 above).

young women before marriage (Hebrew *betulah*), especially Christian girls who are betrothed and have an agreement with their fiancés not to marry (7:25-38). It seems that more women than men are choosing not to marry. What is the problem with marriage? Why are these women holy because they are not married? Married people can also live in holiness, but their way is more diffi-cult. The danger to holiness does not stem from sexuality. Sexual activity in a legal marriage is not sin and does not destroy holiness according to Jewish tra-dition. From Paul we learn this indirectly in 1 Cor 6:12-20 (sexual relations of married men with prostitutes destroy the relation of the men's body with Christ, and we can conclude that sexual relations with their wives would not), and directly from 1 Cor 7:1-7. When sexual activity is between married people it does not destroy holiness—so what is the problem?

Married people (though the passage is primarily addressed to men) are in-structed in 7:29-34 how to preserve holiness. Paul teaches them to live *hōs mē*—as if not married. Then he adds that they may weep, rejoice, buy and pos-sess, and use the world in this same way, "as if not." I find this list of the pa-triarch's activities in a patriarchal household to be similar to the lists of activities in Matt 24:37-39; Luke 17:26-30; 14:18-21. Parts of these lists go back to *Q*—a hypothetical source used by Matthew and Luke—and probably existed already in Paul's time. The patriarchal activities include marrying and giving in marriage, eating and drinking. Luke adds buying, selling, planting, building houses (Luke 17:28), buying fields, buying oxen, and, once again, marrying (Luke 14:19). These lists show that patriarchal marriage was re-garded from an economic rather than a sexual perspective. The economy binds people into a structure that Paul and many others of his time call the *kos-mos*/world. This structure destroys the bond and commitment to God. Behind the exhortation to live "as if not," *hōs mē,* are life experiences of being de-stroyed by the dynamics of violence in which people are entangled by the pa-triarchal household and the economy of the time. Even laughter and tears are parts of a structure denying and destroying the life of the people of God (cf. Luke 6:21). But be not afraid, Paul says; God is very near to us. We live in the hour of God's coming (1 Cor 7:29; cf. Mark 13:20; 14:1). We can reach out to God. God is near and helps us not to drown in the structures that kill body and soul, destroying what binds them to God, the source of life.

The problem with marriage for these women we encounter in 7:34 is not sexuality. The structures of this world, to which patriarchal marriage is bind-ing them, are the reason for them not to marry, or to leave their marriages. We see that in its literary and rhetorical context 1 Cor 7:34 presupposes that both sexes can find ways of coping with the structures of the world, but that men are more interested in patriarchal marriage than women, and therefore the principle of "as if not" is more important for them to live by. Christian communities were of enormous relevance particularly for women, because they were the alternative to the patriarchal household. For women the communities offered independence from "the structures of the world," from which they suffered more than men.

Now I need to ask what happens to holy women during the time of menstruation. In the rule enunciated in Leviticus 15 they are impure for at least seven days a month. To me, 1 Corinthians 7 implies that this impurity does not change the holiness of their bodies. If women had to leave the holy community during menstruation, Paul would have had to mention it. This means that the laws for ritual impurity and purity in the sense of Leviticus 15 are observed, but impurity in this sense does not affect the relationship to God and to the holy community.[7] This fits the picture feminist scholars have developed of the impurity laws in Leviticus 15 and the bleeding woman in Mark 5:25-34.[8] This woman, or any woman, could be part of the holy community and the people of God even without being healed.

The Christian perspective on Jewish purity rules according to Leviticus 15 needs to be looked at very critically. The idea that this ritual impurity destroys social relations and the relationship to God is derived only from a Christian perspective. We have to distinguish between the ability to take part in cultic actions in the Temple and the relationship to God and God's people. In everyday life the right to approach holy ground is not an issue, and menstruation requires abstaining from intercourse, nothing else.

Mary Douglas's famous and influential 1966 book, *Purity and Danger,*[9] exemplifies a perspective informed by Christian assumptions about Jewish purity laws: that women's impurity helps to oppress women.[10] Impurity means dirt, and dirt disturbs the order of society; impurity is transferred by touching another person. Douglas does not discuss her presuppositions; hence I do not critique the many details in her book, but the basis of her assumptions, which

[7] The fact that Paul does not discuss ritual purity in the sense of Leviticus 15 could raise the question whether he thinks this part of the Law is irrelevant for Gentiles who are baptized in the name of Christ. But in light of the ongoing *halakhic* discussion with regard to Gentile Christians in Paul this proposal is not convincing.

[8] See the articles by Gerburgis Feld, Ina Johanne Batmartha (Petermann), and Brigitte Kahl in Luise Schottroff and Marie-Theres Wacker, eds., *Von der Wurzel getragen* (n. 3 above).

[9] Mary Douglas, *Purity and Danger: An Analysis of Concepts of Pollution and Taboo* (New York: Praeger, 1966). The influence of this book cannot be overestimated. That influence continues, even though Mary Douglas revised some of her assumptions, especially those about menstruation in Leviticus 15. See Mary Douglas, *Leviticus as Literature* (Oxford: Oxford University Press, 1999) 178–79.

[10] *Purity and Danger,* 147.

she takes to be self-evident. We Christians have to learn that ritual impurity in Jewish tradition (related to Leviticus 15) does not mean dirt, and impurity laws as such do not add anything to women's oppression. The humiliation of the second sex is not brought about through menstruation, giving birth, or women's bodies. These ideas were imported at a later time and as a result of later developments, especially in Christianity.

A new reading of 1 Cor 7:34 can aid our critique of Douglas's fundamental principles. If she is right, menstruation would destroy the holiness of women. But it is obvious that menstruation is not a factor for the holiness of women's bodies, according to Paul. They are holy by God's calling, even when they are bleeding.

In 1 Cor 7:34 the holy bodies and spirits of women exemplify life lived according to God's will in the midst of a society that coerces people to desire possessions, amid the cares of the world and the impurity brought about by Gentile practices such as idolatry. Holiness should not be narrowed to sexual asceticism. The word holiness describes a way of life without lust for wealth and the concomitant desire for a neighbor's death; holiness, rather, is life according to God's will, the Torah. From 1 Corinthians we learn that Christian women in Corinth aspired to a radical and consistent practice of this way of life. It was not the way of "as if not," because they left marriages, patriarchal households, and their structures. Nevertheless, the intention of their way of life was not perfection but the struggle for life, the life of God's creation.

4. FIRST CORINTHIANS 11:29: ENDANGERING HOLINESS

To be holy means to be part of a holy community, the body of Christ. Holiness is not possible for the lone individual. But the holiness of Christ's body is endangered by individuals or groups not living according to the Torah (e.g., 1 Cor 5:11, 13, the man living with the wife of his father, contrary to Lev 18:18). In 1 Cor 11:17-34 Paul wants to influence a group within the Corinthian community that, according to Paul, is endangering the holiness of the body of Christ and all the bodies belonging to the community.[11] This is not only Paul's conviction, but that of other groups within the community, especially the poor people who form the majority. They feel humiliated by the behavior of the rich during the Eucharist, a common meal. The rich do not want to share the food they bring or partake of the meager food the poor have brought to the community meal. The rich say: our food is our private property. Paul and other groups

---

[11] The following assessment of 1 Cor 11:17-34 presupposes an analysis I published in 2000, "Holiness and Justice: Exegetical Comments on 1 Cor 11:17-34," *JSNT* 79 (2000) 51–60.

say: then please eat your private property at home. The food we share is the property of God. It becomes such when the first prayer is spoken during Eucharist. This means that the rich do not discern (11:29) what is holy and what is not holy (profane). To put it another way: The opposite of private is "holy" (not "public," as some interpreters say). The behavior of the rich in Corinth can be compared with the transgression of Ananias and Sapphira (Acts 5:1-11). They transgress the Torah because they do not share their bread with the poor. There is no need for Paul to quote explicitly from Isa 58:7. The consequence of the injury thus done to the body of Christ is that some members are sick and others have died (11:30). These sick and dead people need not themselves be offenders against the body of Christ. They may well be innocent persons.

For those of us who live with the traditions of the Enlightenment this concept of holiness is hard to understand. It seems like comparing apples and oranges—mixing what we would call ethics with what is cultic and material. Perhaps we can relate to this seemingly foreign concept by remembering encounters with the structures of our own days, times when we have fought for a world that can give life to the next generations. It takes only one thoughtless action to destroy air and water, but the struggle to preserve life and justice is long and complicated. Perhaps reflecting on experiences in this context may enable us to understand why the holiness of the community is vulnerable, and why innocent persons die when justice is not done.

As feminist discussions have shown, and shown extensively, the horizon of Paul's speech about gender differences and women is quite narrow. I need to mention here a new aspect of his anti-women assumptions. For him 1 Cor 11:29 is a complete parallel to 11:10, because he lines up the behavior of women refusing symbolic subordination to men with the behavior of the rich during Eucharist. He wants women to cover their heads "because of the angels." I really do not know the meaning of these words. I am not convinced that what Paul has in mind is the sexual desire of the angels. Perhaps he presupposes that the holiness of the angels requires women's subordination: otherwise their holiness and that of the communities could be endangered. The time of prayer, of prophecy, and of Eucharist is both a time for celebrating holiness and a time of vulnerability and danger. Holiness can be injured, and people can be damaged.

I am happy to read that Paul feels insecure because not all people in the community share his opinions about women's subordination (11:16). Nevertheless, I am impressed by the consequences the Corinthian people *and* Paul drew from the Torah for the Eucharist and for the holiness of Christ's body. Here again, we encounter Paul's ambiguity.

5. HOLINESS AND RESURRECTION AS THE WAY TO GOD

Christians of Western culture are used to reading resurrection traditions in a dualistic way: first, here in this world I live as a physical body, *sōma psychikon* (15:44), but after death and God's judgment I will live as a spiritual body, *sōma pneumatikon*. This dualism makes all of us forget that according to Christian belief the turning point in life is not our individual death but the transformation of our life by God.[12] Only in this context can we understand why Paul names holiness in terms of our physical bodies, in this life: temples of the Holy Spirit (6:19), holy in body and spirit, members of Christ's body, transformed as if resurrected (Rom 6:13). This means that the hope to become a spiritual body is not focused on the time after death, but on the time or experience when we fulfill God's will without being destroyed by the structures of this world, the *kosmos*. Paul and many other Jews and Christians of his time did not fear physical death; they feared the death caused by the worldwide power of sin. They were convinced that God did send the Messiah, Jesus, to set people free from the structures of the *kosmos* and from all that causes us to be dead before God. They were certain that Christ freed them to fulfill the Torah. We ought not to read traditions about holiness and resurrection with a hermeneutic of dualism; we should, rather, read them with a hermeneutic of experience: the experience of death and of freedom, of the destruction of bodies and the resurrection of the body. We experience already what we are yearning for. But all these experiences are not the culmination of the process of holiness or a fixed stage on a scale; they are the beginning. In Paul's letters this beginning has a name: now, *nyni*.

I find two rabbinic parables describing this process of holiness and resurrection. The first is this: our lives depend on God's commandments and our fulfilling them. One should be cautious in handling the lists of God's commandments, because our lives depend on them. The parable: A person falls into deep water. The helmsman gives that person a rope and says: hold on to this rope with both hands and don't let go. If you let go, you will lose your life. And so God spoke to the people: hang on to the rope of my commandments; don't let go of them (*Midrash Tanḥ. B, ad Num.* 15:39, 215b.32; *Num. R.* 17.182b).[13]

---

[12] For a feminist understanding of resurrection see especially Claudia Janssen, "Bodily Resurrection (1 Cor 15). The Discussion about Resurrection in Karl Barth, Rudolf Bultmann, Dorothee Sölle and Contemporary Feminist Theology," *JSNT* 79 (2000) 61–78; Luzia Sutter Rehmann, Sabine Bieberstein, and Ulrike Metternich, *Sich dem Leben in die Arme Werfen. Auferstehungserfahrungen* (Gütersloh: Kaiser/Gütersloher Verlagshaus, 2002).

[13] See Hermann L. Strack and Paul Billerbeck, *Kommentar zum Neuen Testament aus Talmud und Midrasch.* 6 vols. in 7 (Munich: Beck, 1922–61) 4:289.

The second parable is this: Rabbi Abun said: A king had a wine-cellar. He had men sit in the cellar to watch the wine. One group was Nazorean; the other group were drunkards. At the end of the long day the king paid the guards and gave double to the drunkards. The Nazoreans protested: why do you give them twice what you gave us? The king answered: they're drunkards and used to drinking wine. They had to struggle hard to watch the wine, while you Nazoreans had no struggle with the evil desire. This is why God used the word holy only once when addressing the angels, but used it twice when speaking to the people: you shall be holy because I am holy (Lev 19:2; *Lev. Rabb.* 24.123ᵃ).[14]

Holiness depends on living according to God's will. The picture of the drunkards in the wine cellar fits the image Paul paints of men living "as if not," *hōs mē*. They have the bottles of wine within their reach. The picture of the person clutching the rope over deep water may be an image for women holy in body and spirit. The structures of the world are menacing as deep water, because women were more exposed to violence against body and soul. Therefore they were happy to hold the rope in their hands and experience what resurrection means: to be holy, to become *sōma pneumatikon*.

CONCLUSION

In the Corinthian community holiness is a concept for life in all its aspects—and for both women and men. To live in holiness means to leave behind the structures of violence and death, the world, the *kosmos* with its idolatry.[15] People discuss whether the rich should give up private property. Giving up marriage as a consequence of holiness plays a dominant role, not for sexual reasons but because marriage is the foundation of the patriarchal system of economy and orientation toward property and inheritance.

Women embraced this concept more actively than men. They were willing to leave their nonbelieving husbands and even their impure children. Obviously more women than men lived free from marriage, holy in body and spirit. Women expressed their bonds to Christ and God by praying and prophesying openly in the communities' worship services. Paul, and perhaps some other men, tried to hinder those women, arguing that their symbolic equality to men contradicted their subordination ordained by God and nature.

[14] Ibid. 4:492.

[15] The word "idolatry" as used in the ancient sources refers to other religions from a Jewish perspective. Today it could be understood as discriminating against other religions. But we should take into account that this Jewish perspective on other religions included the critique of life *praxis* in the sense I have tried to describe.

Holiness is a concept for life, hotly debated, and employed aggressively especially by women. Leviticus 19:2 is not quoted here, but the notion of holiness in Scripture is, of course, the basis of the early Christian concept.

In identifying consequences for feminist hermeneutics I find inspiration in 1 Corinthians as a text stemming from women and men and one secretary: Paul. I am impressed by the ability of the Corinthians, mainly the women, to bring together questions of holiness and justice, thereby shaping and transforming their lives. We need to abandon Christian dualism between spirituality and justice, between holiness and everyday life, and discover ways to be holy. What does Lev 19:2 mean for us today? The answer to that question cannot be given by one person. To experience holiness means to experience the nearness of God, the transformation of life. This is "the beauty of holiness," which for me, as a Prussian Protestant, echoes most fully in memories of music.

Placing the Text in Context

Accusing Whom of What?
Hosea's Rhetoric of Promiscuity

Marvin L. Chaney

❧

INTRODUCTION

Reading the text of Hosea is a bit like looking into a kaleidoscope. One image tumbles into the next, often with little or no boundary or transition. Trope is layered upon trope, leaving to the reader's discernment the many complexities of preunderstanding and interdependence. Such material demands of its interpreter both a sharp eye and a light hand—not to mention a healthy dose of humility. Failure to focus sharply enough the myriad analogues of Hosea's metaphors and similes will rob them of both analytical and evocative power. Too literal or heavy-handed a treatment risks killing the rich symbols outright.

Social scientific tools can render an important service in effecting the desired balance, because the vast majority of Hosea's metaphors and similes involve social institutions. The clearer our understanding of the institutional structures and dynamics to which allusion is made in the text, the sharper the focus of our reading and the defter our discernment of the polyvalent and interactive tropes. The text of Hosea, however, most often excoriates by metaphoric allusion rather than by direct description. In the interpretation of such a text, overarching presuppositions about the social world addressed tend to be controlling. Commentators find in the complexities and difficulties of this most complex and difficult text what their presuppositions lead them to expect.

For many decades the primary *Gestalt* presupposed was some version of a "Canaanite fertility cult" in which "sacred" or "cultic" prostitution figured prominently.[1] More generally, interpreters understood Hosea to be exercised

---

[1] William F. Albright, *Archaeology and the Religion of Israel* (4th ed. Baltimore: Johns Hopkins University Press, 1956) 68–94; Francis I. Andersen and David Noel Freedman, *Hosea*. AB 24 (Garden City, N.Y.: Doubleday, 1980); Helgard Balz-Cochois, *Gomer: Der Höhenkult Israels im*

about the adulteration of Israelite "religion" through the "syncretistic" influences of "debased, Canaanite" beliefs and practices. This focus upon "religious" institutions and dynamics in Hosea was further shaped by a frequent heuristic contrast between Hosea and Amos. As recently as late 2002 this definition-by-contrast finds reiteration by David L. Petersen in what promises to be a widely used introduction to the prophetic literature.

> . . . Amos and Hosea try to explain to those in Israel why they are to suffer such a dire fate. Interestingly, the reasons they offer are diverse. Amos inveighs against social and economic practices in the northern kingdom, whereas Hosea focuses on religious and political misdeeds.[2]

Read through this lens, Hosea's metaphors and similes—many of which are less than self-evident—are unlikely to be understood as involving "social and economic practices." Moreover, this perspective tacitly separates "economic" and "political" institutions and dynamics into different realms.

Recent scholarship has subjected the aptness of this *Gestalt* for interpreting Hosea and the accuracy of its several presuppositions to increasingly sharp criticism. I find that critique compelling and wish to build upon its alternative presuppositions. Space precludes all but the briefest review here. Readers unfamiliar with the growing discussion may consult the details of the literature cited in the following summary.

CRITIQUE OF A *GESTALT* OF "CULTIC PROSTITUTION"

1. There is little or no unambiguous evidence for "sacred" or "cultic" prostitution in biblical Israel. While long a fixture of Hosea studies, notions of "sacred prostitution" in biblical Israel and its *Umwelt* today appear to be largely a figment of scholars' imaginations, nourished by brief but sensationalist accounts in Herodotus. Later accounts in Greek and Latin authors frequently cited in this regard now appear to be derived from Herodotus, whose narrative of Babylonian practices has long been viewed with skepticism by scholars spe-

---

Selbstverständnis der Volksfrömmigkeit. Untersuchungen zu Hosea 4,1-5, 7. Europäische Hochschulschriften XXIII/191 (Frankfurt and Bern: Peter Lang, 1982); Graham I. Davies, *Hosea.* Old Testament Guides (Sheffield: Sheffield Academic Press, 1993) 38–51; Philip J. King, *Amos, Hosea, Micah—An Archaeological Commentary* (Philadelphia: Westminster, 1988) 97–101; James Luther Mays, *Hosea: A Commentary.* Old Testament Library (Philadelphia: Westminster, 1969) 25–26; Hans Walter Wolff, *Hosea.* Hermeneia. Translated by Gary Stansell (Philadelphia: Fortress, 1974) 14.

[2] David L. Petersen, *The Prophetic Literature: An Introduction* (Louisville: Westminster John Knox, 2002) 10.

cializing in the study of his writings. In their stricter definition so-called "sacred marriage" texts from Mesopotamia come only from the limited periods of Ur III and Isin. Upon closer examination they are viewed by many cuneiformists as concerned to present the king as a son of the gods and hence divine. Cultic prostitution is nowhere in view in these texts. In short, "sacred prostitution" is not at all the constant it was once presented as being in the Ancient Near East.[3]

2. Phyllis Bird has argued persuasively that Hosea's identification of Israelite cults with prostitution was polemical, symbolic, and innovative.[4] In linking prostitution with the cultus Hosea more likely presents us with an interpretive *novum* than with an allusion to a ubiquitous cultural artifact. The Deuteronomistic historian, Jeremiah, and Ezekiel probably amplify what Hosea began. They should be read in light of Hosea's innovation rather than Hosea's being read in light of their "evidence." Conversely, virtually all agrarian religion— including ancient Yahwism—is much concerned with the fertility of fields, flocks, herds, and the human community. Were it not, it would be truly irrelevant to the agrarian context.

3. Hosea 4:11-14, long considered bedrock for the "cultic prostitution" model because of its mention of *qᵉdēšôt,* has been demonstrated instead to be a parade example of Hosea's polemical and innovative "intercourse" between

---

[3] Elaine June Adler, *The Background for the Metaphor of Covenant as Marriage in the Hebrew Bible,* Ph.D. diss., University of California at Berkeley, 1989; Phyllis Bird, "'To Play the Harlot': An Inquiry into an Old Testament Metaphor," in Peggy L. Day, ed., *Gender and Difference in Ancient Israel* (Minneapolis: Fortress, 1989) 75–94; Phyllis Bird, "The End of the Male Cult Prostitute: A Literary-Historical and Sociological Analysis of Hebrew *qadeš-qedešim,*" in *Congress Volume: Cambridge, 1995,* VTSup 66 (Leiden: Brill, 1997) 37–80; Christina Bucher, *The Origin and Meaning of ZNH Terminology in the Book of Hosea,* Ph.D. diss., Claremont Graduate School, 1988; Jerrold S. Cooper, "Heilige Hochzeit, B. Archäologisch," *Reallexikon der Assyriologie* V.4 (Berlin: de Gruyter, 1975) 259–69; Eugene J. Fisher, "Cultic Prostitution in the Ancient Near East? A Reassessment," *BTB* 6 (1976) 225–36; Mayer I. Gruber, "Hebrew *qᵉdēšāh* and her Canaanite and Akkadian Cognates," *Ugarit-Forschungen* 18 (1986) 133–48; Stephen Hooks, *Sacred Prostitution in Israel and the Ancient Near East,* Ph.D. diss., Hebrew Union College, 1985; Alice A. Keefe, "The Female Body, the Body Politic and the Land: A Sociopolitical Reading of Hosea 1–2," in Athalya Brenner, ed., *Feminist Companion to the Latter Prophets.* FemCB 8 (Sheffield: Sheffield Academic Press, 1995) 70–100; eadem, *Women's Body and the Social Body in Hosea.* Gender, Culture, Theory 10. JSOTSup 338 (London: Sheffield Academic Press, 2001); Robert Oden, *The Bible without Theology: The Theological Tradition and Alternatives to It* (San Francisco: Harper & Row, 1981); Johannes M. Renger, "Heilige Hochzeit, A. Philologisch," *Reallexikon der Assyriologie* V.4 (Berlin: de Gruyter, 1975) 350–59; Joan Godnick Westenholz, "Tamar, *Qᵉdēšā, Qadištu,* and Sacred Prostitution in Mesopotamia," *HTR* 82 (1989) 245–65.

[4] Bird, "'To Play the Harlot.'"

prostitution and cult. A *qᵉdēšāh* was a "hierodule" or "female cult functionary," not a "cult prostitute."[5]

4. The "cultic prostitution" paradigm has made far too facile and simplistic an equation of female cultic personages, female deities, and sacralized sexuality in Canaanite religion in specific and Ancient Near Eastern religion in general.[6] The data base, epigraphic and anepigraphic, and more recent research into dimensions of gender in Ancient Near Eastern religion do not support this generalizing conflation.

5. The "religious syncretism" believed by the older *Gestalt* to be rampant in eighth-century Israel finds scant support in the extra-biblical, epigraphic record, as the studies of Jeffrey H. Tigay and Jeaneane D. Fowler have made clear.[7] The notable absence of anthropomorphic idols from the archaeological excavations of Israelite shrines of the period seems to point in the same direction.[8]

6. The separation of ancient Israel into religious, social, economic, and political dimensions more or less discrete from one another flies in the face of everything known by sociology and anthropology about agrarian societies as a generic type on the basis of comparative study. Even to speak of their "integration" may be a dangerous anachronism. The far more probable assumption is that they were quite incompletely differentiated in Hosea's Israel. If, as seems patent, all three of Hosea's prophetic contemporaries decry what they regard as abuses in the political economy, should not the default position be to ask if Hosea in any way reflects the same conditions and how his critique of Israel's "religion" is related thereto?

7. Critics of the older set of assumptions in Hosea studies have offered a compelling sociology-of-knowledge analysis of how the model arose, why it persisted for so long unchallenged, and why challenges have now surfaced when and how they have.[9]

---

[5] Phyllis Bird, *Missing Persons and Mistaken Identities: Women and Gender in Ancient Israel.* Overtures to Biblical Theology (Minneapolis: Fortress, 1997) 229–36; Gruber, "Hebrew *qᵉdēšāh* and her Canaanite and Akkadian Cognates;" Keefe, *Woman's Body and the Social Body in Hosea,* 54–55, 100–01; Ziony Zevit, *The Religions of Ancient Israel: A Synthesis of Parallactic Approaches* (New York: Continuum, 2001) 462–63 and nn. 52 and 53.

[6] Keefe, *Woman's Body and the Social Body in Hosea,* 60–61.

[7] Jeffrey H. Tigay, *You Shall Have No Other Gods: Israelite Religion in the Light of Hebrew Inscriptions.* HSS 31 (Atlanta: Scholars, 1986); Jeaneane D. Fowler, *Theophoric Personal Names in Ancient Hebrew: A Comparative Study,* JSOTSup 49 (Sheffield: JSOT Press, 1988).

[8] Keefe, *Woman's Body and the Social Body in Hosea,* 121.

[9] Ibid. 62–65, 140–89; Yvonne Sherwood, *The Prostitute and the Prophet: Hosea's Marriage in Literary-Historical Perspective.* Gender, Culture, Theory 2. JSOTSup 212 (Sheffield: Sheffield Academic Press, 1996).

Even this all-too-brief summary suggests why the once-dominant *Gestalt* of "cultic prostitution" and its concomitants can no longer be regarded as probable, though it continues to have distinguished proponents and is likely to endure in certain quarters for some time into the future. But destruction by critique is proverbially easier than the construction of a new interpretive paradigm. That is particularly true in a field like Hosea studies, where so many issues are interdependent, and changing assumptions about one element changes what it is possible to assume about others. My tentative proposal of an alternative interpretive paradigm is therefore, of necessity, multifaceted, though in essence relatively simple.

AN ALTERNATIVE HYPOTHESIS

Building on the work of Phyllis Bird and Alice Keefe, though differing from both in ways I shall try to specify, I propose that "promiscuity" in the book of Hosea is primarily a figure for dynamics in the political economy of Israel, most particularly for the dynamics of agricultural intensification.[10] To the extent that "religious" institutions and practices come within the purview of that figure they involve the sacral legitimation of agricultural intensification, its architects and short-term beneficiaries.

Viewed through this lens, Hosea's "wife of promiscuity" becomes a sarcastic trope for the male urban warrior elite of Israel and for the land whose agricultural priorities and techniques they increasingly dictated. The bastard children, whose illegitimacy is a function of the "promiscuity" of this "mother," are primarily a metaphor for the Israelite lower classes. Just as illegitimate children in agrarian, patriarchal societies share their mother's ill-treatment while being innocent of her guilt, so these Israelite peasants suffer innocently from the various results and punishments occasioned by the elite's "promiscuous" pursuit of agricultural intensification.

Presuppositions of the Alternative Paradigm

The reasoning that supports this thesis presupposes several vectors in previous scholarship. While each is the subject of ongoing research, strictures of space prohibit all but a brief epitome here. Please note, however, that they are systemically interdependent. If one changes the pre-understanding of any one of them, what is possible or impossible for several of the others tends to shift accordingly.

---

[10] Bird, "'To Play the Harlot'"; eadem, *Missing Persons and Mistaken Identities;* Keefe, "The Female Body, the Body Politic and the Land"; eadem, *Woman's Body and the Social Body in Hosea.*

1. I have argued elsewhere[11] in concert with many others[12] that agricultural intensification and its concomitants were stark facts in eighth-century Israel and Judah, and are clearly reflected and reflected upon in the books of Amos, Isaiah, and Micah. As a policy, agricultural intensification was initiated and engineered by the urban-based ruling elite of both nations in close coordination with one another. While it greatly enhanced the wealth and power of the pinnacle of the social pyramid in the short term, it impoverished the burgeoning peasant masses and destroyed both the web of their social relations and their risk-spreading, subsistence agriculture. Nor was it sustainable in the longer term.

[11] Marvin L. Chaney, "Systemic Study of the Israelite Monarchy," *Semeia* 37 (1986) 53–76; "Bitter Bounty: The Dynamics of Political Economy Critiqued by the Eighth-Century Prophets," in Robert L. Stivers, ed., *Reformed Faith and Economics* (Lanham, Md.: University Press of America, 1989) 15–30; "Bitter Bounty: The Dynamics of Political Economy Critiqued by the Eighth-Century Prophets," in Norman K. Gottwald and Richard A. Horsley, eds., *The Bible and Liberation: Political and Social Hermeneutics* (Maryknoll, N.Y.: Orbis, 1993) 250–63—a slightly revised republication of the 1989 paper; "Whose Sour Grapes? The Addressees of Isaiah 5:1-7 in the Light of Political Economy," *Semeia* 87 (1999) 105–22.

[12] Robert B. Coote and Mary P. Coote, *Power, Politics, and the Making of the Bible: An Introduction* (Minneapolis: Fortress, 1989) 45–51; John Andrew Dearman, *Property Rights in the Eighth-Century Prophets: The Conflict and Its Background.* SBLDS 106 (Atlanta: Scholars, 1987); Moshe Elat, "Trade and Commerce," in Abraham Malamat, ed., *The Age of the Monarchies: Culture and Society,* vol. 4.2 of Benjamin Mazar, ed., *The World History of the Jewish People* (Jerusalem: Massada, 1979) 173–86; Shulamit Geva, "Archaeological Evidence for the Trade between Israel and Tyre," *BASOR* 248 (1982) 69–71; Norman K. Gottwald, *The Politics of Ancient Israel.* Library of Ancient Israel (Louisville: Westminster John Knox, 2001); Larry G. Herr, "The Iron Age II Period: Emerging Nations," *BA* 60 (1997) 114–83; John S. Holladay, Jr., "The Kingdoms of Israel and Judah: Political and Economic Centralization in Iron IIA-B (ca. 1000–750)," in Thomas E. Levy, ed., *The Archaeology of Society in the Holy Land* (New York: Facts on File, 1995) 368–98; David C. Hopkins, "The Dynamics of Agriculture in Monarchical Israel," *SBLSP* 22, ed. Kent Harold Richards (Chico: Scholars, 1983) 77–202; idem, "Bare Bones: Putting Flesh on the Economics of Ancient Israel," in Volkmar Fritz and Philip R. Davies, eds., *The Origins of the Ancient Israelite States,* JSOTSup 228 (Sheffield: Sheffield Academic Press, 1996) 121–39; Bernhard Lang, "The Social Organization of Peasant Poverty in Biblical Israel," in *Monotheism and the Prophetic Minority: An Essay in Biblical History and Sociology.* SWBA 1 (Sheffield: Almond, 1983) 114–27; Devadasan N. Premnath, *The Process of Latifundialization Mirrored in the Oracles Pertaining to Eighth Century B.C.E. in the Books of Amos, Hosea, Isaiah and Micah,* Ph.D. diss., The Graduate Theological Union, 1984; idem, "Latifundialization and Isaiah 5.8-10," *JSOT* 40 (1988) 49–60; idem, *Eighth Century Prophets: A Social Analysis* (St. Louis: Chalice, 2003); Lawrence E. Stager, "The Finest Oil in Samaria," *JSS* 28 (1983) 241–45; idem, "The Archaeology of the Family in Ancient Israel," *BASOR* 260 (1986) 1–35; cf. Shunya Bender, *Social Structure of Ancient Israel.* Jerusalem Biblical Studies 7 (Jerusalem: Simor Ltd., 1997); Paula McNutt, *Reconstructing the Society of Ancient Israel.* Library of Ancient Israel (Louisville: Westminster John Knox, 1999) 148–81; J. David Schloen, *The House of the Father as Fact and Symbol: Patrimonialism in Ugarit and the Ancient Near East.* Studies in the Archaeology and History of the Levant 2 (Winona Lake: Eisenbrauns, 2001).

Eighth-century Israel and Judah saw an increase in international trade, in which their leaders imported luxury goods, military *matériel,* and the where-withal of monumental architecture. To pay for these imports, foodstuffs—particularly the triad of wheat, olive oil, and wine—were exported. Imports benefited mostly an elite minority, while exports necessary to procure them cut deeply into the sustenance of the peasant majority. Urban elites, whose priorities called for the maximally efficient production of the three preferred export commodities over the short term, pressed for a regional specialization of agriculture. Villagers' traditional priorities for the long-term sufficiency of mixed, subsistence agriculture and its penchant for risk spreading were overwhelmed by these pressures, and land consolidation proceeded apace. Not only were agricultural labor and land ownership increasingly separated, but the various other factors of production were segmented and each subjected to separate rent. Absentee landlordism proliferated. Many peasants were left no alternative to survival loans at *de facto* interest rates usurious by any standards. Foreclosure on family land and family members pledged as collateral was often at the discretion of the creditor. The courts of law called upon to process such foreclosure proceedings came increasingly under the control of the urban elites who had initiated the agricultural intensification. These courts gave a façade of legality to foreclosures regarded as illegal by most peasants and their prophetic defenders. The prophets declared that actions by YHWH's court of last resort had vindicated the poor peasants' cause and had found the urban elites guilty regarding the matters under adjudication.

Not all parts of the country were equally affected by these dynamics. The land best suited to wheat lay in the plains and the Shephelah, where most of it had long since been garnered into the large estates of the wealthiest and most powerful landlords. The conflict over agricultural priorities, techniques, and land took place primarily in the hill country, where the villagers' preference for the sustainability and sufficiency of mixed, subsistence cropping constituted a major impediment to the urban elites' desire for the "efficient" production of ever-greater quantities of wine and oil.

The conflict within the political economy of upland agriculture was not fought on equal terms. As noted above, survival loans with hill-country peasants' plots pledged as collateral gave urban elites a powerful tool to consolidate into their own hands lands from which they desired oil and wine, not mixed subsistence. This same small but powerful class also controlled state policies, including those of taxation. To further several of their goals at once, all they had to do was to levy a heavy tax on grain produced "inefficiently" by the subsistence farmers of the hill country. In the short term such a tax secured them one of their three preferred commodities, but in the longer run it also gave

powerful incentive to convert into vineyards and olive orchards what had previously been multipurpose land. This conversion accomplished the increased
production of wine and oil desired by the elite, both for domestic conspicuous
consumption and for export. In the process, of course, many previously free-
holding villagers lost their land and were ruined. Amos 5:11 probably reflects
this process and its causal linkages in its indictment and futility curses:

> Therefore, because you impose cereal tax[13] upon the poor one,
>   And exactions of grain you take from him,
> You have built houses of hewn stone,
>   But you shall not dwell in them as lord;
> You have planted delightful vineyards,
>   But you shall not drink their wine.

Nor is archaeological evidence lacking for the intensification of wine and
oil production in the hills. While rock-cut olive- and grape-processing installations are probably almost as old as agriculture itself in Palestine, archaeological surveys suggest a proliferation of and innovation in such installations in the
eighth century B.C.E.[14] Some ancient terracing can probably also be traced to
this time,[15] though such installations are notoriously difficult to date with certainty. The Samaria ostraca—despite all the controversies surrounding their
exact dating and interpretation—"evidence the flow of oil and wine, probably
to officials of the royal court"[16] in the eighth century. A survey of west Samaria
by Shimon Dar reports not only the founding of new villages on virgin sites in
Iron II but the presence in and near them of wine- and oil-processing installations.[17] While the best exemplars date from later periods, massive and well-

---

[13] This translation of the *hapax legomenon bšs* is supported both by the parallel line and by a
probable Akkadian cognate, *šabāšu/šabāsa,* as seen already by Harry Torczyner (Tur-Sinai)
("Presidential Address," *JPOS* 16 [1936] 6–7). Numerous commentators, translators, and lexicog-
raphers have since adopted this reading (Shalom Paul, *Amos.* Hermeneia [Minneapolis: Fortress,
1991] 172–73). Whether or not the Hebrew term here involves a wordplay on *bws,* "tread down,
trample," must remain a matter of conjecture, though the suggestion is thoroughly plausible.

[14] Edward F. Campbell, Jr., *Shechem II: Portrait of a Hill Country Vale. The Shechem Regional
Survey.* ASOR Archaeological Reports 2 (Atlanta: Scholars, 1991) 109–12; Shimon Dar, *Landscape and Pattern: An Archaeological Survey of Samaria 800 B.C.E.–636 C.E.* BAR International
Series 308 (Oxford: Biblical Archaeological Review, 1986) 147–90; David Eitam, "Olive Presses
of the Israelite Period," *Tel Aviv* 4 (1979) 146–54; Carey Ellen Walsh, *Fruit of the Vine: Viticulture
in Ancient Israel.* HSM 60 (Winona Lake: Eisenbrauns, 2000) 142–62.

[15] Gershon Edelstein and Mordechai Kislev, "Mevasseret Yerushalayim: The Ancient Settlement and Its Agricultural Terraces," *BA* 44 (1981) 53–56.

[16] Premnath, "The Process of Latifundialization," 62.

[17] Dar, *Landscape and Pattern.*

constructed "towers" are frequently associated with these installations. Dar traces the antecedents of these towers to Iron II and interprets them as centers for the fermentation and storage of wine. Only wine's need for darkness and moderately low, constant temperatures, he argues, can explain the unique features of these towers, whose construction required an enormous expenditure of labor. Carey Ellen Walsh now appears to agree with this interpretation,[18] after earlier seeing the towers as primarily defensive.[19] Towers in Jordan dating to the Iron II period, not discussed by Dar and Walsh, seem easiest to interpret as agricultural in function, though some role in defense cannot at present be excluded.[20]

The population estimates of Magen Broshi and Israel Finkelstein for Iron II Palestine, based on archaeological surveys and anthropologically standardized coefficients of density, offer striking evidence for rapid population growth in eighth-century Israel and Judah.[21] Even more significant, perhaps, they document such rapid growth in the population of the hill country that for the first time in history it exceeded that of the lowlands. One need not solve the old chicken-and-egg debate in demographic and economic theory about population growth and agricultural intensification[22] to note that one usually witnesses the other.

To reiterate, then, agricultural intensification was a stark fact in eighth-century Israel and Judah. It is clearly a major issue addressed by all Hosea's prophetic contemporaries. Is it sound method to assume, *a priori,* that Hosea ignored it or that the religious realities he addressed in no way interfaced with it?

---

[18] Walsh, *Fruit of the Vine,* 128–36.

[19] Carey Ellen Walsh, "God's Vineyard: Isaiah's Prophecy as Vintner's Textbook," *BRev* 14/4 (1999) 49.

[20] Henry O. Thompson, "Some Towers in Jordan," in *The Archaeology of Jordan and Beyond: Essays in Honor of James A. Sauer.* Studies in the Archaeology and History of the Levant 1 (Winona Lake: Eisenbrauns, 2000) 482–89; Randall W. Younker, "Towers in the Region Surrounding Tell ʿUmeiri," in Lawrence T. Geraty, et al., eds., *Madaba Plains Project: The 1984 Season at Tell el-ʿUmeiri and Vicinity and Subsequent Studies* 1 (Berrien Springs, Mich.: Andrews University Press) 195–98; idem, "Architectural Remains from the Hinterland Survey," in Larry G. Herr, et al., eds., *Madaba Plains Project: The 1987 Season at Tell el-ʿUmeiri and Vicinity and Subsequent Studies* (Berrien Springs, Mich.: Andrews University Press, 1990) 335–42; idem, "Preliminary Report of the 1994 Season of the Madaba Plains Project: Regional Survey, Tall El ʿUmayri and Tall Jalul Excavations (June 15–July 30, 1994)," *AUSS* 34 (1996) 65–92.

[21] Magen Broshi and Israel Finkelstein, "The Population of Palestine in Iron Age II," *BASOR* 287 (1992) 47–60.

[22] Ester Boserup, *The Conditions of Agricultural Growth* (London: Allen and Unwin, 1965); David B. Grigg, *Population Growth and Agrarian Change: An Historical Perspective.* Cambridge Geographical Studies 13 (Cambridge: Cambridge University Press, 1980); Robert McC. Netting, *Smallholders, Householders: Farm Families and the Ecology of Intensive, Sustainable Agriculture* (Stanford: Stanford University Press, 1993).

2. Agricultural intensification exacerbated male dominance in Israel, as it has and does in most traditional agrarian societies. By agrarian society I mean a human society in which the economic base is provided by a tillage of fields, that knows the plow and traction animals in some form, but not the extensive use of inanimate energy sources associated with the industrial revolution.[23] Virtually all agrarian societies known to history are patriarchal. A major perspective in current economic anthropology sees the primary cause for this correlation in the incompatibility of the activities associated with plowing and those associated with the care of infants and small children. Protracted warfare also exacerbates gender inequities. Drafting and rewarding only men for state undertakings that are distant and dangerous offers less chance that agricultural production and human reproductive levels will be disrupted. The rewarding of men with control over family land and labor promotes their loyalty to the state and maintains their incentive to serve in its levies. Experience in such activities gives men more leverage in negotiating with the state. Once ensconced for these reasons, male dominance tends to reproduce itself socially and to create elaborate ideological justifications for its being how things "ought" to be.[24]

3. The Hebrew verb *zānāh,* and particularly the plural abstract noun, *zᵉnûnîm,* favored by Hosea, refer to sexual activity that is "promiscuous," as David Noel Freedman, Francis Andersen, and Phyllis Bird have shown.[25] In a patriarchal agrarian context the primary concern about such behavior is that it places in doubt the *paternity,* and hence the *legitimacy* of any children born to a "promiscuous woman." Because her focus is elsewhere when treating this term, Keefe—in an otherwise trenchant discussion—misses the importance of paternity and legitimacy in Hosea's rhetoric.[26]

4. The rhetorical vector of much of the book of Hosea presumes a male audience. To quote Bird, "By appealing to the common stereotypes and interests of a primarily male audience, Hosea turns their accusation against them."[27] This technique has marked affinities with the juridical parable, a genre that I have elsewhere argued is applied exclusively in the Hebrew Bible to elite addressees.[28]

---

[23] Gerhard E. Lenski, *Power and Privilege: A Theory of Social Stratification* (2d ed. Chapel Hill: University of North Carolina Press, 1984) 190–296.

[24] Laurel Bossen, "Women and Economic Institutions," in Stuart Plattner, ed., *Economic Anthropology* (Stanford: Stanford University Press, 1989) 318–50; Carol Meyers, *Discovering Eve: Ancient Israelite Women in Context* (New York: Oxford University Press, 1989) 189–96.

[25] Andersen and Freedman, *Hosea,* 157–69; Bird, "'To Play the Harlot,'" 80–82.

[26] Keefe, "The Female Body, the Body Politic and the Land"; eadem, *Women's Body and the Social Body in Hosea.*

[27] Bird, "'To Play the Harlot,'" 89.

[28] Chaney, "Whose Sour Grapes?"

The obvious example in eighth-century prophecy is Isa 5:1-7. Hosea's dense literary allusiveness—much remarked upon by commentators—also requires a formally educated, and therefore probably upper-class, male audience. Bird has emphasized the gender dimension of the audience that Hosea's rhetoric presumes,[29] Keefe the class dimension.[30] Only when the two are combined in discerning the foil of Hosea's polemic can a major vector of his rhetoric be discerned with clarity.

5. While redaction criticism has, in my opinion, proved highly efficacious in the study of Amos, Isaiah, and Micah, I cannot term successful any of the full-scale redaction-critical analyses of Hosea. I say this despite the great learning of several studies and their obvious contributions on individual points.[31] To be sure, the book bears clear signs of Judahite editorial activity that took place after the fall of Samaria. Although I would not argue that material in the book apparently antecedent to this Judahite editorializing gives direct access to the historical prophet, I do believe that the basic metaphors it preserves refer to institutional dynamics in roughly the third quarter of the eighth century B.C.E. and that these metaphors derive from the named prophet.

6. The Judahite circles in which Hosea was preserved were intensely nationalistic. Certainly from Josiah on, the critique of all the eighth-century prophets was understood as applying to the nation as a whole, with little or no distinction of various classes of inhabitants. But just as obviously materials in Amos, Isaiah, and Micah that were preserved in this nationalist guise express quite a different perspective. Much of the critique is addressed exclusively to members of the ruling urban elite. Far from being their perpetrators, the peasant and lower-class majority are seen as the innocent victims of the activities excoriated.[32] Given the history of composition and interpretation of the book of Hosea, is it not likely that it, too, has seen critiques that earlier applied only to elite classes broadened to include the whole of Israel?

7. Older scholarship tended to view the much-noted obscurities of the book of Hosea as occasions for text-critical or philological operations—or some combination of the two—to vouchsafe the true, *singular* meaning of the text.

[29] Bird, "'To Play the Harlot.'"

[30] Keefe, "The Female Body, the Body Politic and the Land"; eadem, *Women's Body and the Social Body in Hosea.*

[31] Grace I. Emmerson, *Hosea: An Israelite Prophet in Judean Perspective.* JSOTSup 28 (Sheffield: JSOT Press, 1984); Gale Yee, *Composition and Tradition in the Book of Hosea: A Redaction Critical Investigation.* SBLDS 102 (Atlanta: Scholars, 1987).

[32] Robert B. Coote, *Amos Among the Prophets: Composition and Theology* (Philadelphia: Fortress, 1981); Mays, *Micah;* Marvin A. Sweeney, *Isaiah 1–39, with an Introduction to Prophetic Literature.* The Forms of the Old Testament Literature 16 (Grand Rapids: Eerdmans, 1996).

More recent literary studies, particularly when pursued in conversation with the conceptual matrix sketched here, suggest a different initial approach to such obscurities. Commentators should first ask, I believe, if the received Hebrew text witnesses a coining of words or phrases, a bending of forms beyond their usual malleability, an audacious paronomasia, and/or a jarring juxtaposition of universes of discourse elsewhere deemed to be mutually exclusive. All these phenomena can evoke several realities simultaneously, such that they interpret one another in language that is intrinsically multivalent. This is not at all to posit a completely inerrant received text, but rather to argue that "difficult" passages should be scrutinized for exemplars of the devices just noted before the "difficulties" are emended or explained away to achieve a single, referential meaning.

The anomalous form *ʾĕhî* in Hos 13:7, 10, 14, for example, is likely a play between and among *ʾehyeh*, "I am, I shall be, I shall become," *ʾayyēh*, "where?" and *ʾEhyeh*, the form of the divine name in Hos 1:9 and Exod 3:14.[33] Thus, for instance, v. 14b would read "I am/*ʾEhyeh* is/where are your plagues, O Death; I am/*ʾEhyeh* is/where is your destruction, O Sheol?" If this reading is cogent, its "meaning" inheres in the "semantic innovation" elicited by the "tension" between and among the several semantic fields involved. Resolving that tension, either by textual emendation or morphological explanation, destroys the essence of the text.

8. Ronald Hendel's analysis of the aniconic tradition in early Israel argues that its rejection of sacral kingship as a fundamental orienting structure demanded also a rejection of the divine images that symbolized the authority of the king.[34] Building upon that analysis, Keefe reasons that Hosea's repeated invectives against idols, bull icons, priests and sanctuaries may be read convincingly as an attack upon a whole complex of ritual activity that legitimated and collaborated with structures of political and economic power.[35] His attacks upon the "promiscuities" of these cults thus concern their role in the dynamics of political economy, and do not constitute a pervasive critique of a putative "fertility religion."

While each of these presuppositions begs for fuller discussion, I now turn to the analysis of several problems occasioned when the "promiscuous wife" of Hosea is understood primarily as a trope for the nation of Israel as a whole.

[33] Andersen and Freedman, *Hosea*, 635; Francis Landy, *Hosea*. Readings: A New Biblical Commentary (Sheffield: Sheffield Academic Press, 1995) 160–67.

[34] Ronald Hendel's analysis ("The Social Origins of the Aniconic Tradition in Early Israel," *CBQ* 50 [1988] 113–48).

[35] Keefe, *Women's Body and the Social Body in Hosea*, 95–96, 118–30.

*Problems with Understanding "Gomer" as the Whole
of Israel and Alternatives Thereto*

1. Such interpretation tends to forget about the children. They are emphasized by the biblical text, both in chs. 1–2 where the promiscuity metaphor is
prominent, and in chs. 4–14 where it moves in and out of view. In a number of
Hosean texts the children are clearly a metaphor for Israel.

Keefe surfaces this problem only to dismiss it. Early in her study she writes,

> There have been all manner of theories broached which hope to make sense
> of these children as symbolic presences within the extended metaphor. The per-
> ceived problem revolves around a confusion regarding the allegorical corre-
> spondences intended here: if the mother symbolizes Israel, then what of the
> children, whose names indicate that they also symbolize Israel?

> The search for a clear set of allegorical correspondences to assign to the parts of
> the metaphor ends in frustration as it is based upon the faulty premise that the
> trope is an allegory, rather than a complex metaphor, which draws upon a set of
> symbolic associations tied up with the intertwining images of woman, children,
> land and nation.[36]

She continues to distinguish—à la I. A. Richards [37] and Paul Ricoeur [38]—between "tropes of substitution" and "tropes of invention," ". . . where the 'tension' between semantic fields elicits a 'semantic innovation' which does not
simply clothe an idea in a new image, but reveals 'something new about the
reality.'"[39] "Thus the vehicle is not dispensable, and the meaning of the metaphor may not be resolved by neatly assigning the correct tenor to it. This is the
case only in allegory or analogy, where a resemblance serves to illustrate the
point in a new manner, but the point remains essentially the same. But unlike
allegories, 'real metaphors are not translatable.'"[40]

I agree with Keefe on the theoretical level, but believe that she misapplies
metaphor theory to the point at issue in Hosea's rhetoric. Hosea's "wife of promiscuity" and her "children of promiscuity" are indeed—as I hope to show—not
simply allegories or analogies, but parade examples of "tropes of invention."
They are complex and interactive metaphors by the most stringent definitions
of the term. But for the "tension" between semantic fields to elicit the brilliant

---

[36] Ibid. 22.

[37] Ivor A. Richards, *The Philosophy of Rhetoric* (Oxford: Oxford University Press, 1971;
reprint of 1936 edition).

[38] Paul Ricoeur, "Metaphor and Symbol," in idem, *Interpretation Theory: Discourse and the
Surplus of Meaning* (Fort Worth: Texas Christian University Press, 1976).

[39] Ibid. 53.

[40] Ibid. 52; Keefe, *Woman's Body and the Social Body in Hosea,* 23 n. 14.

"semantic innovations" that all but the most ham-handed of commentators know to be Hosea's signature, it must "work" without undue confusion. The ambiguities articulated by the "tropes of invention" must reveal new richness *and* clarity, not merely obfuscate all semantic fields involved. I suspect that Keefe's failure to see paternity and legitimacy as important dimensions of these metaphors has been detrimental to her discernment on this particular point.

2. Viewed through the lens of modern marriage customs and morality, the principal valence of the promiscuity metaphor is often understood as adultery and fidelity. But as we have already seen, Hosea's parlance clearly emphasizes promiscuity over adultery. The verb *zānāh* and its related nouns occur twenty-one times in the book (1:2, 2, 2, 2; 2:4, 6, 7; 3:3; 4:10, 11, 12, 12, 13, 14, 15, 18, 18; 5:3, 4; 6:10; 9:1), *nā'ap* and its cognate noun only six (2:4; 3:1; 4:2, 13, 14; 7:4). When the two "roots" occur together (2:4; 4:13, 14), *zānāh* always enjoys priority in their poetic pairing. For the male Israelites of Hosea's time, particularly those of the upper classes, the issue highlighted by this language is that of *paternity*.

In the days before *in vitro* fertilization the *maternity* of a child was never in question. The mother was always present at birth. The Ancient Near East, in fact, lacked a modern understanding of reproductive physiology. The entire fetus was thought to derive from the father's semen, the mother's womb providing only the nurturing "matrix." But the *paternity* of a child could be insured only when the mother's sexuality had been the exclusive domain of one man. Female promiscuity placed paternity in doubt. To guarantee paternity, strict sanctions were laid against female promiscuity, thereby creating a double standard between the sexes for sexual behavior.

But why was paternity such an issue for men, particularly those of the ruling elite, and what had it to do with agricultural intensification? Paternity was the nexus where the two most basic functions of any agrarian society—production and reproduction—came together. Arable land, the means of production, passed from generation to generation patrilineally. Inheritance went only to "legitimate" sons, those whose paternity was beyond question.

For the elite latifundializers such legitimacy became a virtual obsession. No stricture on their women was too great if it insured that their inherited and accumulated land and wealth, their political and military power, and their social prestige passed only to sons guaranteed to be born of their own seed. In the elite male sodality know as the *marzēaḥ*—mentioned in Amos (6:7) and Jeremiah (16:5) and mirrored in Isaiah and Hosea[41]—both the boundaries of this

---

[41] Coote, *Amos among the Prophets,* 36–39; John L. McLaughlin, *The Marzeah in the Prophetic Literature: References and Allusions in Light of the Extra-Biblical Evidence.* VTSup 86

elite class and the continuities between and among its generations, living and dead, were celebrated and reinforced by the voluptuous consumption of the preferred commodities of agricultural intensification.

3. I have already hinted at another problem with understanding Hosea's "promiscuous wife" principally as a metaphor for the whole nation of Israel. Such interpretation ignores class divisions and their importance in Hosea's world and in the oracles of his prophetic contemporaries.

Class and gender, moreover, intersected powerfully as salient categories in eighth-century Israel's patterns of stratification. The language of elite male virility in Hosea's world and diction was the language of power and privilege in the political economy. Status sex was a potent symbol of authority and prestige, as Absalom and Ahithophel understood when, in the process of Absalom's attempted usurpation of David, they made a public display of his assumption of his father's harem (2 Sam 16:20-23). Conversely, when the aging David flunked the virility test administered by "Miss Israel," Abishag the Shunammite, it was yet another sign that the struggle for succession was on in earnest (1 Kgs 1:1-4).

Military institutions added an important dimension to this mix of class and gender stratification. The urban elite males were also a military elite. Much of their identity was wound up in their role as warriors, a role for which they practiced long hours. This identity as elite male warriors spawned a culture of *machismo* that fed back into their obsession with guaranteeing the paternity of their offspring. The more completely they controlled and dominated their women's sexuality, the more they not only insured the paternity of their children, but the more status and honor they gained in their macho fraternity. Failure to control their women's sexuality, on the other hand, led to dishonor and humiliation. For members of Israel's urban male warrior elite, therefore, few things could be more abhorrent than for one of *their* women to be sexually promiscuous. When they defeated other warrior elites, however, one of the major ways of humiliating their vanquished enemies was through the violation of their women.[42]

Each of the several facets of urban male warrior elite identity that I have discussed is part of the semantic field of one word in biblical Hebrew, *ba'al*.

(Leiden: Brill, 2001); Taek Joo Woo, *The Marzeah Institution and Rites for the Dead: A Comparative and Systemic Study with Special Attention to the Eighth-Century Prophets,* Ph.D. diss., Graduate Theological Union, 1998.

[42] David D. Gilmore, *Manhood in the Making: Cultural Concepts of Masculinity* (New Haven: Yale University Press, 1990); Alice A. Keefe, "Rapes of Women/Wars of Men," *Semeia* 61 (1993) 79–97; Ken Stone, *Sex, Honor, and Power in the Deuteronomistic History,* JSOTSup 234 (Sheffield: Sheffield Academic Press, 1996).

Whatever the exact identity and content of the divinity or divinities and cults evoked by this title in Hosea's parlance, they served to grant sacral legitimation to one class of elite men and their activities. In religious terms, *ba'al* was the "lord" of land, women, and political, military, economic, judicial, and social power and privilege writ large. *Ba'al* was the urban male warrior elite projected to infinity, and all attempts to understand "baalism" in Hosea must reckon with that fact. "Baalism" sanctioned agricultural intensification and the powerful few who instigated it and benefited from it.

Numerous details in the text of Hosea 1 and 2 and beyond confirm this analysis or can be viewed with greater nuance because of it. Space permits mention of only a few. The text itself interprets the trope of the promiscuous wife in 1:2: "Go, take for yourself a wife of promiscuity and children of promiscuity, for *the land* commits great promiscuity from after YHWH." The "gifts" the promiscuous wife seeks from her lovers are the preferred products of agricultural intensification, headed by the triad of grain, new wine, and new oil. As Bird has rightly argued, Hosea links the trope of promiscuity polemically with that of prostitution to castigate the greed of this agricultural intensification.[43] Vines and fig trees are called *'etñāh,* "(harlot's) hire." The term occurs only in Hos 2:14 and was probably coined as a pun with *tᵉʾēnāh,* "fig (tree)," and perhaps with *taˣⁿāh,* "rutting time." Elsewhere, including Hos 9:1, the form is *'etnān.*

In the context of ch. 9 "Israel" is accused of having loved a "harlot's hire" on all the threshing floors of grain. As commonly recognized by students of the subject[44] and evidenced in detail in Assyrian sources,[45] activities at the threshing floor constituted a climax and point of control in cereal production. Payment of peasants' survival loans and rents was most often due in grain delivered at harvest time to the threshing floor. Even the threshing floors themselves were sometimes pledged and foreclosed upon in the process of agricultural loans.

With regard to the gender dimension of the class-gender nexus under discussion, Gomer's name in Hosea probably deserves a second look. In the genealogies of Gen 10:2, 3 and 1 Chr 1:5, 6, as well as in Samaria ostracon 50:1, Gomer is a *male* name. Whatever its etymology and meaning—and both are

---

[43] Bird, "'To Play the Harlot.'"

[44] Victor H. Matthews. "Entrance Ways and Threshing Floors: Legally Significant Sites in the Ancient Near East," *Fides et Historia* 19 (1987) 25–40.

[45] *The Assyrian Dictionary of the Oriental Institute of the University of Chicago,* vol. 1, A, part 1, ed. A. Leo Oppenheim (Chicago: The Oriental Institute, 1964) 129–30 under *adru;* J. Payne Smith (Mrs. Margoliouth), *A Compendious Syriac Dictionary* (Oxford: Oxford University Press, 1903) 4, for cognate Syriac sources.

disputed[46]—can its *gender* in Hosea's rhetoric really be regarded as either neutral or irrelevant,[47] particularly when that rhetoric is so stridently polemical with regard to gender, and male gendering of the name is witnessed by a source as proximate geographically and chronologically as the Samaria ostraca? At least the alternative paradigm being developed here permits a new and rhetorically potent perception of Gomer's gender.

4. My final problem with the usual understanding of Gomer as a trope for all Israel regards modern obsession with personality and interpersonal relations. As long recognized by some students of the book, the text of Hosea grants almost no access to the *persons* of the prophet, his wife, or her children. These characters serve rather as tropes to convey the prophet's *message*. Thus the primary task of exegesis is not to speculate about personal details that are inaccessible but to elucidate Hosea's tropes in the socio-historical context of his time.

The male urban warrior elite of Hosea's time, if confronted with wives guilty of sexual promiscuity, would have reacted by meting out some combination of beating, confinement, public stripping, humiliation, divorce, exile, injury, deprivation of food and water, induced illness, and death. In Hosea's parlance each of these actions becomes a figure for what the Assyrian army was doing to Israel's elite male warriors and to the land and agricultural production they dominated. Rhetorically they are hoist with their own petard, their fate interpreted to them as being that which their macho culture knew only too well was what a "promiscuous woman" richly deserved. This bitterly sarcastic inversion shares much with the self-condemnation into which the juridical parable tricked powerful men, long accustomed to passing judgment on women and their social inferiors. It loses most of its punch if Gomer is a figure for all Israel or even for all male Israelites.

Focusing the trope of the promiscuous wife more sharply facilitates a concomitant clarification of the identity and significance of the illegitimate children. In patriarchal agrarian contexts bastard children are routinely marginalized and abused. They are innocent of their mother's guilt, but they share her fate and punishment. Thus the peasants and other members of the lower classes are innocent of responsibility for agricultural intensification; they are instead its victims. But they share their "mother's" punishment in the form of Assyrian military activity and ecological degradation. The trope works at another level as well. Bastards cannot inherit; they are landless. That was precisely the state into which the promiscuity of agricultural intensification forced growing numbers

[46] Andersen and Freedman, *Hosea*, 171.
[47] Andrew A. Macintosh, *Hosea*. ICC (Edinburgh: T & T Clark, 1997) 11–12.

of peasants in Hosea's Israel, as they were dispossessed by foreclosure and land consolidation proceeded apace.

This interpretation of Hosea's promiscuous wife and children whose legitimacy is in question grants the tropes a power and nuance they otherwise lack, not only in the texts that pronounce judgment but also in those that proclaim salvation. In a reversal unthinkable in the macho culture of the warrior latifundializers, Hosea says these bastard children will be granted legitimacy and inheritance in a world where the depredations of the warring classes are abolished and the earth yields its bounty in the subsistence village agriculture that YHWH intended all along. In such a world, where *grace* requires as its *prerequisite* that the presuppositions of patriarchy and hierarchy be overthrown, even the male urban warrior elite can be redeemed. They can become the faithful wife, free of the promiscuity of agricultural intensification, who knows that her divine husband is not her * baʾal* but her *ʾîš* (2:18). Changes in social systems are usually accompanied by concomitant changes in their legitimating religious symbol systems.

The names of the bastard children figure as well in the dialectic between judgment and salvation. Jezreel is the firstborn son (1:4), and his name also serves as the punch line in Hosea's verbal picture of healing and restoration (2:24). A name more pregnant with meaning or more multivalent can scarcely be imagined. It is, of course, a pun on Israel, and thus an added indication that the children, not the promiscuous mother, are the more frequent figure for most of the nation's population. But Jezreel also evokes Jehu's bloody usurpation of the Omrids (1:4), a bloodbath pitched by its legitimating apology as necessary to end the Omrids' oppressive drive for agricultural intensification and the "baalism" that sanctioned it (1 Kings 21; 2 Kings 9–10).[48] Hosea and his audience knew, however, that Jehu's dynasty, still on the throne in Hosea's early years in the person of Jeroboam II, had outdone the dynasty it usurped in both offenses. The literal sense of Jezreel, "God sows/inseminates," evoked understandings of both agriculture and paternity that the prophet regarded as "legitimate," but could also carry the double-entendre of God's sowing destruction.

CONCLUSIONS

Thus the literary figures of Hosea's text, salvific as well as judgmental, provide a sweeping critique of agrarian Israel's systemic integration—those who rule it "benefit" from it and legitimate it. Hosea says the urban male military elite are "promiscuous women" who achieve just the opposite of what

---

[48] Marsha C. White, *The Elijah Legends and Jehu's Coup.* BJS 311 (Atlanta: Scholars, 1997).

they purport: instability, not stability; infertility, not fertility; illegitimacy, not legitimacy; infidelity, not fidelity; insecurity, not security; impotence, not potency; dishonor, not honor; sickness, not health; want, not prosperity; defeat, not victory; frenetic titillation on the way to destruction, not intimate understanding and loyal relationship.

The Parable of the Ten Virgins (Matthew 25:1-13): The Integrity of Identity and Activity

Herman C. Waetjen

꒱

Of all the parables attributed to Jesus in the synoptic gospels, none is more ambiguous in terms of its origin and meaning than the Parable of the Ten Virgins.[1] Everything depends on the correspondence between content and context, and especially the issue of literary form and function, regardless of whether the story is interpreted in terms of its present location in Matthew's Gospel or in an earlier setting.[2] No one denies that the parable appears to have a certain allegorical character, but is it an allegory in its form and function? And is the content of the story so completely determined by the crisis of the delay of the *parousia* that its conception as an allegorical illustration must be allocated in the context of Matthew 24–25 or the early church?[3] The application of 25:13, an admonition

---

[1] My great thanks to Dr. Cornelia Cyss-Wittenstein for the ongoing dialogue about this parable that we shared and the new insights that emerged from it.

[2] Illustrative of an investigation of the correspondence between content and context is the redaction-critical analysis of Wolfgang Schrenk, "Auferweckung der Toten oder Gericht nach den Werken: Tradition und Redaktion in Matthäus 25:1-13," *NovT* 20 (1978) 278–98. He concludes that the original tradition of the parable consisted of vv. 1, 2, 6, 7, 10, and intended, in the dialogue related to 1 Thess 4:15-17, to give an answer to the problem of the resurrection of the dead in the context of the delay of the *parousia*. Matthew, on the other hand, redacted that tradition to illustrate the beatitude of 5:6 and at the same time to forewarn that there will be no awakening from the sleep of death for those who do not have a store of good works. See especially pp. 294–98.

[3] The literature on this story may be classified under two distinguishing perspectives: First, those who ascribe the allegorical features of the story to Matthew's redaction or the early church but nevertheless acknowledge its authenticity as a parable of Jesus: Adolf Jülicher, *Die Gleichnisreden Jesu*. 2 vols. (2d ed. Tübingen: J.C.B. Mohr [Paul Siebeck], 1899; reprint Darmstadt: Wissenschaftliche Buchgesellschaft, 1963) 456–59; Charles H. Dodd, *The Parables of the Kingdom* (London: Nisbet, 1935) 172; Joachim Jeremias, *The Parables of Jesus* (rev. ed. London: S.C.M.,

that concludes the story, supports such a possibility but, as everyone recognizes, it is a Matthean redaction. If, however, the narrative is predetermined by its apparent Christian motifs, its dismissal as an allegorically fashioned story originating within the context of the early church would appear to be justified.

On the other hand, the features of the story only appear to be allegorical because of the narrative's placement in the context of Jesus' eschatological discourse in Matthew's Gospel. Originally the story may have been a parable of Jesus and therefore without an allegorical orientation of its content to the futuristic eschatology of the *parousia*. Consequently, its function as a parable would be unlike that of an allegory and, if the characterization of parable formulated by C. H. Dodd is adequate, it would "arrest the hearer by its vividness or strangeness, and leaving the mind in sufficient doubt about its precise application . . . tease it into active thought."[4]

One criterion that has been proposed to determine whether the story is a parable, and therefore most likely authored by Jesus, or whether it is an allegory originating in the early church, is that of the authenticity of the wedding customs the story conveys.[5] If those details correspond to the cultural conven-

---

1963) 51–52, 171–75; Dan O. Via, Jr., *The Parables: Their Literary and Existential Dimension* (Philadelphia: Fortress, 1967) 123; Schrenk, "Auferweckung der Toten oder Gericht nach den Werken," 294–98; Armand Tarrech, *La parabole des dix vierges.* AnBib 28 (Rome: Biblical Institute, 1983) 143–79; and Arland J. Hultgren, *The Parables of Jesus: A Commentary* (Grand Rapids: Eerdmans, 2000) 176–77. Second, those who consider the story to be an allegorical formulation of Matthew or early Christianity: Rudolf Bultmann, *History of the Synoptic Tradition,* trans. John Marsch (Oxford: Basil Blackwell, 1972) 119 (3d German ed. 125): "This is a church formulation completely overgrown by allegory . . . ." See also Günther Bornkamm, "Die Verzögerung der Parusie: Exegetische Bemerkungen zu zwei synoptischen Texten," in Werner Schmauch, ed., *In Memoriam Ernst Lohmeyer* (Stuttgart: Evangelisches Verlagswerk, 1951) 125; Erich Grässer, *Das Problem der Parusieverzögerung in den synoptischen Evangelien und in der Apostelgeschichte* (Berlin: Alfred Töpelmann, 1960) 125–27. Eta Linnemann, *Jesus of the Parables* (New York: Harper & Row, 1966) 126–27, claims that the parable is a creation of the early church but refuses to regard the story as an allegory. See Karl P. Donfried, "The Allegory of the Ten Virgins (Matt 25:1-13) As a Summary of Matthean Theology," *JBL* 93 (1974) 415–28; James Breech, *The Silence of Jesus: The Authentic Voice of the Historical Man* (Philadelphia: Fortress, 1983) 217; Bernard Brandon Scott, *Hear Then the Parable: A Commentary on the Parables of Jesus* (Minneapolis: Fortress, 1989) 70–72. William R. Herzog II, *Parables As Subversive Speech: Jesus As Pedagogue of the Oppressed* (Louisville: Westminster John Knox, 1994) omits the parable.

[4] Dodd, *The Parables of the Kingdom,* 16. Dan O. Via, Jr.'s characterization of parable is also worth citing in this context: "The parable is not a literal description of what is literally and finally true for all men but is a hypothetical and imaginative work with existential implications (*The Parables,* 125).

[5] John H. Donahue, *The Gospel in Parable: Metaphor, Narrative and Theology in the Synoptic Gospels* (Philadelphia: Fortress, 1988) 101. In his judgment the story is an allegory by which "Matthew summons his community to responsible discipleship in the face of the delay of the parousia."

tions of a Palestinian wedding at the time of Jesus, the story is very likely a genuine parable of Jesus. If, on the other hand, those elements are unrealistic, the story should be regarded as an allegorization of the early church's expectations of the *parousia*.

Features of narrative, however, whether realistic or unrealistic, are not necessarily valid criteria by which the literary genre of a story is to be determined. Empirical narrative, such as history and biography, has an allegiance to reality, while fictional narrative tends to be oriented to the ideal and to ideology.[6] "The eye [of the writer of fiction] is not on the external world but on the audience which he [she] hopes to delight or instruct, giving it either what it wants or what he [she] thinks it needs."[7] Fictional narrative that employs figurative language, such as parable, allegory, and myth, functions metaphorically by referring to one subject and intending another. But two different functions are involved, and it is precisely those functions that separate parable from allegory. As John Dominic Crossan has observed,

> One is to illustrate information so that information precedes participation. The other is to create participation so that participation precedes information. The former function produces allegories and examples, pedagogic devices which are intrinsically expendable. The latter produces *metaphor* on the verbal level and *symbol* on the nonverbal level. At their best they are absolutely inexpendable and even at their worst they are dormant rather than dead.[8]

Accordingly, if the narrative of the Ten Virgins is an allegory, the information that is already known to its audience, and therefore precedes their participation, is the scheme of apocalyptic eschatology that is presented in Matthew 24.[9] Consequently the story is illustrative of Jesus' exhortation in 24:42 and 44 "to watch" and "be prepared." In response to his disciples' question of 24:3, "Tell us, when will this be, and what will be the sign of your coming and of the close of the age?" Jesus cites the apocalyptic portents that will precede the reconstitution of all things. But he culminates his apocalyptic discourse with an emphasis on the unknowability of the end-time and the coming of the Son of the Human Being:

---

[6] Robert Scholes and Robert Kellogg, *The Nature of Narrative* (New York: Oxford University Press, 1966) 13–14.

[7] Ibid. 14.

[8] John Dominic Crossan, *In Parables: The Challenge of the Historical Jesus* (New York: Harper and Row, 1973) 15.

[9] See also Donfried, "The Allegory of the Ten Virgins," 419.

> Keep on watching, therefore, for you do not know on what day your Lord is coming. But know this, that if the householder knew in what watch of the night the thief comes, he would watch and would not permit his house to be broken into. Therefore you also must be ready; for the Son of the Human Being is coming at an hour you do not expect. (Matt 24:42-44)

In view of the unknowability of the end-time, Jesus confronts his disciples with the existential question, "Who then is that 'faithful and wise slave' who serves as a responsible householder?" It is, as he submits in a response to his own question, the one who discharges the duties and obligations of the household in fulfillment of the Master's will. In contrast, "the wicked slave" is the one who takes advantage of the Master's delayed return by behaving unethically toward his fellow slaves and by dissolute living.

It appears that it is the correspondence between the delay of the *parousia* and the delay of the bridegroom that establishes a circumstantial relationship between the story of the Ten Virgins and its context. Concomitantly, the tenable allegorical identifications of the bridegroom as the Christ, the marriage feast as the messianic banquet, and the exclusion of the five foolish virgins as the final judgment, all Christian motifs of the early church, enhance the possibility that the story belongs to the genre of allegory and illustrates information the Christian community already possesses.

But the correspondence between the narrative and its Matthean context is flawed by the absence of watchfulness in the story.[10] Jesus' admonition to watch is not observed by the ten virgins as they wait for the bridegroom: "Now as the bridegroom was delayed, they became drowsy and fell asleep." Moreover, the conduct Jesus prescribes in view of the delay of the *parousia* is to be fulfilled *prior* to the coming of the Son of the Human Being. The failure of five of the ten virgins to serve as bearers of light occurs *after* the bridegroom has arrived and is to be escorted to the wedding feast. Coincidentally there is nothing unethical about their conduct. They are victims of their own lack of foresight and preparation.

In all probability, therefore, the narrative of the Ten Virgins, in spite of its apparent allegorical character, is a parable and not an allegory.[11] The verb of the introductory formula in 25:1, "Then the reign of the heavens ὁμοιωθήσεται (will be like)," has been cast in the future passive indicative in order to ac-

---

[10] It may be conceded that "watching" metaphorically signifies "being prepared." See Schrenk, "Auferweckung der Toten oder Gericht nach den Werken," 282.

[11] See also Joachim Jeremias, *The Parables of Jesus*, 52. Hultgren (*The Parables of Jesus*, 177) is hesitant to identify the story as a parable of Jesus because of its allegorical elements, yet he appears to embrace that conclusion.

commodate the story to its Matthean setting.[12] But if the story had a similar introductory formula during its transmission as a tradition of Jesus in the early church, its more original form may have been the adjective of comparison, ὁμοία (similar, like) or the aorist passive indicative, ὡμοιώθη (it is like), both of which have been used in the formulations of Jesus' parables in earlier contexts in the gospel.[13] On the other hand, if Eta Linnemann is right, parables, as "freely composed stories" that tell of "interesting particular cases" or recount an event that happened only once, may have been introduced without any formula at all.[14] Typical of many such parables is the beginning of the story in Luke 15:11-32, "A certain human being had two sons."[15] The story of the Ten Virgins may have been introduced in a similar fashion, without the formula.

A parable, in contrast to an allegory, creates audience participation by "articulating a referent so new or so alien to consciousness that this referent can only be grasped within the metaphor itself."[16] In its function as an extended metaphor the parable conveys "a new possibility of world and of language so that any information one might obtain from it can only be received *after* one has participated through the metaphor in its new and alien referential world."[17] In that process, however, a parable not only opens up the possibility of "a new world"; it simultaneously subverts the "world" of the present social construction of reality.[18] In this respect it is the opposite of myth.[19] While myth builds

---

[12] This verb ὁμοιωθήσεται (it will be like) is used in a similar manner in Matt 7:24 and 26, but nowhere else in Matthew's Gospel.

[13] Bultmann, *History of the Synoptic Tradition* (3d German ed. 190–91) 176, attributes this introductory formula as well as the others of the parables in the Gospel of Matthew to the evangelist. For other occurrences of ὁμοία (like), see 13:31, 33, 44, 45, 47, and 20:1. For other uses of ὡμοιώθη (it is like), see 13:24; 18:23; 22:2.

[14] Linnemann, in her differentiation between "similitude" and "parable," characterizes them as follows: "What the similitude gains from the authority of what is generally known and recognized, the parable replaces by perspicuity. The parable is even a higher form, because it is more subtle, and its bias less obvious. The similitude uses words like 'no one,' 'no . . . ,' 'everyone,' 'whenever,' 'as often as,' etc.; it tries to overwhelm the listener by the weight of its generalization. . . . The parable gently gives up this use of force; it says: 'Listener, let me tell you just one story; if it doesn't win you over I will be silent . . .'" (*Jesus of the Parables,* 3–4).

[15] See also Mark 12:1; Matt 21:28; Luke 10:30; 12:16; 13:6; 14:16; 16:1, 19; 18:2.

[16] Crossan, *In Parables,* 13.

[17] Ibid.

[18] John Dominic Crossan, *The Dark Interval: Towards a Theology of Story* (Niles, Ill.: Argus, 1975) 59. There is a later edition of this book bearing the same title (Sonoma, Calif.: Polebridge, 1988) 42.

[19] Ibid. Argus ed., 55; Polebridge ed., 38.

"world," parable subverts "world." "Myth proposes, parable disposes."[20] "To live in parable means to dwell in the tension of myth and parable."[21]

The parable of Matt 25:1-12 begins with a tantalizingly significant number of virgins who are to function in the story as bearers of light for a wedding procession: "The rule of the heavens is like *ten* virgins." Ten is not simply "a favorite round number to describe a fair-sized group of people."[22] It is the number of the *minyan,* the quorum of ten required for the establishment of a synagogue, the basic Jewish community of fellowship in prayer, liturgy, Scripture reading, and interpretation.[23] But at the time of Jesus, and indeed in some synagogues today, a congregation, in order to be a legally constituted body of Israel, must be established by ten men. "Women could not be counted to make up a quorum *(minyan)* for public worship in the synagogue, for which ten free adult males were required."[24] At the very beginning of the parable there is already a shattering of expectations, indeed a subversion of the legality of constituting a synagogue. Ten women have replaced men as a *minyan* to form the basic religious community in Judaism, the institution of the synagogue.

It is this subversion that may have contributed to the introduction of another reversal, namely the substitution of the coming of the groom and groomsmen in place of the procession of a bride to the home of the groom. According to Safrai and Stern,

> The principal stages of the wedding celebration were: (1) preparation of the

---

[20] Ibid. Argus ed., 64; Polebridge ed., 47.

[21] Ibid. Argus ed., 59; Polebridge ed., 42.

[22] Linnemann, *Jesus of the Parables,* 124; also Adolph Jülicher, *Die Gleichnisreden Jesu,* 450: ". . . die Zehnzahl ist bloss gewählt worden, um der Anschauung festes Material zu bieten; hier war es wohl die kleinste für solche Umstände mögliche Zahl" (. . . the number ten is simply chosen to illustrate fixed material; here it was probably the smallest possible number for such circumstances).

[23] As far as I can determine only one other scholar has related the number *ten* to the legal quorum of the *minyan* to constitute a synagogue: J. Massingberde Ford, "Parable of the Foolish Scholars: Matt 25:1-13," *NovT* 9 (1967) 115–16. Unfortunately, she does not let this reversal lead her further into the parable. Working from the early rabbinic traditions on Canticles, she claims that the parable is directed against the Jewish teachers who are symbolized by the ten virgins and whose study of the Torah is represented by the lamps, but who lacked the oil of good deeds. See pp. 113–14 and 116–17.

[24] George Foote Moore, *Judaism in the First Centuries of the Christian Era: The Age of the Tannaim.* 2 vols. (Cambridge: Harvard University Press, 1954) 2:131 and 1:300. On the synagogue and the quorum of ten men see also Shemuel Safrai and Menachem Stern, in cooperation with David Flusser and W. C. van Unnik, *The Jewish People in the First Century* (Philadelphia: Fortress, 1987) 2:908–44.

bride, (2) transfer of the bride from her father's house to that of the groom, (3) the bride's introduction into the home of the groom, and (4) blessings and festivities within the husband's home.[25]

The bride was accompanied on her journey to the groom's home by "the most highly respected people" and "the sages even interrupted their study so that they and their students could meet a bridal procession and dance before the bride."[26] "Wedding processions and festivities were held towards evening, and it was customary to accompany the bride with torches to the festivity."[27]

If this was the general protocol of weddings at the time of Jesus, the story of the Ten Virgins is an unusually "interesting case." It is a freely composed narrative, perhaps of an incident that occurred only once, "whether or not other people would do it the same way," and Jesus tells it in order to achieve his purpose of subverting a particular feature of contemporary ideology.[28]

The identification of the women as virgins must also be significant, for there is no reason why the task of providing light for a wedding procession requires the employment of virgins. Women and men of all ages would have participated. Their identification, therefore, as "virgins" intimates a symbolic identity that links them to the prophetic representation of the people of God.[29] They are the embodiment of the true Israel. They are "the Daughters of Zion" who are admonished and denounced, pitied, and lamented by the prophets.[30] They can be faithful or faithless in their allegiance to God and their observance of the regulations of the covenant. Whatever they may be—disobedient, willful, recalcitrant, or dedicated, loyal, stalwart—they remain "the virgin daughters of Zion," and although they may be disciplined, they are never abandoned by God. As virgins, then, they constitute an inimitable *minyan.*

---

[25] Ibid. 2:757.

[26] Ibid. 2:758.

[27] Ibid. But see Hultgren, *The Parables of Jesus,* 170–71. His delineation of the two stages of Jewish marriage customs is somewhat similar to that of Safrai and Stern, but he apparently assumes that the procession of the groom to the wedding feast was the usual protocol of Jewish weddings.

[28] Here again I am subscribing to the characterizations of parable in Linnemann, *Jesus of the Parables,* 3–4; and Crossan, *The Dark Interval,* Argus ed., 59; Polebridge ed., 42.

[29] For prophetic references to Israel as the "virgin" see Amos 5:2; Isa 37:22; Lam 2:13; Isa 7:14 LXX. Jeremiah particularly referred to Israel as "the virgin"; see Jer 14:17; 18:13; 31(38):4, 21. Sometimes the designation "virgin" is combined with "the Daughter of Zion," as in Isa 37:22 and Lam 1:6; 2:13.

[30] References to "the Daughter of Zion" in the singular and the plural, or "Daughter of Jerusalem" or "Daughter of My People" abound in the prophets: Mic 4:8, 10, 13; Zeph 3:14; Isa 1:8; 3:16-17; 4:4; 10:32; 16:1; 22:4; 37:22; 52:2; 62:11; Jer 4:31; 6:2, 23, 26; 8:19, 21, 22; 9:1; 14:17; Zech 2:10; 9:9; Lam 1:6, 15; 2:1, 4, 10, 11, 13, 15, 18; 4:22.

Disturbing, however, is the immediate distinguishing characterization of the virgins as "foolish" and "prudent." The narrator is committing the mistake of "telling" rather than "showing," a literary technique that appears to be foreign to the art and style of Jesus' storytelling.[31] Most, if not all the parables of Jesus in the synoptic tradition "show" rather than "tell" and consequently permit the audience to make the implied determinations.[32] On the basis of the earlier differentiation between "the prudent man who built his house on the rock" and "the foolish man who built his house on sand" that is attributed to Jesus in Matt 7:24, 26, it seems valid to assign this partition to Matthew. But there is no need for it, and very likely Jesus did not include it in the story. The foolishness of the five who did not take an additional supply of oil with them will be manifested soon enough.[33]

The ten virgins have a calling, a vocation. They are to serve as bearers of light in the festive celebration of a marriage. The circumstance of marriage as the context for the exercise of this vocation also appears to have a symbolic significance. Both pre-exilic and post-exilic prophets utilized marriage as a metaphor to envision a new relationship between God and Israel.[34] Hosea anticipates a time in the future when God will enter into a marriage union with Israel.

> And in that day, says YHWH, you will call me "My Husband," and no longer will you call me "My Baal." For I will remove the names of the Baals from her mouth, and they shall be invoked by name no more. And I will make a covenant for you on that day with the beasts of the field, the birds of the air, and the creeping things of the ground; and the bow, the sword, and war I will abolish from the land; and I will make you lie down in security. And I will betroth you to me forever. I will betroth you to me in righteousness and in justice, in steadfast love,

---

[31] Via notes: "This is one of the few cases in Jesus' parables (cf. also Luke 18:6) where a figure is characterized directly by the narrator's use of an adjective—'wise' and 'foolish'—rather than by simply relating his deeds and words" (*The Parables,* 124).

[32] Any example will suffice to establish this. The Parable of the Father and the Two Sons in Luke 15:11-32 is especially illustrative of this principle. Nothing is said about the alienation between the two sons, but it is already intimated at the beginning of the story when the older son does not interfere as the younger son asks his father for his share of the inheritance, gains the right of disposition, and proceeds to turn his assets into cash. See Kenneth E. Bailey, *Poet and Peasant: A Literary Cultural Approach to the Parables in Luke* (Grand Rapids: Eerdmans,1976) 163–69.

[33] According to Günther Schwarz's analysis of the story's vocabulary in "Zum Vokabular von Matthäus 25:1-12," *NTS* 27 (1981) 270–73, but especially 270 n. 5, the word ἔλαιον does not refer to olive oil but to butter. Olive oil was used for the lamps in the Temple, but butter for lamps like those in the parable. But see also Safrai and Stern, *The Jewish People in the First Century* 2:745–46: "All oils may be used in the lamp, but olive oil is preferred."

[34] See Ford, "Parable of the Foolish Scholars," 113–15, for rabbinic texts that interpreted Canticles in terms of the nuptial relationship between YHWH and bride Israel.

and in mercy. I will betroth you to me in faithfulness; and you shall know Y HWH. (Hos 2:16-20)

In his vision of a new heaven and a new earth, Third Isaiah characterizes the new conditions that will result when God and Israel will be united in marriage.

> You shall be a crown of beauty in the hand of Y HWH, and a royal diadem in the hand of your God. You shall no longer be named "Forsaken," and your land shall no longer be named "Desolate." But you shall be called "Hephzibah" (my delight is in her), and your land "Beulah" (married). For Y HWH delights in you, and your land shall be married. For as a young man marries a virgin, so shall your Builder marry you; and as the bridegroom rejoices over the bride, so shall your God rejoice over you. (Isa 62:3-5)

Israel's future of a union with God in marriage denotes a new creation, the inauguration of a new moral order. It corresponds to Daniel's vision of the reign of God (2:44-45) and the ascent of "one like a human being" to receive dominion, glory, and the reign of God. If, as Jesus asserts in his introduction to this parable, "the reign of God is like ten virgins who, taking their lamps, went out to meet the bridegroom," the marriage feast in which the parable culminates signifies the actualization of this long-awaited eschatological reality of God's reign. Consequently, the responsibility that is entrusted to these virgins is momentous. As virgins, and therefore the embodiment of the true Israel, they are serving in this eschatological moment as the bearers of light. That is their identity. But will they fulfill their identity in activity? Will they provide the needed light that will enable the bridegroom to arrive at his destination and enter into the marriage feast?

As the ten women await the arrival of the bridegroom they grow drowsy and fall asleep.[35] For some reason he has been delayed, but no account or excuse is given for his tardiness. In spite of the conjectures that have been offered (a lengthy dispute over the marriage settlement, or a disagreement over the bride price) no explanation is necessary.[36] The original audience would have been

---

[35] Jülicher, *Die Gleichnisreden Jesu,* 453, appears to be alone in recognizing that one does not let oil lamps burn for long hours needlessly. Moreover, he adds, "how can one fall asleep with a burning lamp in hand?" Yet the story requires that the lamps continue to burn while the virgins are sleeping so that the supply of oil in the lamps will be diminished, and a crisis will result.

[36] Jeremias, *The Parables of Jesus,* 172, 174. According to Safrai and Stern, "Both families had the responsibility of helping the young couple to establish its household; it seems, however, that it was particularly the groom who was interested in his in-laws' accepting the obligation, as it was in the household of the groom's parents that the couple would begin its married life and the major expenses therefore fell upon the groom and his father" (*The Jewish People in the First Century,* 752–53).

able to fill that gap from their own experience. A loud clamor in the middle of the night announces the arrival of the bridegroom, and the women are awakened from their sleep: "Look, the bridegroom! Come out to meet him!" All ten respond immediately. They arise and put their lamps in order by trimming the wicks and replenishing the supply of oil.[37] But five of them find themselves in a critical situation: their lamps are going out, and they did not make provision for such a contingency by bringing additional oil with them. They are obliged to ask the other five to share some of their extra oil, "Give us of your oil, for our lamps are going out."

It is at this point that another startling surprise occurs, a surprise that may evoke a painful disappointment and perhaps even disillusion, especially for women.[38] The five who brought an extra supply of oil in their flasks refuse to share with the five who did not. As ten virgins, they are a community representing the institution of the synagogue. They are united, therefore, in a common calling as women, to serve as bearers of light. It would seem that their natural inclination would be to share their supply of oil with each other. But they refuse with a response that is reinforced by a triple negative: μήποτε οὐ μὴ ἀρκέσῃ ἡμῖν καὶ ὑμῖν. "Certainly there never would be enough for us and for you."[39]

There is, however, another manuscript tradition of their reply in which only a double negative is used: μήποτε οὐκ ἀρκέσῃ ἡμῖν καὶ ὑμῖν. In this reading the negatives would neutralize each other, and the negation would be weakened to such a degree that their initial use of μήποτε would introduce something conjectured, a *probably* or a *perhaps*.[40] Accordingly, the women's reply to the request to share oil would express a degree of uncertainty: "There is probably not enough for us and for you."

The manuscript tradition is more or less evenly divided between the two readings: μήποτε οὐ μὴ ἀρκέσῃ ἡμῖν καὶ ὑμῖν and μήποτε οὐκ ἀρκέσῃ ἡμῖν

---

[37] The employment of the resurrection verb, ἐγείρω (arise), leads Donfried ("The Allegory of the Ten Virgins," 424–25) to conclude that the language of 25:5-7 is allegorical and "refers to the death and resurrection of the virgins." It is another factor in his treatment of the parable as an allegory composed by Matthew.

[38] I am grateful to Dr. Cornelia Cyss-Wittenstein for elaborating this perspective.

[39] This is the translation offered in Walter Bauer's *A Greek-English Lexicon of the New Testament and Other Early Christian Literature*. 3d ed., rev. and ed. Frederick W. Danker (Chicago: University of Chicago Press, 2000) 649. See also Friedrich Blass and Albert Debrunner, *A Greek Grammar of the New Testament and Other Early Christian Literature,* trans. and rev. Robert W. Funk (Chicago: University of Chicago Press, 1961) 223.

[40] Bauer, *A Greek-English Lexicon of the New Testament and Other Early Christian Literature,* 649; and Blass and Debrunner, *A Greek Grammar of the New Testament and Other Early Christian Literature,* 223.

καὶ ὑμῖν. Of the two, however, the former may be the more difficult reading, and therefore also the preferable one. It is the reading of the twenty-seventh edition of Nestle-Aland's *Novum Testamentum Graece.* Accordingly, the conviction of the five who have extra oil is that sharing the oil would make it impossible for the ten of them to fulfill their vocation as light bearers, and therefore the groom and his party would be unable to find their way to the marriage celebration. Nevertheless, as Adolf Jülicher contends, the alternative phrase, μήποτε οὐκ ἀρκέσῃ, is more sensitive and solicitous and fits appropriately into the situation, and it may well have been the original reading.[41] The only alternative is for the others to obtain more oil from another source: "Go rather to those selling and buy [some] for yourselves." Evidently, in spite of the time of night, it is presupposed that oil will be obtainable even if the shop owners will have to be roused out of bed in order to sell oil to these five women. Somehow the five succeed in acquiring the oil they need, but it is too late to enable them to serve as light bearers for the wedding procession.

In the meantime the groom and the groomsmen appear, and the five who were prepared with an extra supply of oil are able to provide the light that is required to enable them to reach their destination. Together they enter into the marriage feast, "and the door is shut." Somewhat later the other five virgins arrive and, as they proceed to knock on the door, they call out, "Master, Master, open for us!"

In view of Jesus' encouragement to his disciples in the Sermon on the Mount (7:7-8), the expectation, at least of the readers of Matthew's Gospel, would be the opening of the door for admission to the marriage feast.

> Keep on asking, and it will be given to you; keep on seeking, and you will find; keep on knocking, and it will be opened to you. For everyone who asks receives, and everyone who seeks finds, and to the one who knocks, it will be opened.

When, however, the door is opened to these five who did not provide light for the wedding procession, it is only to inform them that they are inadmissible to the wedding festivities. Unable to recognize them because they were not among the virgins who provided light for the wedding procession, the Master, who must be the bridegroom, turns them away with an asseveration, "Amen, I tell you, I don't know you!"[42]

---

[41] Jülicher, *Die Gleichnisreden Jesu,* 451.

[42] As noted by Via, the solemn declaration, "Amen," generally does not appear in Jesus' parables, but there are some exceptions (*The Parables,* 123). Compare Matt 18:13 and Luke 12:37 with Luke 11:8; 14:24; 18:14. In view of the thirty-one uses of "Amen" in Matthew's Gospel, it seems likely that it was added by the evangelist.

Five of the ten virgins who represented the institution of the synagogue and who in their virginity embodied the true Israel are excluded from the wedding feast and simultaneously, therefore, from participation in the reign of God that is symbolized by the wedding feast. Their use of the double address, "Master, Master" (or "Lord, Lord"), as they knock on the door, expresses their desire to be admitted to the celebration. Its employment here recalls another saying of Jesus in the Sermon on the Mount: "Not everyone who says to me, 'Lord, Lord' (or 'Master, Master') will enter into the reign of God, but the one who does the will of my Father in heaven."

If God's reign is comparable to ten virgins, its concrete reality is not being manifested by all of them. Only five fulfill the purpose of their calling, specifically those who had prepared for contingency by taking with them an extra supply of oil that subsequently enabled them to provide the light that was needed to escort the groom and his wedding party to the marriage feast. But it is not the sufficiency of oil that constitutes their integrity, or that symbolizes their obedience to God's will and therefore admits them to the marriage feast.[43] It is the integrity of identity and activity! It is the identity of discipleship within the eschatological reality of God's reign that is validated by the activity of bearing light. But that integrity can only be established individually in and through individual performance. It would seem, therefore, that the only rationale for sharing oil would be a carefully calculated amount that would suffice to enable all ten virgins to fulfill their vocation as bearers of light and thereby establish their integrity individually. Such a determination is impossible in this context. Yet even if it were possible, codependency cannot establish the integrity of individual personhood. No one can claim or appropriate the integrity of identity and activity from another human being. Participation in the wedding feast, and therefore in the reign of God that it symbolizes, requires the individual human being to express the identity of being a bearer of light in terms of concrete activity. If Jesus entrusted God's reign to his disciples, as Matt 16:19; Luke 12:32 and 22:29 attest, the response-ability of exercising that rule involves both the identity of being God's surrogate and the activities it requires for the fulfillment of that identity. That, in fact, is the identity Jesus conferred on his disciples in Matt 5:14: "You are the light of the world."

John the Baptizer, in Matt 3:9, had already proclaimed that identity in and of itself cannot qualify one for participation in the reality of God's reign: "And do not think to say in yourselves, 'We have father Abraham.' For I say to you, God is able to raise up children to Abraham from these stones." The true char-

---

[43] As claimed by Donfried, "The Allegory of the Ten Virgins," 423, 425; and Schrenk, "Auferweckung der Toten oder Gericht nach den Werken," 294.

acter of Israel as God's people who participate in the reign of God must be manifested in incarnational activity.

The story of the Ten Virgins proves to be a parable, an extended metaphor drawn from common life that arrests the hearer by its vividness and strangeness, and teases the mind into active thought.[44] It is an "interesting particular case," perhaps "freely composed," and all of its reversals function as a parable that subverts the world of male domination and its nationalistic ideology of ethnic identity as God's elect people.[45] Attendantly, in a mirror-like fashion it compels its hearers—and readers—to scrutinize their discipleship within the eschatological reality of God's reign in order to determine if and to what extent their identity is validated by their activity.[46] And finally, at the same time, the parable discloses "a new possibility of world" that is symbolized by the marriage feast in which the bearers of light participate. But all that this new possibility signifies depends of course on the individual hearer—or reader—and the extent to which that eschatological reality is construed in the light of the prophetic expectations of texts like Hos 2:16-20 and Isa 62:3-5.

[44] Dodd, *The Parables of the Kingdom,* 16.

[45] From Linnemann, *Jesus of the Parables,* 3–4 and Crossan, *The Dark Interval,* Argus ed., 59; Polebridge ed., 42.

[46] As far as I have been able to determine, the mirror-like character of parable was introduced by Antoinette Clark Wire, *The Parable Is a Mirror,* 1983–84 Bible Study Book (Atlanta: The Office of Women, General Assembly Mission Board, Presbyterian Church, U.S.A., 1983).

De-colonizing Ourselves as Readers: The Story of the Syro-Phoenician Woman as a Text

Hisako Kinukawa

༭

I. A GROUP JOURNEY TOWARD BECOMING POSTCOLONIAL SUBJECTS

Who would imagine that I would start writing my article for this book at San Francisco Theological Seminary, where Anne Wire has been teaching New Testament for many years and where she worked with me when I wrote my dissertation in 1989 and 1991. This year marks the tenth anniversary of my graduation. I am privileged to have been on the SFTS campus again, teaching a course—Feminist Hermeneutics of the Gospels—for the Doctor of Ministry program.

The members of the class (eleven women and one man) were a diverse group consisting of representatives from many countries: Argentina (originally from the Netherlands), Ghana, India (presently located in Switzerland), Indonesia (formerly doing ministry in the Philippines), Korea (presently in the U.S.), Japan, Puerto Rico (presently in Colombia), Samoa (presently in Fiji), and the U.S. The diversity gave an ecumenical and global perspective to all phases of the class readings, reports, and discussions. It engendered powerful dynamics as we tried to create a critical, constructive community of learning. Needless to say, most of us had bi- or tri-cultural experiences, so that we had no difficulty in grasping the idea of the hybrid-ness of our reality in the contemporary sociopolitical world as well as in the religious world. In addition, many were aware of the dire need for decolonizing our way of reading texts and

131

even our classmates, if we could consider them as living texts. Each showed sensitivity and receptiveness as we listened to the stories of her/his classmates as "flesh and blood" readers,[1] which prepared us to be engaged with the methodological articles and the text.

It was my first experience teaching a course in English at the graduate level, although quite a number of opportunities had been given to me in the past to read papers and lecture in English. This new adventure was exciting, meaningful, and enriching in many senses. It was such a challenge to listen to various accents of English and to figure out the meaning and implications of what was spoken. Although our common language was English, we spent much time learning what each person meant in her/his expressions from her/his social locations. Since Anne was away in China for her research, I kept feeling I was missing the right person to give my experience the final touch.

Steps We Have Trodden Together as a Group

My course consisted of three major components: social locations, critical methods, and interpretation of the story of the Syro-Phoenician/Canaanite woman recorded in Mark and Matthew respectively. At the end of the first presentation of our individual social locations I asked the group what our goal is when we do exegesis of biblical texts. We had already discovered that there is no value-neutral document or person. Each book in the Bible is a profoundly social document that was born in the context of concrete faith communities. Specific people in particular times and places were deeply involved in the creation of each document. In turn, each document was written in response to specific issues, problems, conflicts, and turbulences in the life of specific community/ies.

As each writer/author/editor wrote his gospel he was provoked by a sense of urgency. Something was burning inside him, pushing him to communicate the stories of the gospel to the community/ies. In writing the gospel he undertook three tasks: First, confronting the realities facing his community/ies, he engaged the issues with which they were struggling. Second, urged and inspired by his community/ies, he wrote/edited his gospel looking back on the life of Jesus. Third, in writing his gospel he hoped to give the community/ies a vision for the future.

Because our documents embody particular social locations, it is important

---

[1] The term is used by Fernando Segovia in his article, "Toward a Hermeneutics of the Diaspora: A Hermeneutics of Otherness and Engagement," in Fernando F. Segovia and Mary Ann Tolbert, eds., *Reading from This Place* (Minneapolis: Fortress Press, 1995) 1:57. The group read his article as one of the major resources. Most in the group resonated with his distinctive idea of intercultural criticism born out of redefining his social location as one in the diaspora.

that we also consider our own social locations. In this way we can clarify for ourselves the vantage points and perspectives which we bring to our reading and interpreting of the social documents in the Bible. It is necessary to identify two dimensions of our social locations: (1) that determined by birth/circumstances and (2) that determined by our commitments. From our birth/circumstances, we are given, for example, race, class, nationality, education, gender, sexual orientation, and age. We accept them as they are or we challenge them and transform their meanings for our lives as our commitments are made. By commitments we choose who we want to be/become. In this category may be counted faith, world views, vocation, marriage/union/singleness, political or social commitments, and the like.

An important question to ask is how we see our social locations in relation to the power to be. Social locations raise questions concerning advocacy and engagement. Social locations define the position from which we act politically and socially and on the basis of which we identify ourselves in relation to the social, political, and economic aspects of our society/ies and the world. A key question we asked in class is whether we are able to discern whom we are oppressing and by whom we are oppressed.

The group experienced some critical moments when we revealed that some of us have been colonized and marginalized while some of us have been associated with colonizing, regardless of wanting or not wanting to do so. The group struggled, searching for ways to understand the differences arising from the power relationships between the nations as well as the histories behind us. Personal encounters through group discussion as well as private conversations (that were not without bitterness as well as efforts at being perceptive) engendered among us a deeper comprehension of the situational differences between us as well as a greater incentive to understand the experiences of others that were different from anything we had experienced. Thus the second presentation of our social locations took place, which turned out to be far deeper and more complex.

The reason we asked the question about social location is that the Jesus movement was a social praxis. Both the writing and reading of the gospels are, therefore, social actions. As "flesh and blood" readers with particular social locations who are aware of the various forms of oppression surrounding us in the world, we are called to make clear the oppressive messages hidden in the documents of the Bible. We are asked to uncover ways in which the colonizing power structures of the time are evidenced in the texts. We are asked to undertake interpretations that bring forth liberation and justice for the marginalized and dehumanized in our society/ies. I asked the group: "What is the urgency for us in reading the documents in the Bible? What compels us to read them? What motivates us to get involved with the social praxis of reading them?"

Reading carefully each chapter of the book *Mark and Method: New Approaches in Biblical Studies,*[2] the group grasped the main ideas of narrative, reader-response, deconstruction, and feminist criticism. Since each article dealt with various texts in Mark, it gave the students a good background in the gospel before we became more deeply involved in one story. At this point we added another article, "The Doubly Colonized: Decolonizing Method," by Musa Dube in her book, *Postcolonial Feminist Interpretation of the Bible,*[3] to introduce us to postcolonial criticism. Dube describes herself and women of the two-thirds world as being under "double colonization." That means "they are oppressed by two structural systems: imperialism and patriarchy."[4] She problematizes the fact that white middle-class women have only paid attention to patriarchy. She proposes that biblical feminist discourses also "need to adopt decolonizing feminist practices, given the pervasiveness of imperial biblical oppression in the global structures of the past and present."[5] The proposal caused some additional critical moments among the students because those who were from colonized countries comprised half of the group while the rest were from colonizing countries. However, a voice saying that neither group needs to defend her/himself healed a sort of pain running through the group. Everyone came to the point where all were eligible to uncover the power structures of patriarchy and colonization in the texts we read.

According to Dube, "Decolonizing feminist biblical practices describes the commitment and the methods of reading the Bible that resist both patriarchal and imperial oppression in order to cultivate a space of liberating interdependence among nations, genders, races, ethnicities, the environment, and development."[6] She proposes a subversive hybrid approach, which identifies the location of colonized women as the first point of contact for the colonizers and at the same time rejects "the privileging of imperial texts and institutions as the standard for all cultures at all times."[7]

This aroused some sensitivity, especially among those from the U.S., who asked how they could be decolonized or how they could be conscious of being part of the colonizers. Because "feminist discourse also theorizes women as

---

[2] Janice Capel Anderson and Stephen D. Moore, eds., *Mark and Method: New Approaches in Biblical Studies* (Minneapolis: Fortress, 1992).

[3] Musa Dube, "The Doubly Colonized: Decolonizing Method," in eadem, *Postcolonial Feminist Interpretation of the Bible* (St. Louis: Chalice, 2000).

[4] Ibid. 113.

[5] Ibid. 115.

[6] Ibid. 111.

[7] Ibid. 115–16.

colonized landless citizens,"[8] it seemed easier for the women to understand the meaning of being colonized. That resulted in leaving my only male student out of our solidarity. However, he was very perceptive in his efforts to comprehend what it meant to "re-read the master's canonical texts."[9] The class was carried on with a certain effective tension and inevitable discourse, including the work of re-acknowledging each one's own social location with a new vocabulary. That meant, in practice, reading the texts from differing angles, which Dube names "Rahab's reading prism."[10]

II. MY RE-VISIT TO THE STORY
OF THE SYRO-PHOENICIAN WOMAN (MARK 7:24-30)

The class read articles on the story of the Syro-Phoenician/Canaanite woman in Mark and Matthew written from different perspectives and social locations by fifteen scholars, fourteen of whom were women. It is beyond the scope of this paper to articulate what the class found, discussed, and decolonized through the journey of reading together the two versions of this story of a woman. Here I would like to reflect in hindsight on my own encounter with the story of the Syro-Phoenician woman recorded in Mark. It is, for me, a re-encounter with this particular story, since I wrote a chapter on it in my book, *Women and Jesus in Mark: A Japanese Feminist Perspective,* using the lenses of historical and rhetorical criticism. Here I will concentrate on the social location of the story of the Syro-Phoenician woman and then ask why Mark put such a bitter phrase ("Let the children be fed first, for it is not fair to take the children's food and throw it to the dogs") in Jesus' mouth. My goal is to uncover the power relationships that are reflected overtly and covertly in the story. My approach to the story will be multi-axial, as proposed by postcolonial criticism.[11]

Mark sets the story of the woman on an occasion when Jesus "went away to the region of Tyre" (7:24). In speaking of the "region of Tyre," Mark indicates that Jesus did not visit the city of Tyre, which is located on an island just off the coast in the Mediterranean Sea, but the rural hinterlands surrounding the city. The woman is introduced as "a Greek (ʹΕλληνίς) of Syro-Phoenician origin" (v. 26). The story begins with the woman's plea for the healing of her

---

[8] Ibid. 111.

[9] Ibid.

[10] Dube writes: "Rahab's reading prism is a postcolonial feminist eye of many angles and of seeing, reading, and hearing literary texts through resisting imperial and patriarchal oppressive structures and ideologies" (ibid. 123).

[11] Kwok Pui-lan, *Discovering the Bible in the Non-Biblical World* (Maryknoll, N.Y.: Orbis, 1995), 79.

little daughter who has an unclean spirit, but it is clear that the miracle is not reported for its own sake. The discourse between the woman and Jesus centers around eating bread at the table of fellowship. At first glance the story raises several questions for us as readers. We wonder: What is presupposed by the storyteller and hearers? What did they know about the region of Tyre and the woman, a Greek of Syro-Phoenician origin? Why does Jesus respond to her by using the language of bread, even though he knows her main concern is in the healing of her sick child?

There is much discussion about whether Jesus actually went out of Israel, even to the region of Tyre, and whether he actually intended an evangelizing mission to foreigners. Because the community of faith Mark was related to already contained both Jews and foreigners, it is probable that he set two parallel cycles of stories (4:35–6:44 and 6:45–8:26) in his gospel. The first cycle is located in Galilee and the second cycle, in which our story is included, in foreign lands.

In the Old Testament, Tyre is said to be proud and a threat to Israel. It is always named with Sidon (Isaiah 23; Jer 47:4; Ezekiel 27, 28; Joel 3:4-8; Zech 9:2) and described as polluted by materialism.[12] At the time of Jesus both Galilee and Tyre were part of the territory occupied by the Roman empire. Their cities and regions were under imperial control and oppressed by colonial politics. Despite this fact, it is said that the cities of Tyre and Sidon were two of the wealthiest and most important ports on the coast. In contrast, the peasant population in Galilee suffered under threefold oppression: (1) Roman imperialism, (2) the Herodian monarchy, which fawned on Rome, and (3) Temple politics in Judea. Jonathan Reed, in his recent book, draws our attention to the fact that Tyre was closer to Capernaum than Capernaum was to Jerusalem.[13] Tyre might not sound too foreign or distant to those residing in Galilee.

Relationships between Tyre and Galilee

The phrase "the region of Tyre" in Mark 7:24 implies the rural territory surrounding the city of Tyre, which borders on Galilee. According to Mark, Jesus seems to have restricted his visit to this rural area (see also 3:8). Gerd Theissen, who has carried out extensive research on the cultural context and

---

[12] Some important manuscripts such as Sinaiticus, Alexandrinus, Vaticanus, and others add "and Sidon" after "Tyre" (Gail R. O'Day, "Surprised by Faith: Jesus and the Canaanite Woman," *List* 24 [Fall, 1989] 291).

[13] Jonathan L. Reed, *Archaeology and the Galilean Jesus: A Re-examination of the Evidence* (Harrisburg: Trinity Press International, 2000) 185–87. See also Masahiro Yamaguchi, *Iesu Tanjo no Yoake* (Tokyo: Nihon Kirisuto Kyodan Shuppankyoku, 2002).

historical situation of the regions of Tyre and Galilee, analyzes the relationship between the two regions from six angles.[14] Following my review of Theissen's analyses on Tyre and Galilee, I will revisit the social location of the story of the Syro-Phoenician woman in the hope that it may offer clues to assist us in answering our questions.

(1) ETHNIC RELATIONSHIP

In describing ethnic relationships in the region, Theissen states that "Anyone who looks closely at the geographical relationship will discover that, both in the rural hinterland of Tyre and in the territory of the Decapolis, Jesus could find Jews living next to Syrians and Phoenicians."[15] Villages inhabited by Jews existed right next to the villages inhabited by Syrians and Phoenicians, where the hinterland of Tyre intersected the hinterland of Galilee, with no clear borders separating the two. We may plausibly imagine that villages of different ethnic groups were intermingled in such areas. According to Reed, "archaeological evidence, especially recent studies on pottery and clay sources, have shown that Syro-Phoenician settlements emanated from the cities of Tyre and Sidon and extended considerable distances inland."[16] Reed further points out that "Tyrian territory and Syro-Phoenician settlements were closer to Galilee than is often recognized. Kedesh, a key Tyrian site on its border with Upper Galilee, was only twenty-five kilometers north of Capernaum, and archaeological evidence of Syro-Phoenician settlements has been uncovered at several sites in the Huleh Valley, and isolated evidence has been found even in southern Golan."[17] Theissen comments on this geographic proximity, "Thus the 'journey into gentile territory' described by Mark only touches places where Jews lived. This favors the idea that Mark gave an entirely new meaning to some of the place-designations he received from tradition: Jesus' going to the places mentioned gives the appearance of a mission to the Gentiles, of whose legitimacy and necessity Mark is convinced."[18] Though Mark may have used Tyre and Syro-Phoenicia for the purpose of associating Jesus with the mission to foreigners, the names may be more historically plausible, bearing existential significance because Jews and foreigners lived in close proximity.

---

[14] Gerd Theissen, *The Gospels in Context: Social and Political History in the Synoptic Tradition*, trans. Linda M. Maloney (Minneapolis: Fortress, 1991) 61–80.

[15] Ibid. 68.

[16] Reed, *Archaeology and the Galilean Jesus*, 185–86.

[17] Ibid. 163

[18] Theissen, *The Gospels in Context*, 68; Reed, *Archaeology and the Galilean Jesus*, 185–86.

(2) Cultural Circumstances

Of the cultural circumstances, Theissen writes, ". . . there was [a] long-standing contrast between Phoenician and Jewish culture. On top of this was imposed a Hellenistic culture that undoubtedly made a much greater impact in the cities than in the hinterland, in which we may include the Jewish-populated areas of Palestine."[19] The designation of the woman points to these circumstances. She would have known Greek, at least, and probably was thoroughly integrated in Greek culture. Nevertheless, she would have been able to communicate easily with Jesus if she used her native Phoenician language, which is very close to Palestinian Aramaic. In the woman's encounter with Jesus, two different "social worlds" meet. If we recognize the proximity of Phoenician inland settlements to Jewish settlements along Galilee's northern border we must expect, as Reed points out, much more cultural contact as well as tensions between villages in the peripheral areas of Galilee.[20]

(3) Social Status

With respect to the woman's social status and the Hellenistic culture that influenced the life of the Phoenicians, Theissen points out, "knowledge of Greek language and culture point to a member of the upper class, since Hellenization had first affected the people of higher status everywhere. And for a long time there would be many among the simple people who did not understand Greek."[21] Though he admits that Greek must have penetrated the lower classes, he asserts that a woman who is called *"Hellenis"* would be someone of higher social status. He goes a step further and adds that she may be relatively affluent and belong to the privileged group of *"Hellenes."*[22]

On the other hand, the use of *"Hellenis"* to describe the woman with a sick child may simply have been intended to indicate that she was not a Jew, but a foreigner. This would be consistent with usage of the term by most New Testament writers.[23] Thus we should exercise caution in describing the woman as relatively affluent and privileged. Mark may have used the word simply to make a clear distinction between the woman as a foreigner and Jesus as a Jew for the purpose

---

[19] Theissen, *The Gospels in Context,* 68.

[20] Reed, *Archaeology and the Galilean Jesus,* 163–64.

[21] Theissen, *The Gospels in Context,* 70.

[22] Ibid. 70–72.

[23] It is interesting to observe that this is the only place where Mark uses the word "Greek" in his gospel, and no other synoptic gospel writer uses the word at all. In the whole Christian Testament the word is used twenty-seven times. Half of these uses are found in Acts and the other half are in Pauline letters, as we would expect. Exceptions are in John 7:35 and 12:20, and in Col 3:11. In almost all cases the word is used to designate foreigners in contrast to the Jews.

of suggesting the possibility of Jesus' foreign mission. Since Mark specifies that Jesus was in the "region of Tyre," it is possible that the woman may be from one of the peripheral villages of Tyre, where people's lives were not as easy as the lives of those in the urban cities—that is, not at all a member of the elite.

(4) ECONOMIC CONDITIONS

The fourth aspect discussed by Theissen is economic conditions in the border regions of Tyre and Galilee. The city of Tyre was well known for "its wealth based on metal work, the production of purple dye and an extensive trade with the whole Mediterranean region. Its money was one of the most stable currencies in circulation at this period . . . . This was certainly one reason why the temple treasury was kept in Tyrian coin, even though this meant accepting the fact that the coins of Tyre depicted the god Melkart."[24] Because the city of Tyre had very little space for farming, it depended on importing agricultural products from Galilee and other places. "The Galilean hinterland and the rural territory belonging to the city (partly settled by Jews) were the 'breadbasket' of the metropolis of Tyre."[25] Most of the produce was purchased by rich city dwellers, while the peasants in the hinterlands were always in want.[26] Galilean peasants must have been resentful when they saw the ruling class taking their produce for sale to the urban population of Tyre. Agricultural crops produced by the peasants did not return to their daily table to satisfy their own basic need. The peasants experienced a constant shortage of food and money, even though they labored from dawn to dusk all through the year. Under their threefold exploitation, the Galilean peasants were deprived of a stable life.

Taking into consideration the bitter economic relationship between affluent Tyre and exploited Galilee, we can see that Jesus' bitter words in Mark 7:27 would have had a powerful impact. The saying, which is so offensive to the woman, would reflect the humiliating power relationship that Galileans had to endure with respect to urban Tyrians: "First let the mouths of the poor people in the Jewish rural areas be satisfied. For it is not good to take poor people's food and throw it to the rich Tyrians in the city." Heard this way, the words overtly express the reality of the destitute Galilean peasants and show

---

[24] Theissen, *The Gospels in Context,* 73.

[25] Ibid. 74.

[26] Ibid. 72–75. Pointing out that popular coins used in Israel were with Tyrian imprint, Reed says they "were a daily reminder of Tyre's economic influence on Galilean commerce" (*Archaeology and the Galilean Jesus,* 186). Paula Fredriksen, in her book *Jesus of Nazareth, King of the Jews: A Jewish Life and the Emergence of Christianity* ([New York: Alfred A. Knopf, 1999] 208), also points out that the Temple in Jerusalem relied on the Tyrian coins and so there were money changers who converted the currencies of pilgrims from various places to this standard coinage.

their resistance against the power exercised by the urban people of Tyre. Theissen says, ". . . when people mentioned food in the border regions of Tyre and Galilee, and also spoke of children (= Jews) and dogs (= Gentiles), they simultaneously addressed the general economic situation, determined by a clear hierarchy that was just as clearly reversed by Jesus' words. Perhaps Jesus, in replying, was able to make connections with a well-known saying shaped by this situation."[27] Those Tyrians who hungered for and devoured the agrarian produce of Galilee are analogized to "dogs" by Jesus. Jesus' reply represents the popular feeling of the Galilean peasants toward the Tyrians whom they viewed as rich, representing the Hellenistic culture of the elite.

Yet if the Syro-Phoenician woman in this story is from one of the villages in the hinterland of Tyre, which is plausible, the village is surely peripheral from the perspective of the urban elite in the city of Tyre. Compared to them, the woman might not be so rich or so privileged. Assuming this to be the case—that the woman with her sick child is from the hinterland, with only limited access to the life of the urban rich, and is socially ostracized because of the unclean spirit in her child—then it is easier for us to understand why she is not knocked down by Jesus' words. She does not identify herself with those to whom Jesus' bitter words are thrown and whom he criticizes. She is from a village in the vicinity of Galilee where the life may not be so different from that of the Galilean peasants.

(5) Political Relationships

The fifth aspect discussed by Theissen is the political relationships between Tyre and Galilee. According to Theissen, "The lands of these Jewish and gentile regions merged gradually into one another. The temptation to expand at the expense of the Jewish hinterland was powerful."[28] Similarly, Sean Freyne observes that since there was no natural border between Tyre and Galilee, "Tyre . . . [had] a history of personal encroachment into Galilean territory from the days of Solomon to Caesar. Thus it [posed] the threat not of the invader but of the permanent aggrandizer."[29] The expansion is also fairly well attested in the Old Testament and the writings of Josephus. This pattern of expansion means that Galilean peasants were subjugated and oppressed politically and economically by one of the rival colonies of the Roman empire.[30]

---

[27] Theissen, *The Gospels in Context*, 75.

[28] Ibid. 76.

[29] Sean Freyne, *Galilee from Alexander the Great to Hadrian, 323 B.C.E. to 135 C.E.: A Study of Second Temple Judaism* (Notre Dame: University of Notre Dame Press, 1980) 120.

[30] Theissen, *The Gospels in Context*, 75–77. According to Reed, "from Josephus and the New Testament we know that Tyre's wealth and economic stature cast a shadow over Galilee: imperial

(6) Social-Psychological Relationships

The last aspect of Theissen's analysis is concerned with social-psychological relationships. As has been illustrated in the analyses above, there were significant differences in terms of power between Tyre and Galilee, despite the close proximity of their villages. It can easily be imagined that there were aggressive prejudices on both sides.[31]

In summary, we may conclude with Reed that "Tyre is not arbitrarily chosen, but it was the closest foreign city to Galilee that was part of their epic traditions and that is still powerfully influencing their present social and economic situation."[32]

Who Is This Woman?

The woman is said to be ethnically Syro-Phoenician and culturally Greek. Her religious identity is not apparent from these representations. Although it is plausible to assume she believes in the Tyrian god Melkart and other gods, we do not hear her own voice in this respect. We do not know if she has any interest in Jesus' itinerant movement. She hears that Jesus is nearby and dares to come meet him. We may only infer that she might be socially stigmatized because her daughter is possessed by an unclean spirit. The woman may see Jesus as offering a chance to have her sick child healed.

She enters the house where Jesus is and falls down at his feet, asking for a favor. Just like the demon-possessed man (5:6) and Jairus, the synagogue leader (5:22-23), she assumes a subordinate position in relation to Jesus. However, in contrast to his reaction to these two men, Jesus shows great reluctance to respond to her request. Mary Ann Tolbert describes Jesus in this scene as using "a highly disparaging metaphor, likening her to a dog."[33] As I have previously mentioned, this metaphor reflects the power relationships between Galilee and Tyre. Jesus sides with the Galilean destitute peasants and thus defends them over against the Tyrians who benefit from the Galilean peasants.

Some find the reason for the rebuff in the fact that the Syro-Phoenician woman is a foreigner, but we have read earlier in Mark that Jesus has healed a

decrees warned Tyre against encroaching too far into Jewish lands in Galilee (e.g., *Ant.* 14.190-216), and on at least one occasion, in 43 B.C.E., Tyre seized considerable Galilean territory from the Jews under the Tyrant Marion (*War* 1.238-39). Tyre was dependent on and hungry for the produce of Galilee (Acts 12:20), a point that the Galileans certainly resented whenever the ruling elite sold their produce to the highest bidder" (*Archaeology and the Galilean Jesus,* 186).

[31] Theissen, *The Gospels in Context,* 77–78.

[32] Reed, *Archaeology and the Galilean Jesus,* 186.

[33] Mary Ann Tolbert, *Sowing the Gospel: Mark's World in Literary-Historical Perspective* (Minneapolis: Fortress, 1989) 185.

foreigner, the man with an unclean spirit in the country near Gerasa in the De-capolis (5:1-20). Some say she is rebuffed because she is a woman and see in this the sexism of the time. Yet the analyses above indicate that there are other concerns besides gender at work in this story. Tolbert offers another view, sug-gesting, "His rebuff provides the opportunity for her faith to be fully revealed, for she takes his metaphor and turns it back on him."[34] Although the story may imply that the woman has faith, the woman's response indicates that her inter-est is focused less on faith and more on her child's need to be cured—so much so that she persists even when rebuffed by Jesus. As Kwok Pui-lan says, "The woman, though denigrated by Jesus, speaks in a supportive and affirmative way, for she is concerned with maintaining the relationship."[35]

In order to understand the woman, it is important to bear in mind that she does not identify herself with the rich and privileged people of the city of Tyre. Since she resides in the Tyrian hinterland, she identifies more closely with the Galilean peasants. She does not succumb to Jesus' words that rebuff the pop-ulace of Tyre as a whole. In response, she says, "Yes, it is so, but, sir, even the dogs under the table eat the children's crumbs" (7:28; literal translation of the original). She acknowledges the primacy that the Galilean peasants ought to have. At the same time, she reminds Jesus—who is more concerned about the Galileans who scarcely have food to live on and critically reveals the dominant relationship of the Tyrians over the Jews through his harsh words—of the fact that there are the other kinds of dogs (people of Tyre destitute like her and her child) that also need to be fed. In this expression we may see her raising a se-rious question: can Jesus totally ignore a sick child while talking about feed-ing the "children" of Israel? If Jesus protects the children of Israel, the woman insists, then she and her sick child should also be protected. She insists that Jesus' harsh words do not apply to her and her child. To the contrary, she and her child will be exploited by Jesus if he will not feed them, since they also are suffering. Therefore she does not give up.

Listening to Jesus, she is made aware of the fact that she is from Tyre, a city noted for robbing even the smallest bits of food from Galilean peasants who are forced to sell their produce to Tyre, or hand it over in taxes. On the other hand, in hearing Jesus protect the "others" in Galilee, she is made aware of the fact that she is also one of these "others" in the society of Tyre. There-fore she keeps asking Jesus to expand his mercy to the "others" in Tyre. She questions how it is possible for Jesus to exclude her and her child from his

---

[34] Ibid.

[35] Kwok Pui-lan, *Discovering the Bible in the Non-Biblical World*, 74.

table community. She asks for Jesus to be consistent in giving primacy to the marginalized wherever they are and showing an egalitarian spirit toward those who are destitute. Had she not experienced being the "other" in her society, she would not be able to be as confident as she is in asking Jesus' help. Her tenacity can be read as evidence that she is neither rich nor privileged.

Jesus responds to her with words that fully accept her request: "For your words, you may go . . . ." Jesus affirms her, as if he has learned a new lesson from her. In the first part of the encounter between Jesus and the woman, the distribution of power is apparently in favor of Jesus. Toward the end it is reversed, favoring the woman. The last verse, "So she went home, found the child lying on the bed, and the demon gone," does not say anything about her faith, conversion, or religion. We must abstain from concluding she has become the first foreign woman Christian regardless of how much Mark wants the audience to read the story in this way. We also must admit that it is Mark's redactional activity that puts the story in the context of table fellowship. This story is not originally about table fellowship, but about the power relationships between Tyrian urban people and Galilean peasants.

III. CONCLUDING MY JOURNEY

Two elements—the political and economic relationships between the regions of Tyre and Galilee and the oppressive power of Tyrians over Galilean peasants—provide a context for understanding why Jesus throws such bitter words at the woman: His words reflect the urgent need of Galileans to secure food for their daily lives. His words, then, reveal the story to be about a very basic issue: the unfair distribution of food among rival colonies within the Roman empire. The woman's words, however, demonstrate that she rejects being used as a foil in Jesus' conflict with the affluent urban Tyrians. Her words reveal that Tyrian society also is hierarchical, and therefore Tyrian people are not monolithic. She identifies herself, instead, with the destitute Galilean peasants in the sense that she also is one of those whose needs must be met. When Jesus heals her daughter he acknowledges her claim. In the same way, only after we see her need taken care of may we begin talking about the story as one that encourages a table fellowship inclusive of all those in need, wherever they are.

The woman decolonized Jesus' primary emphasis, which was limited to the Jews. Jesus decolonized the relationship between those within the Tyrian power base and the Galilean peasants. And have I succeeded in decolonizing the story? Perhaps. But the interpretation goes on, and surely for me what I learned from Anne is critical to my interpretation. Certainly she was present with us at San Francisco Seminary as we wrestled with the text and context in our own lives and in the lives of the biblical characters and writers, even though she was physically absent. Her challenge to explore the texts in depth has always been my guide as I interpret the text.

What's the Matter with Nicodemus?
A Social Science Perspective on John 3:1-21

Richard L. Rohrbaugh

The story of Nicodemus in John 3:1-21 has attracted voluminous attention from scholars, clerics, and laity alike, including people of nearly every imaginable theological persuasion. In fundamentalist circles the story serves as the touchstone of a "born again" theology and has thereby motivated innumerable sermons extolling the new birth experience. Among scholars, however, John 3:1-21 has become the classic example of (so-called) double entendre, the misunderstanding and subsequent explanation that appears so frequently in the Gospel of John.[1] It has even been understood as a Johannine literary gem overflowing with ironies[2] (both subtle and heavy-handed) that become nothing less than the occasion for Jesus' self-revelation.[3]

Not only the story, but also the particular character of Nicodemus has been the subject of endless debate. Was he finally, in the end, a believer (19:39)? Was he an inadequate believer, perhaps one who came to Jesus only because he saw "signs" (John 2:23; 3:2; 4:48; 6:2; 6:26; 7:31; 9:16; 11:47; 12:37; 20:30)? Was

[1] A good review of John's (supposed) use of misunderstanding, double meanings, and subsequent explanation can be found in R. Alan Culpepper, *Anatomy of the Fourth Gospel: A Study in Literary Design* (Philadelphia: Fortress, 1983) 152–65. See also Earl Richard, "Expressions of Double Meaning and Their Function in the Gospel of John," *NTS* 31 (1985) 96–112.

[2] Treatments of ambiguity and double meanings as "irony" are especially common in the literature (Duke, O'Day, Culpepper, Gibbons, Snyder, et al.). Sandra M. Schneiders ("Born Anew," *ThTo* 44 [1987] 189–96) argues that John 3 is "profoundly and pervasively ironical." Winsome Munro ("The Pharisee and the Samaritan in John: Polar or Parallel?" *CBQ* 57 [1995] 710–28) assumes the use of irony in John's gospel is a "well-established" scholarly consensus. Our contention is that treating Johannine language as irony represents a serious misunderstanding of Johannine anti-language.

[3] This is the view of Gail R. O'Day, "Narrative Mode and Theological Claim: A Study in the Fourth Gospel," *JBL* 105 (1986) 657–68.

he a "timid half-disciple," as some have called him? Or is Nicodemus perhaps to be understood as an ambiguous figure, a representative of the uncertain response of many to the historical Jesus? Of course, it has also been argued that there is no indication whatsoever in the gospel that Nicodemus is anything other than an outsider, a symbol of those who finally did not become real followers of Jesus.[4]

Interesting as this question may be, we will leave it to others to determine the final state of Nicodemus' faith. Instead, our interest is in Nicodemus' initial approach to Jesus, the moment of the first encounter. What kind of experience is being described here? Does it replicate real experience? Is this strange sort of conversation the kind of thing that actually happened?

This is not, of course, an inquiry about whether the episode in John 3:1-21 is a report of an actual event in the life of the historical Jesus.[5] The story may simply be a literary construct by the author. If that is the case, however, it is still germane to ask about its verisimilitude: does a story like this in some measure reflect the kind of actual social experience that would make it plausible or believable to a Johannine reader? Is it thus a scene an author could use as a device to reflect on the experience of his own community in its encounter with outsiders?

This raises another set of questions that bear on the literary nature of the story. Is this really an example of double entendre, misunderstanding and explanation—as is almost universally assumed? Above all, is it really an example of Johannine irony, a literary technique designed to tease readers into exploring its meaning on more than one level? That, after all, has been the dominant understanding of this text in recent literary criticism.[6]

Our contention will be that it is neither. While misunderstanding is in fact involved, this is not a simple case of double entendre as that is usually understood. And while ironic elements may be present at many points in the Gospel of John, to treat Johannine language as fundamentally ironic is to misunderstand

---

[4] For a review of the various options and arguments see Jouette M. Bassler, "Mixed Signals: Nicodemus in the Fourth Gospel," *JBL* 108 (1989) 635–46. See also Gail R. O'Day, "New Birth as a New People: Spirituality and Community in the Fourth Gospel," *Word and World* 8 (1988) 53–61; Debbie Gibbons, "Nicodemus: Character Development, Irony and Repetition in the Fourth Gospel," in *Proceedings, Eastern Great Lakes and Midwest Biblical Societies* 11 (Grand Rapids: Eastern Great Lakes and Midwest Biblical Society, 1991) 116–28; and Schneiders, "Born Anew," 189–96.

[5] See Raymond E. Brown, *The Gospel According to John* (Garden City, N.Y.: Doubleday, 1970) 1:135–36, for a discussion of the historicity issue.

[6] See especially Schneiders, "Born Anew," 191. There she argues the conversation is "supremely ironical." Also Paul D. Duke, *Irony in the Fourth Gospel* (Atlanta: John Knox, 1985).

the nature of the Gospel's peculiar rhetoric. Moreover, it will be our contention that a by-product of this misunderstanding is to obscure what is actually happening in the Nicodemus episode. But in order to understand our contention it will be necessary to review the basic nature of what anthropologists call "anti-language" and its use in the Gospel of John. (Existing work on that topic makes necessary only a brief summary here.)[7]

ANTI-LANGUAGE AND ANTI-SOCIETIES

A genuine anti-language, as opposed to simple slang or idiom, is the product of an alienated group of people. That is, it derives from an anti-society: a group "set up within another society as a conscious alternative to it."[8] It is not mere affectation or literary flair. It is not a "technique," and certainly not a *literary* technique. It lives only among the genuinely marginalized who protest the values of the society in which they live. Anti-language is an insider way of speaking that functions as a primary boundary marker between those inside an alienated group and all outsiders. An anti-language, along with its anti-society, is therefore a profound form of social protest from the margins of a dominant social order.

Three important characteristics of anti-language are critical for understanding what is happening in the Nicodemus story. The first is what M.A.K. Halliday calls "re-lexicalization."[9] By that he means that old words are given new, insider meanings by a socially alienated group of people. As Halliday puts it, "same grammar, different vocabulary." Moreover, as Halliday's studies make clear, this new vocabulary is concentrated in precisely those areas that are central to the protest of the subculture and distinguish it most sharply from the surrounding society.

---

[7] The initial work on anti-language was done by sociolinguist M.A.K. Halliday, *Learning How to Mean: Explorations in the Functions of Language* (London: Edward Arnold, 1971); idem, "Anti-languages," *American Anthropologist* 78 (1976) 570–84; idem, *Language as Social Semiotic: The Social Interpretation of Language and Meaning* (London: Edward Arnold, 1978). For a full treatment of the Gospel of John as anti-language see Bruce J. Malina, *The Gospel of John in Sociolinguistic Perspective.* 48th Colloquy of the Center for Hermeneutical Studies, ed. Herman Waetjen (Berkeley: Center for Hermeneutical Studies, 1985); idem, "John's: The Maverick Christian Group. The Evidence from Sociolinguistics," *BTB* 24 (1994) 167–84; and Bruce J. Malina and Richard L. Rohrbaugh, *Social Science Commentary on the Gospel of John* (Minneapolis: Fortress, 1998). See also the excellent work by Norman R. Petersen, *The Gospel of John and the Sociology of Light: Language and Characterization in the Fourth Gospel* (Valley Forge, Pa.: Trinity Press International, 1993).

[8] Halliday, "Anti-languages," 570.

[9] Ibid. 571

It is important to stress here that anti-language does not consist of new words. It uses old words, common to the vocabulary of the dominant culture, but gives them distinctive meanings. The result is that insider and outsider use the same vocabulary, but not in precisely the same way.

It is this kind of re-lexicalization that abounds in the Gospel of John. Words like world, grace, truth, light, glory, door, vine, way, life, abide, shepherd, believe, see, above, and below are all common vocabulary in the dominant culture of the first century—but not the way John uses them. His meanings are fundamentally distinctive, and sometimes, at least to us, incomprehensible. Thus while John's special words frequently obfuscate matters for the ordinary reader—secrecy and mystery are *necessary* properties of anti-language—they function as closed communication that fosters solidarity in an anti-societal group. Moreover, in the Gospel of John this social function of the distinctive vocabulary is *at least as important as its "meaning."* In fact, to press for the meaning of the Johannine vocabulary before recognizing its social function, as we exegetes are wont to do, is emphatically to miss the point.

A second characteristic of anti-language is what Halliday calls "over-lexicalization." Think about the way John multiplies synonyms, at least terms that are synonymous for him if not for the dominant society: spirit, above, life, light, not of this world, freedom, truth, love. All are basically synonymous. So also are their opposites: flesh, below, death, darkness, this world, lie, hate. All these terms describe contrasting spheres of existence, opposing modes of living and being. But there are more of them than strictly necessary. John multiplies words, not concepts. Thus with very little appreciable difference in meaning John speaks of believing in Jesus, following him, abiding in him, loving him, keeping his word, receiving him, having him, and seeing him.

Like re-lexicalization, over-lexicalization has an important social function. Part of it is a continuing search for originality vis-à-vis the dominant society. To be an anti-language, a way of speaking must be original and distinctive. It cannot coalesce with ordinary language or it loses its social function. It fails to draw boundaries. Hence John provides the reduplication that draws out, lingers over, extends, and fine-tunes the linguistic differences between his anti-group and all others.

Over-lexicalization also has to do with competition, opposition, and display. Synonymy, the piling up of signposts displaying one's difference from the dominant order, betrays a group with attitude. The Johannine community has it in abundance.

There are several key points here. One has to do with the role of re-lexicalization and over-lexicalization in group boundary-maintenance. If an anti-language becomes comprehensible to outsiders it can no longer function as anti-language. It becomes ordinary language. This can easily be understood with a rough analogy.

Even though it is often more slang than anti-language, "teenager-talk" makes heavy use of both re-lexicalization and over-lexicalization.[10] Take the ordinary English word "cool." In teen talk it means "hot." Both are ordinary words used differently. The original effect was to draw a line between those who talk this way (teens) and those who do not (adults). But eventually adults learned how these words are used in teen talk and began to use them themselves. So teens began to over-lexicalize, to pile up synonyms. Along came "rad." Later it was "the bomb." All are ordinary words given new meanings. All are synonyms. Each creative addition to the vocabulary re-established (for a time) the boundary between generations.

It is our contention that something like this process produced the peculiar language used in the Gospel of John. Its creativity and originality maintained boundaries not only between the Johannine anti-society and the dominant Judean world, but also between John's group and competing Christian groups.[11] Moreover, like other boundary maintenance mechanisms adopted by groups seeking distinctiveness (taboos, behavioral requirements, dress, food regulations, etc.) anti-language is high profile. It is out front and in your face.

Another important point has to do with secrecy and mystery. Members of anti-societies do not explain their peculiar talk to outsiders. They do not teach them how to use it. Outsiders may eventually catch on, but if they do the anti-language users will up the ante by inventing new uses for yet more ordinary words. They will over-lexicalize. Since anti-language is being used to distance its users from all others, the gap between Johannine group members and outsiders is not going to be narrowed by group members openly teaching people anywhere and everywhere how to speak Johannine. That will be reserved only for those who are becoming part of their group.

A third and final point we wish to emphasize before turning to the Nicodemus story is the importance of anti-language in forming identity. Anti-language is an identity marker *par excellence*. As sociolinguists Howard Giles, Anthony Mulac, James Bradac, and Patricia Johnson point out, "When one of an individual's social group memberships is construed as situationally salient, he or she will attempt to differentiate from relevant outgroup individuals on dimensions

---

[10] Halliday's first studies of anti-languages were among prison populations and gangs. Obviously our analogy here is rough and cannot be pushed too far.

[11] Space does not permit a discussion here of what sociolinguists call language "convergence" and "divergence." Language divergence is an important means by which anti-societies maintain their separate group identity. For a discussion of the matter see Malina, "John's: The Maverick Christian Group," 169–72.

that are valued as core aspects of their group identity."[12] That is, in situations where group membership could be construed as important by a Johannine disciple, one would expect some distinctive Johannine identity marker to be on high profile. These sociolinguists then add, "Should *language* (emphasis added) be a salient dimension of that group membership, as it so often is for ethnic groups, then differentiation by means of language or nonverbal divergence will ensue (on one of the following dimensions: language, dialect, slang, phonology, discourse structures, isolated words and phrases, posture, and so on) in order to achieve a positive psycholinguistic distinctiveness."[13] Exactly. Language is exactly what is used by the Johannine group to achieve distance from the Judean world and from other Christians. It is also what they used to signal an identity and thereby gain solidarity and reassurance from each other.

Interestingly, we also have a rough analogy for this in contemporary religious circles. Fundamentalist Christians in the U.S., wishing to draw boundary lines between themselves and the dominant, secular society, use language in just this distinctive way. Their conversation is sprinkled with "Jesus-speak." "Praise Jesus!" Hallelujah!" "The Lord spoke to me . . ." "Glory to Jesus!" Such terms are not part of the vocabulary of mainstream America. But they appear immediately when fundamentalists want to (1) identify themselves to each other or (2) reassure each other that they are in the presence of like-minded friends. The language serves as an identity marker. Among some fundamentalist groups this way of talking has recently come to be called "spiritual Hebrew." Thus when a new guest appears on an evangelical TV talk show it is always just a matter of moments before the distinctive lingo begins to appear. The display is obligatory. The audience thereby knows immediately that the speaker is one they can really trust. As Howard Giles and John Wieman point out, this kind of language is always a key factor in tenuous interpersonal relations.[14]

As an anti-society, then, the Johannine community has a language all its own. It is an anti-language, an original tongue. Any new member of the community had to learn the insider language in order to be part of the group. As persons did so they assumed a new identity, an anti-society identity, that could stand over against "this world" and "the Judeans." Their insider lingo effectively displayed the group's opposition to the values of the dominant society. It may also

---

[12] Howard Giles, Anthony Mulac, James J. Bradac, and Patrick Johnson, "Speech Accommodation Theory: The First Decade and Beyond," in Margaret L. McLaughlin, ed., *Communication Yearbook 10* (Beverly Hills, Calif.: Sage, 1987) 29.

[13] Ibid.

[14] Howard Giles and John M. Wiemann, "Language, Social Comparison and Power," in Charles R. Berger and Steven H. Chaffee, eds., *Handbook of Communication Science* (Beverly Hills, Calif.: Sage, 1987) 351.

have been a form of resistance to competing groups of Christians whose style and language the Johannine group thought remained "of this world."

WHAT'S THE MATTER WITH NICODEMUS?

As we noted above, scholars have spent considerable ink trying to figure out whether Nicodemus was a real believer. A number of scholars puzzling over the strange conversation between him and Jesus have chided Nicodemus for his incomprehension. Raymond Brown is typical. He claims to see ". . . the basic meaning of the interchange that the evangelist reports as having taken place between Jesus and Nicodemus, that is, the meaning that Nicodemus *should have been able to understand* [emphasis added] in the scene *as it is portrayed* [emphasis in original]."[15] This is because, in Brown's mind, the Old Testament background "should have enabled Nicodemus to understand that Jesus was proclaiming the arrival of the eschatological time when men would be God's children."[16] Thus Brown, like so many others, declares that Nicodemus was a timid half-disciple who just didn't get it.

The list of interpreters attributing one failing or another to Nicodemus is a long one. Typical is F. P. Cotterell, who accuses Nicodemus of a "woodenly uncooperative" attitude.[17] To Don Williford he is a sincere inquirer with "limited belief," a "representative of an old order that is passing away."[18] For James Bell, Nicodemus is a man troubled by unanswered intellectual questions.[19] Bryan Born claims he is a person of "insufficient faith."[20] Terence Donaldson thinks he is a figure of ambiguity in a gospel of certainty.[21] One way or another Nicodemus is seen to be inadequate.

Perhaps. But given what has been said above about anti-language and how it functions, it is much more likely that Nicodemus' experience with Jesus was exactly like that of any outsider, whether an inquirer or not, who encountered a Johannine type for the first time. He immediately got hit with anti-language.

---

[15] Brown, *The Gospel According to John,* 137.

[16] Ibid. 139.

[17] Francis P. Cotterell, "The Nicodemus Conversation: A Fresh Appraisal," *ExpTim* 96 (1985) 240.

[18] Don Williford, *"gennēthēnai anōthen:* A Radical Departure, A New Beginning," *RevExp* 96 (1999) 453.

[19] James F. Bell, "An Intellectual's Quest for Christ," *PSB* 1/4 (1978) 237.

[20] Bryan J. Born, "Literary features in the Gospel of John (an analysis of John 3:1-21)," *Direction* 17 (1988) 7.

[21] Terence L. Donaldson, "Nicodemus: A Figure of Ambiguity in a Gospel of Certainty," *Consensus* 24 (1998) 121–24.

Like any other unsuspecting person from the mainstream society, Nicodemus assumed he was hearing ordinary language when in fact he was not. He was hearing Jesus speak "Johannine."

So Nicodemus became confused. Of course anti-language can indeed be confusing; in fact it is *intended* to be so. Thus if Nicodemus had been able to understand Jesus' rejoinder, the language would have *failed in its primary function.* It would not have drawn an immediate boundary or marked a distinct identity. But the story itself pointedly tells us the language functioned precisely the way it was supposed to: it left Nicodemus confused (3:9-10). He did not get it. The story thus describes exactly the way any outsider (Nicodemus is identified as ἄνθρωπος ἐκ τῶν φαρισαίων) would initially react when encountering the (purposely) obscurantist language of the Johannine community.

Of course it may well be that Nicodemus was timid, or inadequate, or any of the other things so often ascribed to him by those who go beyond the text. In the end he may not have been a full or adequate believer. But his *initial* reaction to Jesus is exactly what one would expect of someone encountering a person speaking Johannine for the first time: confusion.

It is important here to be precise about exactly what Nicodemus assumes in v. 4. He assumes an ordinary meaning for ἄνωθεν, a meaning derived from the way the word is used in mainstream society. That is because he does not (yet?) speak Johannine. He does not fail, as Brown puts it, because he cannot see the "higher" meaning in Jesus' words. He does not fall short because he fails to appreciate "the radical difference between the flesh and the spirit," at least not as Brown uses those terms.[22] Like most scholars, Brown uses these terms for what they mean in ordinary language. Ironically, that is precisely the mistake made by Nicodemus! One might say Brown and Nicodemus are on the same page.

Nor is what is going on here to be termed "irony" in the usual sense. As Halliday points out, anti-language is not a *literary* technique. It is a social phenomenon. Johannine language is not so much ironic to the core as it is anti-language to the core. Our task is thus not so much to find the code (meaning) of Johannine language, as would be the case if it were irony, as it is to appreciate the distancing the language was designed to create. To be sure, Johannine language often has meanings of which the characters in the story are not aware. To *us* that looks like irony. To *us* it looks like literary technique.[23] But anti-language is not technique. It is life. It is intended to obscure and confuse,

---

[22] Brown, *The Gospel According to John,* 138.

[23] Brown speaks of the "technique" of misunderstanding (ibid. 130). A full accounting of that common view can be found in Culpepper, *Anatomy of the Fourth Gospel.* Born ("Literary features in the Gospel of John") talks about the "literary technique" of misunderstanding, the "technique of irony," and the "technique of symbolism."

not to tease the hearer/reader into thinking at (higher) levels where the language can be decoded.

The problem is that we who read the language today are not part of an alienated social group. Because we do not speak or relate well to anti-language, we are unlikely to sense its presence. Instead we project our own literary repertoire onto the writings of a group whose social experience (and thus language) is alien to our own.

Above all, the Nicodemus story is not an example of the so-called "revelatory" language in the Gospel of John. It is an example of the obscurantist language in the Gospel of John. Over the years a debate has emerged over the content of the Johannine language. Rudolph Bultmann (who knew nothing of anti-language) argued that it was the fact *(das Dass)* of Jesus' revelation that mattered, not its content *(ihr Was)*.[24] Later Wayne Meeks (who knew nothing about anti-language either) made the point that it is the function of Johannine language that matters most.[25] Gail O'Day picked up on this and then argued that it is critical to see *how* Johannine language functions in order to understand how it goes about *revealing* the Johannine Jesus.[26] Her view is that the language functions as irony, as language with a double meaning, and that by that method the narrative leads the reader to see the "higher" meaning in what is said. Irony, she suggests, is used for the purpose of revelation. Mode (irony) serves the function of content *(Was)*. It reveals.[27]

Norman Petersen, however—one of the first to understand the nature of Johannine anti-language—saw that treating anti-language as irony assumes the language in John, given the right decoding of its second-level meaning, is finally and fully comprehensible. In that manner it can be revelatory. But as Petersen argues, this is to misunderstand. Anti-language is not intended to be decoded or to reveal; it is intended to create distance.[28]

At one level both Meeks and O'Day are right that the function of the Johannine language is the key to understanding the text. But at least in the Nicodemus episode, the function of the language is not to reveal but to obscure.

[24] Rudolph Bultmann, *Theology of the New Testament*, trans. Kendrick Grobel (New York: Charles Scribner's Sons, 1955) 66.

[25] As Wayne A. Meeks puts it ("The Man from Heaven in Johannine Sectarianism," *JBL* 91 [1972] 69), the narrative in John *"functions for the reader in the same way that the epiphany of its hero functions within its narratives and dialogues"* [emphasis supplied].

[26] O'Day writes: "Any study of Johannine revelation that ignores the form, style, and mode of Johannine revelatory language will always miss the mark" ("Narrative Mode and Theological Claim," 662).

[27] Ibid. 664.

[28] Petersen, *The Gospel of John and the Sociology of Light*.

It is intended to display distinctiveness, distance, and boundaries. It is not literary technique, but social experience. It is not irony, but anti-language.

CONCLUSION

To insiders, of course, the anti-language did have a meaning. But in John's narrative it did not yet have a meaning to Nicodemus. In this initial encounter he is still an outsider. He does not understand. Whether he ever does understand and become a believer is something we will leave to others to determine. We simply point out that in the initial encounter he is appropriately confused. By contrast we may note that in the story of the Samaritan woman we do get to see someone being taught to speak Johannine. The woman is in the process of becoming an insider (no ambiguity here), so she gradually learns the lingo. As she does, she assumes a new identity and insiders (readers) could begin to trust her (or those of whom she is a representative) as one of their own.

Of course all that might be true for Nicodemus as well, even though the author gives us no glimpse of further steps he may have taken. All we see is his first encounter and his initial confusion. Therein we learn what it is like to encounter members of an anti-society and their strange way of talking for the first time. Prepare to be confused. Prepare to feel distance. Understand that a flag of distinction is being waved.

Clearly what all this means for the end of the episode is that Jesus is not "explaining" his strange way of speaking in 3:11-21. He is not "clarifying" or "revealing." There is misunderstanding (3:10), but it is not followed by explanation. Jesus simply goes on speaking Johannine. Note how heavily the passage is loaded with the special vocabulary of Johannine anti-language:

> Truly, truly, I say to you, we speak of what we *know,* and *bear witness* to what we have *seen;* but you do not *receive* our *testimony.* If I have told you *earthly things* and you do *not believe,* how can you *believe* if I tell you *heavenly things*? No one has *ascended* into heaven but he who *descended* from heaven, the Son of man. And as Moses *lifted up* the serpent in the wilderness, so must the Son of man be *lifted up,* that whoever *believes in him* may have *eternal life.* For God so *loved* the *world* that he gave his only Son, that whoever *believes* in him should not perish but have *eternal life.* For God *sent* the Son into the *world,* not to *condemn* the *world,* but that the *world* might be saved through him. He who *believes* in him is *not condemned;* he who *does not believe* is *condemned* already, because he *has not believed* in the name of the only Son of God. And this is the judgment, that the *light* has come into the *world,* and men loved *darkness* rather than *light,* because their deeds were evil. For everyone who does evil *hates the light,* and does not *come to the light,* lest his deeds should be exposed. But he who does what is *true comes to the light,* that it may be clearly *seen* that his deeds have been wrought in God (John 3:11-21).

The typical Johannine over-lexicalization is obvious.[29] Note also the strongly oppositional terms here that make it unmistakable that boundaries are the point of the episode (3:18-21). It is us and them. That is what boundaries are about. And they are drawn immediately when outsider first encounters insider. That is what the Nicodemus story comes to in the end.

So, pointedly, there is no indication in the story that after the extended speech of Jesus in 3:11-21 Nicodemus finally "got it." We do not read about a glimmer of recognition or hesitant attempt to use the Johannine language himself. At the end of the story all we really know about Nicodemus is that when he first encountered Jesus and Jesus began speaking Johannine, the anti-language worked.

Sources Consulted

Ashton, John. *Understanding the Fourth Gospel.* Oxford: Clarendon Press, 1991.

Bassler, Jouette M. "Mixed Signals: Nicodemus in the Fourth Gospel," *JBL* 108 (1989) 635–46.

Beasley-Murray, George R. "John 3:3.5: Baptism, Spirit and the Kingdom," *ExpTim* 97 (1986) 167–70.

Bell, James F. "An Intellectual's Quest for Christ," *PSB* 1 (1978) 236–40.

Born, J. Bryan. "Literary features in the Gospel of John (an analysis of John 3:1-21)," Direction 17 (1988) 3–17.

Brown, Raymond E. *The Gospel According to John.* Garden City, N.Y.: Doubleday, 1970.

————. *Community of the Beloved Disciple.* Mahwah, N.J.: Paulist, 1979.

Bultmann, Rudolph. *Theology of the New Testament.* Trans. by Kendrick Grobel. New York: Charles Scribner's Sons, 1951.

Cantwell, Laurence. "The Quest for the Historical Nicodemus," *RelS* 16 (1980) 481–86.

Cotterell, Francis P. "The Nicodemus Conversation: a Fresh Appraisal," *ExpTim* 96 (1985) 237–42.

Cotterell, Peter. "Sociolinguistics and Biblical Interpretation," *VE* 16 (1986) 61–76.

Culpepper, R. Alan. *Anatomy of the Fourth Gospel: A Study in Literary Design.* Philadelphia: Fortress, 1983.

Derrett, J. Duncan M. "Correcting Nicodemus (John 3:2,21)," *ExpTim* 112 (2001) 126.

[29] For a more complete description of the italicized terms as Johannine anti-language see Malina and Rohrbaugh, *Social Science Commentary on the Gospel of John.*

Donaldson, Terence L. "Nicodemus; A Figure of Ambiguity in a Gospel of Certainty," *Consensus* 24 (1998) 121–24.

Duke, Paul D. *Irony in the Fourth Gospel.* Atlanta: John Knox, 1985.

Fowler, Roger, et al. *Language and Control.* London: Routledge and Kegan Paul, 1979.

Gibbons, Debbie. "Nicodemus: Character Development, Irony and Repetition in the Fourth Gospel," *Proceedings, Eastern Great Lakes and Midwest Biblical Societies* 11 (Grand Rapids: Eastern Great Lakes and Midwest Biblical Society, 1991) 116–28.

Giles, Howard, and John M. Wiemann. "Language, Social Comparison and Power," in Charles R. Berger and Steven H. Chaffee, eds., *Handbook of Communication Science* (Beverly Hills, Calif.: Sage Publications, 1987) 350–84.

Giles, Howard, Anthony Mulac, James J. Bradac, and Patrick Johnson. "Speech Accomodation Theory: The First Decade and Beyond," in Margaret L. McLaughlin, ed., *Communication Yearbook 10* (Beverly Hills, Calif.: Sage, 1987) 13–48.

Goulder, Michael D. "Nicodemus," *SJT* 44 (1991) 153–68.

Grese, William C. "'Unless One Is Born Again': The Use of a Heavenly Journey in John 3," *JBL* 107 (1988) 677–93.

Gundry, Robert H., and Russell W. Howell. "The Sense and Syntax of John 3:14-17 with Special Reference to the Use of OYTOS . . . OSTE in John 3:16," *NovT* 41 (1999) 24–39.

Halliday, M.A.K. *Learning How to Mean: Explorations in the Functions of Language.* London: Edward Arnold, 1971.

———. "Antilanguages." *American Anthropologist* 78 (1976) 570–84.

———. *Language As Social Semiotic: The Social Interpretation of Language and Meaning.* London: Edward Arnold, 1978.

Hodge, Robert, and Günther Kress. *Social Semiotics.* Ithaca, N.Y.: Cornell University Press, 1988.

Hymes, Dell. *Foundations of Sociolinguistics: An Ethnographical Approach.* Philadelphia: University of Pennsylvania Press, 1974.

Jonge, Marinus de. *Jesus: Stranger from Heaven and Son of God.* Missoula: Scholars, 1977.

King, J. S. "Nicodemus and the Pharisees," *ExpTim* 98 (1986) 45.

Koester, Craig R. *Symbolism in the Fourth Gospel: Meaning, Mystery, Community.* Minneapolis: Fortress, 1995.

Kysar, Robert. *John: The Maverick Gospel.* Rev. ed. Atlanta: John Knox, 1993.

———. *John's Story of Jesus.* Philadelphia: Fortress, 1985.

Malina, Bruce. *The Gospel of John in Sociolinguistic Perspective.* 48th Colloquy of the Center for Hermeneutical Studies. Berkeley: Center for Hermeneutical Studies, 1985.

———. "John's: The Maverick Christian Group. The Evidence from Sociolinguistics," *BTB* 24 (1994) 167–84.

Malina, Bruce J., and Richard L. Rohrbaugh. *Social Science Commentary on the Gospel of John*. Minneapolis: Fortress, 1998.

McCabe, Robert V. "The Meaning of 'Born of Water and Spirit' in John 3:5," *Detroit Baptist Seminary Journal* 4 (1999) 85–107.

Meeks, Wayne A. "The Man from Heaven in Johannine Sectarianism," *JBL* 91 (1972) 44–72.

Munro, Winsome. "The Pharisee and the Samaritan in John: Polar or Parallel?" *CBQ* 57 (1995) 710–28.

Nicol, George G. "Nicodemus," *ExpTim* 103 (1991) 80–81.

O'Day, Gail R. "New Birth as a New People: Spirituality and Community in the Fourth Gospel," *WW* 8 (1988) 53–61.

———. "Narrative Mode and Theological Claim: A Study in the Fourth Gospel," *JBL* 105 (1986) 657–68.

———. *Revelation in the Fourth Gospel: Narrative Mode and Theological Claim*. Philadelphia: Fortress, 1986.

Osborn, Carroll D. "Some Exegetical Observations on John 3:5-8," *ResQ* 31 (1989) 129–38.

Pazdan, Mary Margaret. "Nicodemus and the Samaritan Woman: Contrasting Models of Discipleship," *BTB* 17 (1987) 145–48.

Petersen, Norman R. *The Gospel of John and the Sociology of Light: Language and Characterization in the Fourth Gospel*. Valley Forge, Pa.: Trinity Press International, 1993.

Richard, Earl. "Expressions of Double Meaning and Their Function in the Gospel of John," *NTS* 31 (1985) 96–112.

Schoenborn, Ulrich, "'Im Wechsel der Worte das Wort' oder: Dialog und Offenbarung in Johannes 3," in Ulrich Schoenborn and Stephan Pfürtner, eds., *Der bezwingende Vorsprung des Guten: Exegetische und theologische Werkstattberichte. FS Wolfgang Harnisch*. Hamburg: Lit, 1994, 108–25.

Schneiders, Sandra M. "Born Anew," *ThTo* 44 (1987) 189–96.

Snodgrass, Klyne R. "That Which is Born of Pneuma is Pneuma: Rebirth and Spirit in John 3:5-6," *Covenant Quarterly* 49 (1991) 13–29.

Snyder, Gradon F. "The Social Context of the Ironic Dialogues in the Gospel of John," in Virginia Wiles and Alexandra Brown, eds., *Putting Body & Soul Together: Essays in Honor of Robin Scroggs*. Valley Forge, Pa.: Trinity Press International, 1997, 3–23.

Stibbe, Mark W. G. *John*. Sheffield: JSOT Press, 1991.

Wieser, Thomas. "Community: Its Unity, Diversity and Universality," *Semeia* 33 (1985) 83–95.

Williford, Don. "*gennēthēnai anōthen:* A Radical Departure, A New Beginning," *RevExp* 96 (1999) 451–61.

Witherington, Ben, III. "The Waters of Birth: John 3:5 and I John 5:6-8," *NTS* 35 (1989) 155–60.

———. *John's Wisdom: A Commentary on the Fourth Gospel.* Louisville: Westminster John Knox, 1995.

Sacrifice No More

Joanna Dewey

I am one of the first wave of academically trained biblical scholars to study and teach New Testament from a feminist perspective. In my teaching I have insisted all along that sacrifice was *only one of the ways* found in the New Testament for understanding Jesus' death; that it was *not* the most common, and it was *not* the earliest. Furthermore, I believe the effects of a theology of sacrifice are detrimental to human life on earth, discriminatory against women and all marginalized people, and thus in my opinion not God's will for humanity. My attention became focused on sacrifice, however, when I discovered I was scheduled to preach in the Episcopal Divinity School chapel on the sacrifice of Isaac (Genesis 22). The result was a sermon passionately arguing against understanding the near-sacrifice of Isaac as the will of God and against interpreting Jesus' death as sacrifice.[1]

The response to the sermon was overwhelming and overwhelmingly positive. I began to focus more and more on sacrifice in my teaching and work. I have read widely on sacrifice among Aztecs, African tribes, Hindus, Hawaiians, Greeks, Romans, Jews, and Christians. I have read anthropological and psychological interpretations. I have grasped early Christianity's categorical rejection of sacrificial practice, and what that entailed socially. I began to study how blood sacrifice crept back in, in the third and following centuries, as part of the repatriarchalizing of the church, indeed as one of the important means for enforcing hierarchy and the marginalization of women. I have grappled with how the understanding of sacrifice has shifted from that of a communal festival to an emphasis on individual self-sacrifice. And I have become even more convinced that sacrificial understandings of Christianity are harmful to people: legitimating hierarchy, encouraging violent behavior, and glorifying innocent victimhood.

---

[1] Joanna Dewey, "An End to Sacrifice," *Christianity and Crisis* 51 (15 July 1991) 213–14.

The rejection of sacrifice is commonplace in Christian feminist theologies.[2] Indeed, much mainstream theology today rejects Anselm's satisfaction theory of atonement, thereby discarding sacrifice. Furthermore, New Testament scholars in general know that sacrifice is not at the heart of the New Testament. Scholars' portraits of the historical Jesus vary, but virtually all totally reject the idea that Jesus understood himself as a sacrifice for sin. Most know how infrequent the New Testament references to Jesus' death as sacrifice are, and how, in some instances, we have read sacrifice into passages the first century would not have understood that way.

In one area, however, sacrificial theology has been gaining ground among Christians. And this area affects most Christians much more directly than biblical or theological scholarship—that is, the area of worship. In the last decades both Lutherans and Anglicans in ecumenical dialogue with Roman Catholics have formally accepted a sacrificial understanding of the eucharist.[3] The understanding of Christ's death as a blood sacrifice and the corollary understanding that what is demanded of Christians is self-sacrifice are reinforced virtually every time a Christian attends church, explicitly in the eucharist in the more liturgical denominations and often in the hymns and prayers of the less liturgical denominations. Sacrifice is alive and well in contemporary American Christianity. It is interesting that in ancient times, when blood sacrifice was the dominant and pervasive religious practice among pagans and Jews structuring both family and state, Christians stood out as non-sacrificers, while today, when family and state are no longer constituted by sacrifice, Christianity continues to embrace it. In what follows I shall first describe the cross-cultural characteristics of blood sacrifice, and then I shall turn to early Christianity and sacrifice, and conclude with a few observations on sacrifice today.

CHARACTERISTICS OF BLOOD SACRIFICE

Cross-culturally, blood or animal sacrifice was frequently *the* way of communicating with a god or gods. The sacrificial ritual functioned as a means of

[2] See, for example, Joanne Carlson Brown and Rebecca Parker, "For God So Loved the World?" in Joanne C. Brown and Carole R. Bohn, eds., *Christianity, Patriarchy and Abuse: A Feminist Critique* (New York: Pilgrim, 1989) 1–30; Elisabeth Schüssler Fiorenza, *Jesus: Miriam's Child, Sophia's Prophet* (New York: Continuum, 1994) 97–128.

[3] The U.S. Anglican-Roman Catholic Theological Consultation (ARC-USA) agreed in 1994, "WE AFFIRM that in the Eucharist the Church, doing what Christ commanded his apostles to do at the Last Supper, makes present the sacrifice of Calvary. We understand this to mean that when the Church is gathered in worship, it is empowered by the Holy Spirit to make Christ present and to receive all the benefits of his sacrifice." Quoted in R. William Franklin, "ARC-USA: Five Affirmations on the Eucharist As Sacrifice," *Worship* 69 (1995) 386–90.

establishing and maintaining patriarchy, that is, a means of constructing society so that power and property descended from father to son or adopted son, while women contributed children but did not hold power or control its transmission to the next generation.[4] Animal sacrifice involves offering and consecration, destruction of the victim, and communal eating. In sociological language, sacrifice is a ritual of a community in which a deity is offered a gift, which is destroyed so that it can no longer be of use to humans, in order to gain some life-effect for the offerer, be it favorable outcome in war, overcoming the "pollution" of childbirth, or the forgiveness of sins.[5] That is to say, we offer the god or gods something that we can no longer use in order to get something from the gods.[6] The practice is very widespread culturally but not universal. Such a practice does not on the face of it have much to do with the establishment of patriarchy. Yet, as Nancy Jay has shown, "In no other major religious institution is gender dichotomy more consistently important, across unrelated traditions, than it is in sacrifice. . . . It is a common feature of unrelated traditions that only adult males—fathers, real and metaphorical—may perform sacrifice."[7] Indeed, Jay summarizes blood sacrifice as "remedy for having been born of woman."[8] Sacrifice is not a gender-neutral practice.

Blood Sacrifice vs. Other Uses of the Term Sacrifice

Blood sacrifice needs to be distinguished from later Christian use of the term "sacrifice" to refer to Christ's death as self-sacrificial, substitutionary, or vicarious, and also from the broader metaphorical use for any sort of giving up, be it chocolate for Lent or one's life in war.[9] Such theological developments have resulted from focusing only on one aspect of the sacrificial ritual, the destruction of the victim, which for ancients was not the central focus. Blood sacrifice also needs to be distinguished from the firstling offerings of hunter-gatherers. In firstling offerings a portion of plants gathered or of a wild animal slain is offered

---

[4] Nancy Jay, *Throughout Your Generations Forever: Sacrifice, Religion, and Paternity* (Chicago: University of Chicago Press, 1992).

[5] Bruce J. Malina, "Mediterranean Sacrifice: Dimensions of Domestic and Political Religion," *BTB* 26 (1996) 37.

[6] This is basically the *"do ut des"* (give in order to get) theory of sacrifice of Sir Edward Burnett Tylor, *Primitive Culture* (London: J. Murray, 1871).

[7] Jay, *Throughout Your Generations Forever,* xxiii.

[8] Ibid. See also Nancy Jay, "Sacrifice as Remedy for Having Been Born of Woman," in Clarissa W. Atkinson, Constance H. Buchanan, and Margaret R. Miles, eds., *Immaculate and Powerful: The Female in Sacred Image and Social Reality* (Boston: Beacon, 1985) 283–309.

[9] For good general discussions of sacrifice see Joseph Heninger, "Sacrifice," in Mircea Eliade, ed., *The Encyclopedia of Religion* (New York: Macmillan, 1987) 12:544–57; and Gary A. Anderson, "Sacrifice and Sacrificial Offerings: Old Testament," *ABD* 5:870–86.

to the spirit world. It is an offering of food rather than of life. The destruction of the animal is not part of the ritual, but is an ordinary or profane event preceding it. Blood sacrifice is not generally found in hunting and gathering cultures.[10] Rather, it is characteristic of agrarian societies, in which the extended family was the basic unit of society, with property in herds or lands to bequeath to the next generation. It occurs precisely in those societies in which the descent of real property to the next generation is a major concern. Firstling offerings continue even as blood sacrifice becomes common. However, firstling offerings do not entail ritual killing and do not have the structural connection to patriarchal hierarchical social organization that blood sacrifice does.

The Role of Killing the Victim in Blood Sacrifice

Ritual killing is not the central focus of blood sacrifice.[11] The priest (the sacrificer) is more important than the sacrificial victim, since it is the priest who mediates between the divine and human realms. The killing is frequently not the work of the priest, but of the offerer or a specially designated functionary, often a slave. Then the priest carries out the crucial act, which is the proper disposal of the blood on the altar. Thus what is offered to the god is not the killing *per se*. Rather, the point is to transfer the ownership of the sacrificial victim from the human to the divine realm. In order to symbolize the transfer, the victim is killed as part of the ritual. What is offered to the deity is life, the life of the sacrificial victim.

Blood Sacrifice and Gender

This taking of life is essential symbolically, for the ritual slaughter is opposed to women's giving birth. Jay writes, "what is needed to provide clear evidence of jural paternity is an act as powerful, definite, and available to the senses as birth."[12] Stanley Stowers writes, "The most fundamental problem in these patriarchal societies is how to eliminate, subordinate, or bypass the claims that women might represent [over their children] with the dramatic and bloody rite of childbirth. Thus, men have employed an equally dramatic and bloody rite of their own, animal sacrifice."[13] Blood sacrifice opposes men's intentional killing to women's giving birth. Deliberate controlled death is opposed to giving of life.

---

[10] Heninger, "Sacrifice," 546.

[11] Richard D. Nelson, *Raising Up a Faithful Priest: Community and Priesthood in Biblical Theology* (Louisville: Westminster John Knox, 1993) 55.

[12] Jay, "Sacrifice As Remedy for Having Been Born of Woman," 291.

[13] Stanley K. Stowers, "Greeks Who Sacrifice and Those Who Do Not: Towards an Anthropology of Greek Religion," in L. Michael White and O. Larry Yarbrough, eds., *The Social World of the First Christians: Essays in Honor of Wayne A. Meeks* (Minneapolis: Fortress, 1995) 330.

In sacrificial cultures not all blood is pleasing to the gods. The blood drained from the animal victims in animal sacrifice is valued as holy and atoning, while the blood connected with women's giving birth is considered polluting and offensive to the gods. In the Hebrew Bible childbirth and menstruation typify pollution in general. Women are allowed only into an outer courtyard of the Temple; women while bleeding are excluded altogether.[14] Among Greeks it is childbirth in particular that is polluting. For ancient Greeks, "childbirth severely polluted anyone who came in contact with the mother or the house where the birth took place. . . . Greeks believed that the pollution caused by women giving birth to children could threaten the very existence of the city."[15] It "is none other than the filth that estranges man from the gods."[16] Greek medical texts draw analogies between the blood of sacrifice and women's blood. Stowers suggests "that these analogies reflect the instincts of Greek men socialized by the environments of sacrificial practice. Intuiting 'obvious' similarities between the birth of a child and the sacrifice of an animal was a reflex of a sacrificially constructed *habitus*." [17]

This *habitus* still exists. It makes intuitive sense to some men today in churches holding to apostolic succession of priests who offer the eucharist as a sacrifice. In the days before the Episcopal Church ordained women, a male student asked Alison Cheek (one of the first eleven women ordained to the Episcopal priesthood in 1974) when she was in seminary, "why did she want to be a priest, she could have a baby."[18] At the 1992 meeting of the National Conference of Catholic Bishops, one bishop said, "It's as impossible for a woman to be a priest as it is for me to have a baby."[19] Even without any experience of actual bloody sacrifice, the logic of sacrifice that opposes superior sacrificing men to inferior polluting childbearing women still holds sway among some.

Blood Sacrifice Brings about What It Signifies

Blood sacrifices are not merely rituals affirming and legitimating social structures created by other means.[20] They actually create the lines of patrilineal descent. Among the Greeks and Romans a child became a member of the

[14] Joan R. Branham, "Blood in Flux, Sanctity at Issue," *Res* 31 (1997) 53–70.

[15] Stowers, "Greeks Who Sacrifice and Those Who Do Not," 300.

[16] Louis Moulinier, *Le pur et l'impur dans la pensée des Grecs d'Homère à Aristote* (Paris: C. Klincksieck) 70; quoted in Jay, *Throughout Your Generations,* 29.

[17] Stowers, "Greeks Who Sacrifice and Those Who Do Not," 309. The concept of *habitus* is derived from Pierre Bourdieu.

[18] Personal communication.

[19] Quoted in Stowers, "Greeks who Sacrifice and Those Who Do Not," 333.

[20] Olivier Herrenschmidt, "Sacrifice: Symbolic or Effective?" in Michel Izard and Pierre Smith, eds., *Between Belief and Transgression: Structuralist Essays in Religion, History, and Myth,* trans. John Leavitt (Chicago: University of Chicago Press, 1982) 24–42.

family not by birth but several days later when the father offered a sacrifice at the purified household hearth. Stowers writes:

> Sacrifices at the hearth, of the *phratry* and *deme* actually caused membership in an all male line of descent through which the initiate received property, power, and status, including citizenship. Pollution and expiatory sacrifices actually caused a separation of women from men. Communion sacrifice actually effected membership and bonds of community in hierarchically ranked groups, both identifying and constituting the group.[21]

Court cases over inheritance entailed arguments about who ate at particular sacrifices. In the Greco-Roman world sacrifice was the means for constituting all of society. It was fundamental for kinship and for politics, for membership in a household, a city, a kingdom, and the empire.

Blood Sacrifice Performs Hierarchical Structure

Furthermore, blood sacrifice served to legitimize and naturalize hierarchical power relations. The whole community, free and slave, male and female, generally participated in sacrificial festivals, but in such a way as to indicate their status in society. In Greco-Roman culture a few elite men functioned as priests. (Very occasionally an elite woman might function as an honorary male in sacrifice.)[22] The elite men received large quantities of the roasted meat of the victim, free men received a very small portion of boiled meat, slaves the same or less or nothing, and free women received meat only as their husbands gave them some of theirs. (Meat was only eaten at sacrifices.) "Only by virtue of attachment to husbands did wives possess any rights. Each sacrifice reinforced this 'pattern of nature.'"[23] Sacrifice mirrored the "proper order" of the dominant society, the few elite over everyone else, men over women, free over slave, as the "proper order" willed by the divine.[24]

EARLY CHRISTIANS AND SACRIFICE

To opt out of sacrificial rites in the ancient world was exceedingly difficult, involving far more than a refusal to worship the emperor. Stowers evokes the difficulty well:

[21] Stowers, "Greeks Who Sacrifice and Those Who Do Not," 328.

[22] Ross S. Kraemer, *Her Share of the Blessings: Women's Religions among Pagans, Jews, and Christians in the Greco-Roman World* (New York: Oxford University Press, 1992) 84–87.

[23] Stowers, "Greeks Who Sacrifice and Those Who Do Not," 327.

[24] Richard Gordon, "The Veil of Power: Emperors, Sacrificers and Benefactors," in Mary Beard and John North, eds., *Pagan Priests: Religion and Power in the Ancient World* (Ithaca: Cornell University Press, 1990) 229–31.

> Imagine a community in the contemporary United States that renounced not only television viewing but also any products, persons, and ideas promoted by television. The group would not vote in elections, drive automobiles, shop in supermarkets, watch athletic contests, or form conventional families. . . . Understanding what it meant for a Greek, Roman, or Syrian to renounce animal sacrifice requires some such act of comparative imagination.[25]

Yet this is what the early Christians did. The Christians were known to the pagans of the Roman empire as those who rejected sacrifice. A Roman historian writes of ascetic cults, including early Christianity:

> The basis of their life is rejection of the ordinary world, above all rejection of the family and private property, the two institutions at the centre of the Greco-Roman sacrificial system. . . . The refusal of sacrifice was, in fact, the most uncompromising possible rejection of the civic model, and it marks off Christianity from all other organized sects of the empire, as the only one to take this stand.[26]

Thus Christian rejection of sacrifice was not just a religious act proclaiming loyalty to the one God, but also an act of resistance to the whole hierarchically ordered social structure of the empire. In their proclamation, "There is no longer Jew or Greek, there is no longer slave or free, there is no longer male and female; for all of you are one in Christ Jesus," early Christians affirmed the end of the sacrificial social order (Gal 3:28).

The New Testament and Sacrificial Interpretations

New Testament passages that suggest an interpretation of Jesus' death as a sacrifice are rare, and generally overemphasized by later Christians. There are many passages that ancient hearers would probably not have understood in terms of sacrifice where modern interpreters have read it in. For pagans and Christians alike, Jesus' crucifixion had nothing to do with sacrifice. Crucifixion was the most shameful means of political execution, reserved for slaves and traitors. It had no connection to religious ritual. While the same elite individuals held both priestly and political power, they sharply distinguished between the holy and the profane. Crucifixion clearly belonged in the realm of the profane. Furthermore, both the combination of the terms "body" and "blood" used in the Eucharist[27] and the fact the Eucharist was a bread and wine meal, not a meat and wine meal, clearly show that the meal was explicitly not sacrificial.

---

[25] Stowers, "Greeks Who Sacrifice and Those Who Do Not," 293.

[26] Richard Gordon, "Religion in the Roman Empire: The Civic Compromise and its Limits," in Beard and North, eds., *Pagan Priests*, 248, 252.

[27] Mack views these two elements as belonging to the "myth of the martyr" (Burton L. Mack, *A Myth of Innocence: Mark and Christian Origins* [Philadelphia: Fortress, 1988] 118).

The existence of the Eucharists described in the *Didache* also suggests that the meal was not initially understood as a sacrifice.[28]

Yet sacrificial ideas did begin to creep in, especially in some of the later New Testament writings such as 1 Peter and Revelation. Sacrifice was ubiquitous in the ancient world, where it was understood as *the means* to communicate with the divine. So it is not surprising that sacrificial metaphors would be used to attempt to express the significance of Christ. Martyrdom, that is, political execution, probably provided the bridge—a bridge made possible by the fact that the sacrificial victim was killed. Occasionally among pagans and Jews sacrificial metaphors would be used to commemorate those who had undergone political executions. Since ancients considered sacrifice effective with the divine, they would ask the deity to treat a political execution as a sacrifice, that is, to consider it as accomplishing the good they understood sacrifice to accomplish. This seems to provide a beginning for later theological developments.[29]

Hebrews and the Logic of Sacrifice

Hebrews was the first and only New Testament text to draw extensively on categories of blood sacrifice. It describes the significance of Jesus as both high priest and victim. Hebrews argues that Christ's once-for-all sacrifice of himself as great high priest is more effective than the repetitive Jewish sacrifices. Indeed, Jesus' high priestly act of offering his own blood is so effective that no further sacrifice is needed. For the author of Hebrews, blood sacrifice has come to an end.[30] So, apparently, has the hierarchical structure created and sustained by sacrifice come to an end. Hebrews reflects minimal hierarchal structuring of the Christian community and no gender distinctions. The only differentiation within the community is between "those who lead" and the community.[31] Hebrews ends sacrifice and the hierarchical gendered sacrificial social order.

Hebrews does not, however, end the *logic* of sacrifice. For Hebrews, forgiveness of sins was obtained through Jesus' high priestly offering. The effects

[28] Chapters 9 and 10. The *Didache* probably dates from around 100 C.E.

[29] See 4 Maccabees, especially 6:26-30. The classic works on sacrifice in the New Testament are Robert J. Daly, *Christian Sacrifice: The Judaeo-Christian Background Before Origen* (Washington: Catholic University of America Press, 1978); and Frances M. Young, *The Use of Sacrificial Ideas in Greek Christian Writers from the New Testament to John Chrysostom* (Philadelphia: Patristic Foundation, 1979).

[30] For a commentary on Hebrews see Harold W. Attridge, *The Epistle to the Hebrews* (Philadelphia: Fortress, 1989). For works that draw on broader understandings of sacrifice see John Dunnill, *Covenant and Sacrifice in the Letter to the Hebrews.* SNTSMS 71 (Cambridge: Cambridge University Press, 1992); and Marie E. Isaacs, *Sacred Space: An Approach to the Theology of the Epistle to the Hebrews.* JSNTS 73 (Sheffield: JSOT Press, 1992).

[31] Heb 13:7, 17, 24.

of Jesus' sacrifice continue to be available for humans. The author of Hebrews, however, twice warns that there is no recourse in the cases of apostasy or serious deliberate sin after baptism since there is no further sacrifice for sin (Heb 6:4-6; 10:26-29). Particular Christians can exhaust, if you will, their own portion of the benefits of Christ's sacrifice. Christians have accepted the benefits of this sacrifice for themselves. If they then turn away, apostatizing or engaging in intentional serious sin, there is no new or additional sacrifice to atone for these new and serious sins.[32] Hebrews suggests rather starkly the consequences of a sacrificial logic: either there is a limit to atonement or one must keep on sacrificing. *Either* an individual can exhaust the benefits of a particular sacrifice, with no way to atone for additional sins, *or* additional sacrifices are needed to make atonement for these sins. If one's understanding of Christ's salvific work is sacrificial, one either follows Hebrews in arguing that the benefits of Jesus' sacrifice can in fact be exhausted for any particular individual, or further sacrifice becomes necessary in order to provide atonement for new sin.

The Reintroduction of Sacrifice

The Christian church chose the latter move, the reintroduction of blood sacrifice, albeit symbolically, into Christianity. By the fourth and fifth centuries we find several related signs of the reincorporation of blood sacrifice into Christianity: (1) the understanding of the Eucharist as a real blood sacrifice, (2) the common naming of Christian leaders as priests, that is, those who offer sacrifice, (3) the restriction of priesthood to males in the proper line of descent, that of apostolic succession, (4) the superiority of priests to the laity, (5) the separation of women from the holy, and (6) the idea of pollution brought about by childbearing women.

The beginnings can be seen clearly in the mid-third-century writings of Cyprian. He is "the first to refer to the body and blood of Christ as the object of sacrifice by Christian priests . . . the first to call the bishop *'sacerdos,'* 'priest,' and the first to make a fully explicit transition from a universal apostolic heritage to a single line of apostolic descent attached to the episcopate."[33] Furthermore, it is at precisely the same time that the debate surfaces over whether or not women who are menstruating can attend the Eucharist. Dionysius of Alexandria, a disciple of Origen, wrote:

---

[32] In the context of Hebrews these passages are clearly warnings against future sin; we do not know how the author would respond to the pastoral issue of those wanting reconciliation after such sin.

[33] Cyprian, Letter 63, quoted in Jay, *Throughout Your Generations,* 116.

> Concerning women in their menstrual separation, whether it is right for them in such a condition to enter the house of God, I think it unnecessary even to inquire. For I think that they, being faithful and pious, would not dare in such a condition either to approach the holy table or to touch the body and blood of Christ.[34]

Christianity, which began with a thoroughgoing rejection of blood sacrifice and the patriarchal social order constituted and sustained by it, had within a matter of a few centuries reincorporated blood sacrifice, as its elite leaders embraced the dominant social structure. In the third century, and even more after the empire became Christian, Christianity was established as a sacrificial religion with all of blood sacrifice's power to order society hierarchically and to marginalize women.

SACRIFICE IN WESTERN CULTURE TODAY

Blood sacrifice in antiquity was generally a celebration, a feast. Participants would have understood themselves to benefit from the deity's acceptance of the sacrifice and from their share, however tiny, of the sacrificial meal. The sacrifice would have made explicit their status or lack of status within the group; it would have made clear women's dependence on men. It effected the superiority of sacrificing men to childbearing women. Today, as a Christian theological doctrine embedded in liturgy and hymnody, it still does much the same work. It still honors blood from deliberate killing and considers women's blood polluting. We continue to struggle with these notions in the church today.

Today, as our culture has become secularized, sacrifice may also have become part of our wider cultural understandings. It is true that blood sacrifice, involving ritual slaughter, is no longer the ritual of the state as it was in Second Temple Judaism and the Greco-Roman world. Fathers no longer offer sacrifices to affirm their paternity of the child. The state no longer offers regular sacrifices for the good of the state or special sacrifices before embarking on war or on returning from a victory. The question is, however, whether sacrifice (and its concomitant, self-sacrifice) has died out, or whether it has been transformed and internalized in the role of war for the creation and maintenance of states.[35] "[W]ith the demise of traditional theodicies the arena of sacrifice has switched

[34] Quoted in Shaye J. D. Cohen, "Menstruants and the Sacred in Judaism and Christianity," in Sarah B. Pomeroy, ed., *Women's History and Ancient History* (Chapel Hill: University of North Carolina Press, 1991) 288. See also Joan R. Branham, "Bloody Women and Bloody Spaces: Menses and the Eucharist in Late Antiquity and the Early Middle Ages," *Harvard Divinity School Bulletin* (Spring 2002) 15–22.

[35] Mary Condren, "To Bear Children for the Fatherland: Mothers and Militarism," in Anne Carr and Elisabeth Schüssler Fiorenza, eds., *Motherhood: Experience, Institution, Theology. Con-*

from the altar to the battlefield and war now plays a major role . . . in the generation of systems of political and cultural legitimation."[36] Mary Condren observes, "throughout Europe, monuments to Jesus 'who gave his life for all' are steadily being replaced by tombs of the Unknown Soldier who 'died for all.'"[37] Sacrificial ritual may have done its work so well, and humans may have so thoroughly internalized its structures and values, that the ritual practice is no longer needed to maintain the "sacrificial contract."[38] The role of sacrifice and its relationship to war and statehood in our present culture, posited by scholars such as Condren and the French feminist theorists Julia Kristeva and Luce Irigaray, goes well beyond the scope of this study. It should be noted, however, that it is not only feminist scholars who see the transfer of the notion to war and the state. Stephen W. Sykes, former bishop of Ely, writes of

> . . . the twentieth-century misuse, or rather equivocal use, of the slogan of sacrifice in the rhetoric of Irish nationalism and the British First World War effort. But precisely the same language was subsequently deployed by Adolf Hitler in his persuasion of the German people to accept economic deprivation and loss of civil liberties as the cost of national revival. . . . It is openly acknowledged by contemporary German theologians that the rhetoric of sacrifice has been defiled to the point where it is unusable in normal Christian preaching.[39]

Its use in the propaganda promoting the United States' Gulf wars has also been evident. I would suggest that the dangers that are apparent to us in its use in war efforts and by Hitler are also dangers inherent in the Christian use of it.

Sacrifice has added over the centuries a new dimension in Christianity and, it could be argued, in the broader culture as a whole. Ancient sacrifice did not exalt the victim, nor did participants identify with the sacrificial victim. As sacrifice was incorporated into Christian practice this changed, for the view of the author of Hebrews that Christ was both high priest and sacrificial victim prevailed. Few people—and those male—could imitate Christ by becoming

---

cilium 206 (Edinburgh: T & T Clark, 1989) 82–90; Mary Condren, "Sacrifice and Political Legitimation: The Production of a Gendered Social Order," *Journal of Women's History* 6:4–7:1 (1995) 160–89.

[36] Mary Teresa Condren, *The Role of Sacrifice in the Construction of a Gendered System of Representation and Gendered Social Order* (Th.D. diss., Harvard University, 1994), Abstract.

[37] Ibid. 339.

[38] The phrase is Julia Kristeva's, from her understanding of modern society ("Women's Time," in *The Kristeva Reader*, ed. Toril Moi, trans. Alice Jardine and Harry Blake [New York: Columbia University Press, 1986] 200).

[39] Stephen W. Sykes, "Introduction," in idem, ed., *Sacrifice and Redemption: Durham Essays in Theology* (Cambridge: Cambridge University Press, 1991) 2–3.

priests. But everyone could imitate Christ by making themselves victims. If imitation of Jesus is at the center of Christian life, and if Jesus' greatest act, indeed his only act of any importance, is his obedient sacrificial death, then the way to imitate Jesus can easily become to sacrifice oneself, even to the point of death. Christian focus on the sacrificial victim suggests that being a victim is pleasing to God, that God wants innocent victims.[40] Christian valuing of victimhood can be seen in the extreme asceticism and early death of some medieval and modern nuns whom the Roman Catholic Church honors as saints. It can also be seen in the lives of many women who remain in violent marriages, believing that their suffering is meritorious before God. This ideal of self-sacrifice, the ideal of making oneself an innocent victim, becomes glorified in much Christian piety. This is harmful to both men and women, but it is particularly harmful to women. For historically, self-sacrifice has been the most acceptable—often the only acceptable—means for women to take initiative in their lives.

I firmly believe that it is time to reject sacrifice as a way to understand Christ's death and to return to the early church's categorical refusal of the practice of sacrifice. Early Christians rejected a near-universal sacrificial system, sometimes at the risk of their lives, and told stories about a Jesus who offered forgiveness to others *during his life*.[41] Jesus' sacrificial death is not needed to atone for sins. There are other ways to interpret Jesus' death, which are in continuity with and give meaning to his life. We do not have to be in bondage to sacrifice. Let us indeed make Christianity a religion of life.

[40] For a critique of the value of innocence see Rita Nakashima Brock, "Dusting the Bible on the Floor: A Hermeneutics of Wisdom," in Elisabeth Schüssler Fiorenza, ed., *Searching the Scriptures: A Feminist Introduction* (New York: Crossroad, 1993) 1:64–75.

[41] See, for example, the story of the healing of the paralytic in Mark 2:1-12, and Jesus' regular association with sinners, which presupposes forgiveness.

Cross-textual, Intertextual, and Inter-Media Readings

Engaging Lamentations
and *The Lament for the South:*
A Cross-Textual Reading

Archie Chi Chung Lee

౩

1. CROSS-TEXTUAL READING
IN BIBLICAL INTERPRETATION

In approaching Lamentations in context, I am confronted with multiple dimensions of the lived experiences of the Chinese people upon whom contemporary socio-political realities have, in recent history, inflicted pain and suffering beginning with the colonial and empire expansion of the West, the resulting humiliating defeat in war, and the loss of geographical integrity. This history of suffering also includes the imperialistic conquest by Japan in Asia during the First and Second World Wars, including the Japanese invasion of China from 1937 to 1945 and the Nanjing massacre during this war period. There are, in addition, incidents such as the Cultural Revolution (1966–1976), initiated by the Chinese Communist Party under the leadership of Mao, and the student demonstrations at Tiananmen Square that ended in bloodshed on June 4, 1989. Public mourning and remembrance of the dead were denied the people on the first anniversary of the June Fourth Incident, with the mass student movement of 1989 being condemned as "counter-revolutionary turmoil" and the soldiers who fired at the students and the ordinary citizens honored as heroes.[1] In China and in the whole of Asia in general it is the people of this "wounded generation"[2] who are the readers engaging Lamentations with their

---

[1] Vera Schwarcz, "'Memory and Commemoration': The Chinese Search for a Livable Past," in Jeffrey N. Wasserstrom and Elisabeth J. Perry, eds., *Popular Protest and Political Culture in Modern China*, 2d ed. (Boulder: Westview, 1994) 170–71.

[2] Vera Schwarcz, "In the Shadows of the Red Sun: A New Generation of Chinese Writers," *Asian Review* 3 (1989) 4–16.

hurts, pains, and above all, the unfailing aspiration to pursue life in the midst of death.

In this paper I have chosen to focus on a literary work, *The Lament for the South (Ai Jiangnan Fu),* which employs a traditional form of lament dating from the Fourth Century B.C.E. Methodologically this paper is an exercise in cross-textual hermeneutics applied to the biblical book of Lamentations and a Chinese poetic book, *The Lament for the South.* In Asia it is the multi-textual reality that constitutes the context for this specific interpretative strategy of reading the Bible. The latter, which originated in the cultural environment of West Asia, was subsequently interpreted and contextualized in the Greco-Roman as well as the Latin worlds, took a detour via Western Christian civilization, and forced its way back to Asian soil as a stranger in its own home and an imperialist book of the empire.[3] The translation and reception history of the Bible among Asian scriptural traditions is, therefore, a significant project in which we biblical scholars in Asia should engage ourselves, in order to recover and understand the hidden phase of biblical interpretation in different global contexts.

In the case of the Chinese, the past four hundred years of biblical interpretation, from the time when the Jesuit Missions arrived in China in the late sixteenth century to the Protestant missionary movements in the early eighteenth century, will be an indispensable area of study if we want to understand the history of Christianity in the Chinese context. It will also shed light on the contemporary scene of biblical interpretation in China. Chinese biblical interpretation has captured the intense attention and passionate interest of Professor Antoinette Clark Wire, to whose fine scholarship this article is humbly dedicated.[4]

The present author proposes adopting the reading strategy of cross-textual hermeneutics to address colonial entanglements and to recontextualize the Bible in the Asian, African, and Latin American cultural milieux.[5] This ap-

---

[3] There are various minor streams of tradition in China and India that are exceptions to the main missionary movements of the eighteenth and nineteenth centuries. The Catholic Jesuit missions also form a separate category. See R. S. Sugirtharajah, *The Bible and the Third World: Precolonial, Colonial, and Postcolonial Encounters* (Cambridge: Cambridge University Press, 2001), and idem, *Asian Biblical Hermeneutics and Postcolonialism: Contesting the Interpretations* (Maryknoll, N.Y.: Orbis, 1998). For a brief history of the Bible in the British Missionary Movement see Brian Stanley, *The Bible and the Flag: Protestant Missions and British Imperialism in the Nineteenth and Twentieth Centuries* (Leicester: Apollos, 1990).

[4] Antoinette Clark Wire, "Chinese Biblical Interpretation since Mid-century," *BibInt* 4 (1996) 101–23.

[5] The method has been expounded with examples in a number of articles written by the present author; see Archie C. C. Lee, "The Chinese Creation Myth of Nu Kua and the Biblical Narra-

proach takes both the Bible and the native text seriously by engaging the two texts in a creative way, making cross-connections between them. In the process the readers' horizons will be widened and their identities formulated at the point of confluence between the two texts. It is hoped that the tension between the two texts will remain adequately ambiguous.[6]

In this paper the biblical Lamentations is read together with the Chinese poem, *The Lament for the South,* written by Yu Xin (513–81), who sees himself as continuing the tradition of an ancient literary creation of Southern China, *The Songs of the South (Chu Ci),* the Chu poetry of Qu Yuan (343–277 B.C.E.). This latter book, which dates from the fourth century B.C.E., is representative of an ancient Chinese lament tradition. The present form of it is generally attributed to Qu Quan.[7] I will first present a brief introduction to *The Lament for the South* before engaging in the cross–textual reading.

II. YU XIN'S *THE LAMENT FOR THE SOUTH*

Yu Xin's *Lament for the South* is composed in a Chu poetic form and consists of two parts: the preface of 72 lines and the body of 520 lines.[8] Many stories and legends have been adopted from the Chinese cultural milieu and refashioned in Yu Xin's own literary style. In expressing his grief, Yu Xin identifies

tive in Gen 1–11," *BibInt* 2 (1994) 312–24; "Death and the Perception of the Divine in Zhuangzi and Koheleth," *Ching Feng* 38 (1995) 68–81; "Exile and Return in the Perspective of 1997," in Fernando F. Segovia and Mary Ann Tolbert, eds., *Reading from This Place: Social Location and Biblical Interpretation in Global Perspective* (Minneapolis: Fortress, 1995) 1:97–108; "Cross-Textual Hermeneutics on Gospel and Culture," *AJT* 10 (1996) 38–48; "Syncretism from the Perspectives of Chinese Religion and Biblical Tradition," *Ching Feng* 39/3 (1996) 1–24; "Feminist Critique of the Bible and Female Principle in Culture," *AJT* 10 (1996) 240–52; "The Recitation of the Past: A Cross-textual Reading of Ps. 78 and the Odes," *Ching Feng,* 38/3 (1996) 173–200.

[6] Jeffery Kuan has provided a good assessment of the method of cross-textual interpretation against the landscape of biblical hermeneutics in Asia in his article "Asian Biblical Interpretation," in John H. Hays, ed., *Dictionary of Biblical Interpretation* (Nashville: Abingdon Press, 1999) 1:70–77. The article also includes a bibliography on the method.

[7] For translation and annotation of *The Songs of the South* see David Hawkes, *The Songs of the South: An Ancient Anthology of Poems by Qu Yuan and Other Poets* (Harmondsworth: Penguin, 1985). Hawkes also provides a very good introduction.

[8] The Chinese text does not have any system of numbering the lines. This paper follows William T. Graham's arrangement and his translation into English in *The Lament for the South—Yu Hsin's Ai Chiang-nan Fu* (Cambridge: Cambridge University Press, 1980). There are, however, places where the present author finds modified renderings more appropriate and retranslations are done accordingly. The transliterations adopted in present-day China will be used in rendering Chinese characters except in quotations and in names where conventional practices are widely accepted. See also commentary on Yu Xin in Ni Fan, *Yu Zishan Ji* (Taipei: Taiwan Commercial Press, 1968).

with a number of great historical characters in the past. He shows both his literary skill and encyclopaedic knowledge in the *Lament*.

From the outset of the lament Yu Xin speaks from the perspective of a survivor—the same perspective found in each of the poems of Lamentations, as pointed out by F. W. Dobbs-Allsopp.[9] Lamentations is accordingly a "most profoundly life-embracing work"[10] and the poet "stubbornly holds onto life and manifests a will to life"[11] although his or her identity remains unknown to us. In contrast to Lamentations, the author of *The Lament for the South* is known, and scholars have no dispute over the authorship of Yu Xin. He was sent, at the age of forty-two, as ambassador from his own country, Liang in the south, to Western Wei in the north when Western Wei attacked Liang and destroyed the capital Jiangling in 554.[12] The enemy, Western Wei, then took him captive. Since Western Wei and the subsequent conquerors and rulers in the north all had great appreciation for his intellectual, literary, and administrative skills, he was forced to serve the enemy rulers in the north till his death at the age of 69 (581 C.E.).

The date of the composition of the *Lament* seems, to many, to be relatively easy to fix. Lines 11–12 refer to the stars completing their twelve-year cycle and a new cycle having started again, but the course of human history remains moving linearly forward. Yu Xin also laments that time has gone on without any sign of him ever returning. Furthermore, there is a description of the very harsh reality of life that his friends and fellow countryfolk experienced as they were captured, exiled to the north, and died one by one over the course of time. It grieves him deeply when he sees himself getting old and being the sole survivor in exile (line 506 and line 510). Taking these general points together, the date of 578 C.E. has been proposed by Ch'en yin-k'o and endorsed by the authors of most commentaries.[13]

---

[9] F. W. Dobbs-Allsopp takes the biblical Lamentations as written from the perspective of the survivors of the calamity of the fall of Jerusalem (*Lamentations: A Bible Commentary for Teaching and Preaching* [Louisville: Westminster John Knox Press, 2002] 46).

[10] Ibid. 2.

[11] Ibid. 3.

[12] The Chinese way of counting one's age is different from that in the West. When a baby reaches the first birthday he or she is regarded as two years old. There is, therefore, an additional year added to the age of a person compared to the general practice.

[13] Ch'en Yin-k'o, "Reading *The Lament for the South*," *Journal of Ch'ing-hua* 13 (1941) 11–16. See the discussion on dating in William T. Graham, *The Lament for the South* (Cambridge: Cambridge University Press, 1980) Appendix IV, 173–74, and in William T. Graham, trans., "Yü Hsin and *"The Lament for the South*,"" *HTAS* 36 (1976) 82–113. There are also other scholars who are in favor of a date close to the fall of Liang in 554; see Lu Tongqun, *A Special Study of Yu Xin*, (Tianjin: Tianjin People's Press, 1997).

During the twenty-eight years of captivity Yu Xin has written many poems of lament articulating his grief and sorrow and eventually his desperation. He bewails the disastrous fall of his own country and the great loss of lives among his people. The fact that he is forced to serve the very enemies who had brought national calamities and catastrophic sufferings upon his people hurts him tremendously. His own family members also were captives of the enemies in the south. The tragedy becomes unbearable when his fellow countryfolk harshly accuse him of betrayal and loss of integrity. In his poems we hear his agonies of self-pity and shame as well as internal conflicts between dynastic loyalty and moral integrity, added to the feeling of pain at the devastating suffering of his people.

Yu Xin's *The Lament for the South* devotes considerable space to the recollection of the past.[14] It recounts the family history of Yu's ancestors going back to the past seven generations, with an emphasis on their contributions and the honors ascribed to them. The loyalty of the family to the imperial rule is duly remembered and narrated. In time of crisis the Chinese usually resort to the past for inspiration and courage. The present is perceived afresh in view of the recounting of historical events.[15] To Yu Xin, "remembering the past" *(huai gu)* has the aim not only of showing the contribution of his family to the Liang Dynasty but also of defending his loyalty and integrity even in his submission to the enemies. There is a detailed account of the good old days when the country was in peace and prosperity.

This is in contrast to the biblical lament with its remembering of the mighty deeds of God to underline the element of hope since "[m]emory and hope are intertwined in prayer and worship in Israel."[16] Brevard Childs also concludes in his study that the Hebrew word for "remember" *(zakar)* is mainly employed in Lamentations according to the genre of complaint psalms, but not necessarily in any cultic setting.[17] In the Chinese lament, exemplified in Yu Xin and Qu Yuan, poetic recitation of the past functions to contrast the royal favor experienced by the lamenter in times of national prosperity with the present misery, and there are no complaints against the deity. On the whole, when compared

---

[14] Remembering the past is usually a theme in lament in the Chinese cultural articulation. Yu Xin himself survived under four different dynasties and nine emperors. He was sent as ambassador to Eastern Wei in a time of cordial relations from 542 to 547. For details of the historical background see Graham, *The Lament for the South,* ch. 2.

[15] There is some truth in Prazniak's idea that "Chinese orthodoxy envisioned an ideal past that it sought to recover" (Roxann Prazniak, *Dialogues Across Civilizations: Sketches in World History from the Chinese and European Experiences* [Boulder: Westview Press, 1996] 183).

[16] Kathleen D. Billman and Daniel L. Migliore, *Rachel's Cry: Prayer of Lament and Rebirth of Hope* (Cleveland: United Church Press, 1999) 32.

[17] Brevard Childs, *Memory and Hope in Israel* (London: S.C.M., 1962) 64.

with the biblical laments, the Chinese do not develop anything like the complaint against God in the face of national calamities. Yu Xin states clearly the aim of composing his *Lament* at the end of the preface:

> Homeless at Xiating,
> A wanderer at Gaoqiao,
> Songs of Chu could not make me happy;
> The wine of Lu was useless in dispelling sorrow.
> So looking back I wrote this song
> That it might serve as a record;
> Not without words of fear and suffering,
> It is still, at the core, a lament.
> The sun is setting; my road is far away;
> How long have I left in this world?
> (Preface, lines 27–36)[18]

Yu Xin imitates and models Qu Yuan, the ancient sage of Chu in the south, in his composition of *The Lament for the South*. The title bears resemblance to the last line of *The Summons of the Soul,* assumed by tradition to be written by Qu Yuan when he was banished from his country Chu by his own government and then exiled in a foreign land due to false accusation by other officials. The last line of *The Summons of the Soul* calls upon the soul to return to the south: "O Soul, come back! Alas for the southern land." Almost eight hundred years later Yu Xin laments for his own exile and the fall of his country at Jiangling, which was the capital of Chu eight hundred years ago.

Their similar historical fate and bitterness at being exiled from the south give rise to a sense of identification between Yu Xin and Qu Yuan, though in the case of the latter his country was not yet defeated, if not far from destruction. In a sense this is a Chinese example of what Tod Linafelt refers to as the survival of literature.[19] Yu Xin not only stands firmly in the line of thought that the suffering people in their pain must sing of their sorrow (lines 69–70), he also renews the tradition of crying to the soul to return. This shamanistic feature of the quest for union with the mystery of life and the power of the cosmos in times of bitterness is preserved in the writings of Qu Yuan. It also survives in the literary form of *The Lament for the South*.

---

[18] Xiating and Gaoqiao are presumably place names, though scholars cannot be certain of their identification. They may be used for contrasting ideas of low/high. The song of the Chu state and the wine of the Lu state are known for dispelling sorrow. These two states may also be chosen for the contrast in the conception of locations in the south and the north respectively. See Graham, *The Lament for the South,* 107 and the translation of these lines on pp. 52–53.

[19] Tod Linafelt, *Surviving Lamentations. Catastrophe, Lament, and Protest in the Afterlife of a Biblical Book* (Chicago: University of Chicago Press, 2000).

Qu Yuan wrote another poem entitled *Mourning for the Lost Capital*,[20] to grieve and bewail the fall of the capital city Ying. The city was the capital of Qu Yuan's Chu in 278 B.C.E. and was renamed Jiangling in Yu Xin's Liang in 554 C.E. The destruction of the same city is the cause of grief and despair in both *Mourning for the Lost Capital* and *The Lament for the South*. The cause of deep sorrow in both cases is, however, the reality of the exile in a foreign land. For Qu Yuan, in *Mourning for the Lost Capital,* the exile had lasted nine years and there was no sign offering any hope of return. In the case of Yu Xin it is a much longer period of twenty-eight years and, coupled with the fact that Yu Xin was then an old man, the hope of ever returning home alive was close to impossibility.

In *The Lament for the South* a strong wish among the exiles to return home is expressed in lines 449–52. Yu Xin, being a desperate and helpless captive from the south, has been longing for return. His being sixty-five years old when the poem was written explains the urgency, anxiety, and fear in the quest for home.[21] To Yu Xin the lament is very real when it is understood in this Chinese context of cultural centrism. This mentality refuses to submit the highly civilized Chinese culture to ruthless and merciless destruction by a less civilized enemy. This explains the great sense of humiliation when the Mongolians defeated the Chinese people in the Song Dynasty in the twelfth century, the Manchurians conquered the Ming Dynasty in the seventeenth century, and again the Western powers overthrew the Qing Dynasty in the nineteenth and twentieth centuries. Yu Xin perceives that the defeat of his country Liang is not only a great shock but a tremendous loss. It grieves his heart to see the empire collapse and the mountains and rivers split asunder by the barbaric enemies from the north:

> And yet they split apart mountains and streams,
> And carved up the empire.
> How could a hundred myriad loyal troops
> All at once discard their armor
> To be moved away and chopped down
> Like grass and trees?
> (Preface, lines 49–51)

Calamity of such an immense magnitude demands a satisfactory explanation. The fall of the capital city of Liang signifies the loss of the ancient center

---

[20] The original title is *The Lament for Ying*. Here I follow the translation of Yang Xian-yi and Dai Nai-die, *The Songs of the South* (Beijing: Foreign Language Publishing Co., 2001) 147.

[21] Yu Xin's quest to return to his homeland must be seen in relation to the deep influence of the conception of the centrality and superiority of Chinese culture in sharp distinction to that of the barbarians. Dying in a "barbaric" foreign land is regarded as one of the greatest curses.

of Chinese civilization to the barbarians. To the cultural centrism of the loyal guardian of Chinese civilization the impact of the capture of the capital city by foreign armies is comparable to the fall of Jerusalem to the Babylonians. The insult of the exile amounts to death and humiliation, being cut off from the source of life in terms of civilization in the Chinese case and the Land for biblical Israel. The personified Zion was concerned with the survival of the people of God and Qu Yuan, in the same way that Yu Xin, who assumes the embodiment of a superior culture, was deeply preoccupied with the future of the Chinese civilization and his people.

The destruction of the capital city and prolonged exile prompted the quest for justification of the tragedy. The author of *The Mourning for the Lost Capital* does not take the blame upon himself, but protests against being accused of sin:

> The birds fly home to their old nests where they came from,
> And the foxes when they die turn their heads toward their caves.
> That I was cast off and banished was truly for no crime.
> By day and night I never can forget.[22]

A large portion of the poem describes the rebellion of the enemies and the cruelty of war. The misery and desolation are lamented in lines 443–48, 453–60. In the description of the sufferings brought about by battles there is a clear anti-war sentiment that permeates the words of the *Lament,* and a condemnation of human suffering. The two seemingly unrelated sentences quoted from *The Book of Changes (The Yi Jing)*—"The greatest gift of heaven and earth is life; the greatest treasure of the sage is the throne"—carry an anti-war ideology. This anti-war sentiment is clearly seen when we consult Yu Xin's citation of the same quotation in another of his poems entitled *A Song of the Sounding of the Horn (Jiaodiao Qu).* Here he adds two words to the above quotation: "Though the greatest treasure of the sage is the throne, the greatest gift of heaven and earth is surely life." Life must be held above the throne, not the other way round. The lives of the citizens are valuable and must not exist merely to serve the throne.[23]

---

[22] David Hawkes, *The Songs of the South,* 166. King Huai entrusted Qu Yuan with great responsibility in running the nation. Unfortunately, after the death of King Huai in the third year of his captivity in Qin in the year 296 B.C.E., the new King Xiang banished Qu Yuan from Jiangling. In 278 B.C.E. the Qin general Bo Qi sacked the capital and the Chu court was forced to move to a new capital in Chen, which was two hundred fifty miles to the northeast (ibid. 162).

[23] Lu Tongqun, *A Special Study of Yu Xin,* 67. In quoting and affirming what *The Book of Changes* proposes (i.e., that life is the greatest gift of heaven and earth and the greatest treasure of the sage is the throne) Yu Xin contrasts the present experience of the agony of the loss of life with the fall of the throne.

Both *The Lament for the South* and Lamentations share this basic critique of war and violence.[24]

Being uprooted and exiled to a foreign land under a foreign rule is a tragic experience. The degree of lament will certainly be intensified if the exiled person dies in an alien land, away from home and without family to mourn the dead and to perform the burial rituals. Yu Xin's cry for home in the south in his old age can be seen in this context. But his personal grief is part and parcel of larger national calamities. The sufferer can never overcome the loss of so many lives in his homeland.

III. THE WILL OF HEAVEN AND/OR HUMAN RESPONSIBILITY

I want to pick up another important issue for discussion. It is the question of agency *in* calamities and the ground for human suffering.

Yu Xin in his lament tries to unlock the mystery of the downfall of the Liang Dynasty: "Neither simply fate nor mistakes in government could explain the destruction of a mighty empire."[25] It seems that according to Yu Xin the fall of his dynasty had been anticipated and portended by natural phenomena.

> Wasn't the royal aura of the south
> To end in three hundred years?
> This would explain why
> Swallowing up the world could not
> Prevent the tragedy at Zhidao,
> And standardizing axles and script
> Could not avert the disaster at Pingyang.[26]
> Alas
> When mountains crumbled
> National calamities seemed inescapable
> As spring and autumn seasons passed
> I grieve for the inevitable destruction
> Heaven's Will—human's doing

---

[24] For the idea of the use of the image of women to depict war's atrocities see Kathleen M. O'Connor, "Lamentations," in Carol A. Newsom and Sharon H. Ringe, eds., *The Women's Bible Commentary, Expanded Edition with Apocrypha* (Louisville: Westminster John Knox, 1998) 187.

[25] Graham, *The Lament for the South*, 55.

[26] On the abdication of the last emperor of Qin at Zhidao and the murder of the two emperors of Jin at Pingyang despite efforts at and policies for unification see ibid. 110. Graham adds a comment: "The fall of the Southern dynasties had also been predicted. Either fate or mistakes in government could explain the destruction of mighty empire" (ibid. 55).

Sorrowful and heart breaking.
(Preface, lines 59–66)

The assumption that the end of the mandate for the royal court and the succession of dynastic rule had been predicted and was comparable to changes in
the natural order and seasonal cycle seems to affirm the dominant view of the
heavenly will. Yu Xin laments the fact that in his family history his ancestry
was originally from the North. Seven generations ago his great-grandparents
settled in the South, but now he is being forced to return to the North. The
heavenly will moves in a full circle and governs people's lives (lines 495–96).
These expressions affirming the heavenly will are significant for understanding the *Lament*. In his other writings, however, Yu Xin is skeptical of the heavenly will.[27] Scholars usually agree that there are two contradictory conceptions
of "Heaven" in Yu Xin's mind: one takes it as the natural order and the other
declares that Heaven represents a personal and willful character in charge of
human affairs.[28]

Seen from the Chinese perspective, the two characteristics of the biblical
Lamentations stand out in contrast: the confession of sin and the complaint
against God. The expression "we have done wrong" does not appear in the
Lament and the pouring out of one's heart before God in terms of accusation
and complaint is not an essential component. When encountering sorrow and
grief, the Chinese lament tends to articulate the mystical dimension of the will
of Heaven *(tian yi)* in conjunction with the social or political factors of the
workings of humans *(ren shi)*. The historical reality of the actions of forefa-
thers and foremothers in the immediate past causes the inevitable suffering
that befalls the present generation. The blame is primarily on human responsibility, but it is always in the larger context of the response of Heaven, which is
said to be reacting primarily to human performance. In the Chinese lament the
will of Heaven is always assumed and implicitly acknowledged. It is in this
sense that the effort to disentangle the tension and dynamics of the will of
Heaven and human responsibility will never be satisfactorily achieved.

The use of the notion of "Heaven" *(tian)* is a more explicit way to articulate this very dimension of the mystery of the divine-human collaboration. In
line 494 the exclamation "How could Heaven have been so drunk!" is intended
to show that something has gone terribly wrong and is beyond our normal
comprehension. The only viable means for making sense of this is to assume
that Heaven, not being of the natural order but an intelligent rational being,
must have been drunk.

---

[27] Tongqun, *A Special Study of Yu Xin*, 52–59.
[28] Ibid. 56.

A survey of the appearance of the word "Heaven" *(tian)* in *The Lament for the South* illustrates Yu Xin's conception of this reality of life. The word is used twenty times in the *Lament*. In the body of the *Lament* it occurs twice in reference to the emperor as "Son of Heaven" and four times in the phrase "heaven and earth" *(tianxia)*. Nine of the remaining fourteen occurrences are in the Preface (four times) and in the concluding paragraphs (five times), and all convey an understanding beyond the natural order of the blue sky. On the one hand, the tragedy of the defeat of the country is attributed to the wrong policy of the royal court in appointing worthless officials to key positions and to the rebellious factions in the country (lines 487–92). But on the other hand, by referring to a popular story in the previous dynasty Yu Xin raises a significant question suggesting that something must be wrong with the whole course of present events. Yu Xin then takes the peculiar position of not laying any blame on Heaven. A few lines after Yu quotes the *Book of Songs (Shi Jing)*—"In death and life [we are] separated and far apart"[29]—he ironically asserts that even in the case of the most miserable and unbearable suffering one may not "question Heaven":[30]

> Though far away in life and death,
> One may not question Heaven.[31]
> Not even though
> The rest have almost all withered and fallen.
> And, another Lingguang, I alone remain.
> (Lines 504–06)[32]

Yu Xin rejects any basis for questioning Heaven even though he is in the midst of national destruction, separated from his family and friends who have died, and far away from those who are still alive at home in the South. As time goes by, his quest for home and the depth of his grief intensify. Therefore at

---

[29] *Book of Songs (Shi Jing)*, no. 31, trans. Bernhard Karlgren, in *The Book of Odes* (Stockholm: Museum of Far Eastern Antiquities, 1950) 19.

[30] Questioning heaven is clearly an allusion to Chu Ci's "Heavenly Questions" ("Tian Wen"). The classical commentary of Wang Yi on the meaning of "Tian Wen" declares that "Heaven is august and may not be questioned," and therefore favors "Heavenly Questions" instead of "Questioning Heaven."

[31] Qu Yuan in his great despair and pain wrote *Questioning Heaven (Tianwen)*, a book of 172 questions addressing a variety of concerns from the creation of heaven and earth to the present-day reality. Hawkes' rendering, "the ultimate Questioning," is another alternative translation (David Hawkes, *The Songs of the South*, 90).

[32] Graham, *The Lament for the South*, 101. Yu Xin alludes to the collapse of all palaces and temples during the rebellion in Han's time except the Lingguang Temple, which alone stands.

the end of the *Lament* he complains about the lack of any person who can comprehend the grief he is trying to articulate.

> The sun is entering its last conjunction,
> The year is about to begin again.
> Constantly driven by fear and anxiety,
> Grieving in my twilight years.
> Among the commoners of Xianyang,[33]
> Not only the prince longs for home.
> (Lines 507–10, 520)

Yu Xin expresses a belief in signs sent by Heaven in the form of the natural order or astronomical portents. Omens are regarded as giving warning to evildoers and sociopolitical leaders, who take no notice of the signals and raise no alarm by their doings. In *The Lament for the South* there are eight references to astrological phenomena (Preface line 12, lines 27–28, 48, 90, 138, 252, 307–08, 390). These, along with natural features such as rivers running dry (line 20) and mountains being shaken to the foundation, constitute a stock of metaphors used to symbolize the fall of a nation. The whole cosmic order was believed to have reacted to dynastic policies and the way the emperor reigned. Omens and portents were signs of nature taking part in human affairs. They joined in the grief of the people at the destruction and the tragic exile of the people to the north.

> A vengeful frost fell in summer;
> Angry springs boiled up in autumn.
> Qi's wife brought down a wall by her cries;
> The Ladies of the Xiang stained bamboo with their tears
> Rivers poisonous as the streams of Qin,
> Mountains as high as the range of Xing,
> Ten miles, five miles,
> Long halts, short halts,
> Driven by hunger after hibernating swallows
> (Lines 433–39).[34]

The constellation and the natural order function metaphorically to express the dimension of the mystery of life and the divine intervention represented by God in Lamentations. Both the Chinese and Hebrew laments have formulated

---

[33] Yu Xin alludes to the story of the captured Chu Crown Prince, hostage in Qin and denied return to his country; see Graham, *The Lament for the South,* 161–62.

[34] These lines depict the plight of the Liang captives who were carried off from their own country to the foreign land. Their cries of lament were indeed echoed in nature. See William T. Graham, *The Lament for the South,* 154.

an expression of "a cry to the beyond" in times of anguish. In Lamentations it is a request to God to look and see the terrible face of human suffering (1:9, 11, 20; 2:20; 3:49-50, 59; 5:1). Here divine violence is the cause of bitter complaint against God from the depths of the human heart (1:13-15; 2:1-8; 3:1-18). Similarly, the Chinese *Lament* also issues a complaint that Heaven has no eyes or that Heaven has not had its eyes open wide enough. The theological assertion in Lamentations is that the LORD has made Lady Jerusalem suffer (1:5), and as a result there *is* none to comfort her (1:9). When YHWH is first mentioned in Lamentations in the context of the harsh treatment of the exiles by the enemy, the emphasis is on YHWH who effected the destruction of Jerusalem, not the enemy. In fact it is YHWH who has become the bitter enemy of the people (2:4-5).[35]

Jannie Hunter observes that the defeat by the enemy is, however, not attributed to YHWH; it was the grave sin of the city that brought about the city's downfall.[36] Here not only are the two agents, YHWH and the enemy, both present, but a grave sin committed by humans is also said to be responsible for the affliction. In Lam 1:12 reference to the day of the fierce anger of YHWH is intended to bring out YHWH's role in inflicting suffering on the people. Hunter assumes that the real cause of it all is definitely the sins of the city (1:14), while YHWH is "the architect of the consequence of sin."[37]

In the Chinese *Lament* the cause of the destruction of the empire is not the sins of the people, but the cruelty of the enemies and the mismanagement of the empire by the wrong officials, who are either incapable or wicked. Human disasters and national calamities are attributed to conflict and factionalism. It is the rebellious forces of Hou Jing that severely slaughtered and massacred Liang's generals, officials, and civilians. The destruction was so drastic and alarming that survivors were left terrified. Internal conflicts in the court further intensified the sense of desperation. Metaphorical phrases are used in the poem to depict the calamities and the civil wars. Yu Xin makes reference to the four ancient states in conflict to drive home his lament for the internal crisis:

> Turbulent, boiling
> Disordered, chaotic
> Heaven and earth were cut off from us

---

[35] The city laments in Western Asia exhibit a similar approach in times of the destruction of cities. Why Enlil destroyed his family and city is the most distressing and searching question the goddesses ever put forward. For a study of the genre in the Hebrew Bible see F. W. Dobbs-Allsopp, *Weep, O Daughter of Zion: A Study of the City-Lament Genre in the Hebrew Bible* (Rome: Pontifical Biblical Institute, 1993).

[36] Jannie Hunter, *Faces of a Lamenting City: The Development and Coherence of the Book of Lamentations* (Frankfurtfurt: Peter Lang, 1996) 113.

[37] Ibid. 115.

> Spirits and humanity were in tragic cruelty
> Jin and Zheng refused to help
> Lu and Wei were not in harmony.
> They struggled to move the gate of heaven,
> Fought to turn the axis of the earth.
> (Lines 217–24)

Yu Xin's concept of Hou Jing and his rebellion is framed in terms of "the civilized" and "the uncivilized." In the poem Hou Jing is seen as a barbarian, a wild ox with a nomadic nature (lines 111–16). Although *The Lament for the South* highlights this human dimension of the calamity and the personal experience of pain in face of the national disaster of the fall of the Liang Dynasty (Preface, lines 13–14), Yu Xin, in his deep lament over the tragic collapse of his country and his miserable situation in captivity, links the socio-political events to a transcendental vision of divine disapproval or heavenly dissent. This is in great contrast to the views of most scholars who stress the human orientation of Chinese culture, which presumably undermines references to the divine.

IV. CONCLUSION

The aim of Yu Xin's *The Lament for the South* is to express his grief and sorrow over the national disaster of destruction of the royal throne and his painful but desperate desire to return to his home in the South. There is no prayer rendered to the divine that brings about the destruction and, therefore, no hope of divine intervention in terms of redemption or revenge against the enemies, as is the case in Lamentations. The transcendental perception of a personal God who can respond in reward and punishment and listen to human cries is not detected in Yu Xin's *Lament*. There is, nevertheless, an articulation of a dimension of mystery that is exhibited in the workings of the natural order, giving signs of disapproval to human endeavors.

As for the discourse explaining the cause of destruction and national calamities, human responsibility in the various failings of the royal court, the corruption of government officials, and human agency in the cruelty and ruthlessness of the enemy are indisputably cited. The political explanations are put in concrete and specific terms, in contrast to the general reference to human sins in Lamentations. There is naturally no place for complaint against God in the Chinese *Lament,* where atrocities are mostly attributed to human workings.

In contrast to Lamentations, the agency of the enemy is not perceived in terms of a divine being who brings about fulfillment of divine intention. The Chinese *Lament* is very critical of the cruelty of the enemy. The accusation against the destructive rebellious force of the enemy, Hou Jing, in the year 548 comes at the beginning of the Preface to the Lament (Preface, lines 1–4) and forms the context of the laments for the people's severe suffering and Yu Xin's subsequent misfortune as a captive in the north (lines 5–8).

The English rendering of the Chinese phrase in the four characters: "Heaven's will human affair" (line 65) is usually expressed in an either/or mentality, while the Chinese original does not suggest making a choice.[38] It is both Heaven's will and human responsibility that brought about the destruction, and this constitutes the core of the lament. The biblical Lamentations is also not clear as to which holds sway when it comes to the controlling factors in human calamities: God's role in punishing and afflicting pain, human sins and rebellion, or the cruelty and arrogance of the enemies? The ambiguity and tension are properly maintained. Lamentations and *The Lament for the South* both resist the temptation to view human sufferings one-dimensionally. The reality of a constant negotiation between the theodic and the antitheodic impulses must be kept alive.[39]

Lament is the language of the lamenter who is not seeking explanation, but the expression of grief. Both Lamentations and *The Lament for the South* provide the sufferer with the means to relate to the profound unknown and the lamenter with a process to discharge the unbearable emotion. They both give the mourner a voice. This language of the lamenter, which is intrinsically characterized by ambiguities and obscurities, is indispensable to those encountering pain and grief in human situations. It gives them a voice to release their grievous and disturbing emotions. Cries of lament, therefore, do not necessarily address God directly, but they are outpourings that "help people to weep over their tragedy and thus release their pain."[40]

These free poetic articulations of the profoundly inarticulable and incomprehensible are a valuable human heritage, which will survive this present wounded generation.

---

[38] Graham translates as: "Whether it was heaven's will or man's doing" (*The Lament for the South*, 56).

[39] F. W. Dobbs-Allsopp, *Lamentations,* 30.

[40] O'Connor, "Lamentations," 187.

Homer and Scripture in the Gospel of Mark

Robert B. Coote and Mary P. Coote

To communicate effectively to their audiences, storytellers must, so to speak, draw ninety percent on old material and ten percent on new, not vice versa. News, even Good News, must in some ways be old for us to make sense of it. In the final analysis there are only one or two good stories, retold in infinite variety from *Gilgamesh* to *The Matrix Reloaded,* in popular as well as elite culture. So too Mark's new story of Jesus rests firmly on old foundations.

One of these foundations, long recognized in New Testament scholarship, would have been stories about Jesus current in Mark's time. Oral storytelling of the past cannot be recovered, of course, and we are forced to reconstruct on the basis of other recorded literary parallels what Mark the writer had to work with in his creation of Jesus' story. Whatever their relation to real events, these stories would have been quickly assimilated to traditional story patterns in order to survive in transmission—as the circulation of jokes and urban legends even in our own time illustrates. Anne Wire's recently published *Holy Lives, Holy Deaths: A Close Hearing of Early Jewish Storytellers*[1] identifies three story types exemplified in Mark's narrative: wondrous provision, prophets' signs, and martyrdom and vindication. As she points out, in a patriarchal society these are the kinds of stories typically told in and about the domestic, private sphere, most often by women. They are legends, closer kin to ballad and folk tale than to epic.

Whatever his debt to women storytellers, the writer of Mark clearly claims another foundation for his story—Jewish Scripture:

Ἀρχὴ τοῦ εὐαγγελίου Ἰησοῦ Χριστοῦ [υἱοῦ θεοῦ]
καθὼς γέγραπται ἐν τῷ Ἠσαΐᾳ τῷ προφήτῃ . . . (1:1)

---

[1] Antoinette Clark Wire, *Holy Lives, Holy Deaths: A Close Hearing of Early Jewish Storytellers* (Atlanta: Society of Biblical Literature, 2002).

Following this opening line he goes on to amalgamate three Scripture texts in a verbatim quotation, the "basis" of his account, and to refer or allude to numerous other Scripture texts in the first fifteen verses.[2] The scriptural foundation, however, consists of more than quotations and allusions. Mark structures his entire story according to the scriptural distinction between Torah and Prophets, delineates his main character in terms of the scriptural figures of king and prophet, bases virtually all his main themes and most of the individual episodes in his story on some Scripture text or set of texts, often quoted verbatim, and writes a work imbued with scriptural style and saturated with scriptural vocabulary. His use of Scripture is not a simple referencing of it, but a contribution to the luxuriant fabric of scriptural exegesis evidenced by the corpus of Hellenistic Jewish writings anchored in Scripture.

Alongside these two major sources, Jesus traditions and Scripture, Mark, writing in Greek under Roman rule in the late first century C.E., must certainly have drawn on non-Jewish Hellenistic literary sources as well. Given that in Mark's culture Homer was the foundation text for education[3] and the prime model for imitation in literature and rhetoric,[4] Mark and the schooled in his audience would have been raised on the epitome of the good story in antiquity, Homer's *Iliad* and *Odyssey*. That Homer was the "primary literary inspiration" of Mark is the contention of Dennis R. MacDonald, who, beginning with discovering the roots of the second-century *Acts of Andrew* in the *Odyssey,* has gone on to search both Mark and Luke for reflections of classical literature. In *The Homeric Epics and the Gospel of Mark,* MacDonald has undertaken to catalog the many episodes and phrases in Mark that mimic Homer. Rejecting the parallels with other contemporary genres (Jewish martyrologies, Plato's death of Socrates, Greek tragedies, aretalogies, folk literature, historical novels, and biographies), he argues that Mark was engaged in "imitation of specific texts of a different genre: Mark wrote a prose epic modeled largely after the Odyssey and the ending of the Iliad."[5] This interpretation puts Mark in touch with the storytelling of the public sphere, the heroic epic of the world of

---

[2] Robert B. Coote, "Mark 1:1: *archē,* 'Scriptural Lemma,'" in Robert P. Carroll, ed., *Text as Pretext: Essays in Honour of Robert Davidson* (Sheffield: JSOT Press, 1992) 86–90.

[3] Ronald F. Hock, "Homer in Greco-Roman Education," in Dennis R. MacDonald, ed., *Mimesis and Intertextuality in Antiquity and Christianity* (Harrisburg: Trinity Press International, 2001) 56–77; Raffaella Cribiore, *Gymnastics of the Mind: Greek Education in Hellenistic and Roman Egypt* (Princeton: Princeton University Press, 2001).

[4] The literature on this point is impressive, not least Dennis R. MacDonald, *Christianizing Homer: The Odyssey, Plato, and The Acts of Andrew* (New York: Oxford University Press, 1994).

[5] Dennis R. MacDonald, *The Homeric Epics and the Gospel of Mark* (New Haven: Yale University Press, 2000) 3.

men, itself originally oral tradition but by Mark's time firmly literary. His purpose is to present a "transvaluation" of the Homeric hero; in persistent "theological rivalry," Jesus' virtues—compassion, strength, nobility, and, most notably, patience in suffering—surpass those of Odysseus and Hector.[6]

Viewed as epic return stories (minus the mandatory wedding in Mark's case), Mark's gospel and the *Odyssey* have remarkable similarities in plot. A hero makes a long journey home on water and land. He demonstrates his cunning, power, and authority on the way. Gathered about him are less-sharp-witted followers who fall away when the going gets tough. He disguises himself before arriving at a home "infested with murderous rivals."[7] These rivals he thrashes in a battle of wit as he readies himself to take his household back. The ending of Mark appears to be very different from the *Odyssey,* but this is a false impression. Jesus leaves no doubt that he will soon, suddenly, and ferociously complete his conquest and rout his rivals by force, just like Odysseus.[8]

Why then, given these similarities and the overwhelming number of echoes and allusions assembled by MacDonald, was the close parallel of Mark with the *Odyssey* not noticed for two thousand years after its promulgation? Even the author of the Gospel of Luke, whose Eutychus story in Acts 20 provides MacDonald's introductory example of Homeric inspiration[9] (Eutychus = Elpenor in the *Odyssey,* the same Elpenor who also corresponds to the νεανίσκος in Mark, and even to Jesus himself[10]), seems to have missed the clues in Mark. Evidently to make the case that Homer rather than Scripture was the "primary literary inspiration" for Mark, one has to discount the obvious scriptural foundation in favor of the obscured, although by no means esoteric, Homeric model.

[6] Ibid. 6

[7] Ibid. 3

[8] MacDonald makes the inventive suggestion that in death Jesus is modeled on Hector: "Jesus dies at the end of the book, his corpse is rescued from his executioner, and he is mourned by three women" (ibid.). The catalogue of similarities with which Macdonald launches his *tour de force* on Homeric influence on Mark sets the pattern for instances of randomness, arbitrariness, vagueness, overvaluation of the commonplace, and verbal sleight of hand that tend to slip into his argument. "Odysseus and Jesus both sail seas with associates far their inferiors, who weaken when confronted with suffering. Both heroes return home to find it infested with murderous rivals that devour the houses of widows. Both oppose supernatural foes, visit dead heroes, and prophesy their own returns in the third person. A wise woman anoints each protagonist, and both eat last suppers with their comrades before visiting Hades, from which both return alive. In both works one finds gods stilling storms and walking on water, meals for thousands at the shore, and monsters in caves . . . interests in the sea, meals, and secrecy . . ." (ibid. 3).

[9] Ibid. 10–14

[10] Ibid. 136, 160.

The intrepid proponents of Mark's use of Homer make short work of this problem. Mark, they argue, knew that literary imitation required subtlety, and his imitations "simultaneously conceal and reveal."[11] As a sophisticated imitator, the writer of Mark "disguised his dependence by writing in prose, altering Homeric vocabulary, rearranging episodes, and borrowing as well from Jewish scriptures."[12] What looks like Mark's reliance on Scripture was actually one of several devices used to disguise his primary dependence on Homer— an extremely successful disguise, as it turned out. Mark's Jesus is presented as Joshua (and Elisha, and the Lord's servant in Isaiah) to cover his true identity as the master of disguises, Odysseus (and Hector, Aeolus, Telemachus, Nestor, Menelaus, Achilles, Elpenor, even Athena and Circe, at various points in the narrative). If this is disguise, one might equally well say that Ronald Reagan was disguised as a conservative, or a Big Mac is disguised as a hamburger. In this view Mark's supposed imitation of Homer then becomes the standard against which Mark's dependence on "tradition, written sources, or Jewish scriptures" is to be measured, and "it necessarily diminishes the extent of such dependence."[13]

Reviewers so far have applauded MacDonald for presenting a fresh, bold, and unique thesis.[14] Approaching Mark intertextually and recognizing the importance of Homer in an education that the writer of Mark is presumed to have shared, he amasses a wide range of examples of varying credibility to support

---

[11] Ibid. 6.

[12] Ibid.

[13] Ibid. 189. The force of this statement is unclear: whatever the extent of Mark's dependence on Homer, Mark's dependence on Scripture remains all-pervading and unmistakable. The proponents of Homeric dependence seem perplexingly content to downplay Mark's use of Scripture. An endnote to MacDonald's first mention of such use gives a single random example, the raising of Jairus's daughter in Mark 5 and "the raising of a woman's son in 2 Kings," and cites, in what appears to be also a random choice, the commentary of Rudolf Pesch (1980) for this parallel, as though Mark's use of Scripture were haphazard and noticing it depended on a chance reference in a solitary commentary (6, 207 n. 27). At the conclusion of *Homeric Epics* MacDonald acknowledges the total of three thousand Scripture citations in the New Testament listed in the two main critical editions, without focusing on Mark and only to decry the relative absence of citations from "pagan literature." In a few places MacDonald seems to treat Homer and Scripture as comparably important for Mark: ". . . one goal of rhetorical mimesis was to feign originality by disguising dependence, especially by employing multiple models, borrowing the best properties from each," in Mark's case "the Greek Bible . . . and the Homeric epics, Mark's two favorite targets for mimesis" (ibid. 172–73).

[14] Ronald F. Hock, review of MacDonald, *Homeric Epics*, in *Bulletin of the Institute for Antiquity and Christianity* 27 (Summer 2000) 12–15; Michael J. Gilmour, review of MacDonald, *Homeric Epics*, in *RBL* (June 2002) [online journal available at www.bookreviews.org].

the claim that Mark's narrative depends substantially on Homer. Critical approval relates mainly to MacDonald's perspective and basic assumptions rather than to the substance of his argument. Sharyn Dowd, for example, sees MacDonald's "most helpful contribution" in his discussion of "mediated influence." "MacDonald draws attention to a few places in Mark that may well reflect an appeal to the general cultural knowledge of Mark's Hellenistic audience." The book is "a useful source of evidence for an occasional allusion that may have been employed by the Evangelist to communicate with his Hellenistic audience." [15]

The biggest problem with MacDonald's argument is that he does not deal with, to say nothing of explain, the relationship between Mark's patent use of Scripture and its veiled use of Homer. Mark is not just subtle in its allusion to Homer; it runs the serious risk of drowning this subtlety in the flood of extremely cogent and significant allusions to Scripture—a Homeric Cassotis Spring swallowed up in a scriptural Niagara Falls. Compared to the wealth of scriptural allusions in the opening verses, there is a paucity of Homeric references until the stilling of the storm in ch. 4; the main parallel between Jesus and Odysseus, the "much-suffering" attribute (*Od.* 1.4), is not raised until ch. 8.[16] Even allowing for present-day ignorance of the conceptual world of the Homeric background, including among professional exegetes,[17] the contrast between the prominence of references to Jewish Scripture and the magnitude of their

---

[15] Sharyn Dowd, review of MacDonald, *Homeric Epics,* in *CBQ* 63 (2001) 155–56. The use of "Hellenistic" here, as in this paper, is not to be understood as contrasting with "Jewish." Cf. Loveday Alexander, *"Ipse dixit:* Citation of Authority in Paul and in the Jewish and Hellenistic Schools," in Troels Engberg-Pedersen, ed., *Paul Beyond the Judaism/Hellenism Divide* (Louisville: Westminster John Knox, 2001) 103–27. On the substance of MacDonald's thesis, Dowd and others question, for example, the validity of MacDonald's criteria for establishing imitation, criteria that often seem to cut two ways. "That some of MacD.'s arguments are less plausible than others is due in part to the slipperiness of his criteria for evaluating parallels. . . . 'This sixth criterion [interpretability] . . . looks for differences between texts as evidence of emulation' (MacDonald, p. 9). In practice, this means that if a passage in Mark has some features in common with a Homeric predecessor, then the differences may also be brought in as evidence for dependence. But the unanswered question is, 'What counts as evidence against dependence?'" (Dowd review, p. 155). Hock and others note the failure to take account of the genre (chasing a chimera, in MacDonald's opinion, p. 204 n. 4) or narrative structure of Mark as a whole. Not satisfied with the emulation argument, Morna Hooker asks, "What was his [Mark's] purpose in 'replacing' or retelling the Homeric myths? . . . MacDonald does not explain Mark's theological motivation in recycling the Greek myths. He sees Mark primarily as an 'artist,' and suggests that hermeneutics should be concerned with 'aesthetics' rather than 'history or tradition' (p. 190)" (Hooker review of MacDonald, *Homeric Epics,* in *JTS* 53 [2002] 196–98).

[16] See the Hock review cited in n. 14.

[17] MacDonald, *Homeric Epics,* 171.

significance and the obscurity of references to Homer—between substantiality and fragility—is extreme.[18]

Mark's plot, return story though it may be, is heavily indebted to the scriptural story of the Exodus, desert trek, and Jordan crossing: Mark begins his story with a recapitulation of the Passover crossing and the gathering of a new Israel, and traces the Torah story backwards through healings and feedings in the desert until it climaxes at a second Passover, during which Jesus is betrayed, captured, deserted by his last remaining lieutenant (at the anniversary moment when Israel viewed Pharaoh's forces dead at the Sea), and crucified. At the same time Mark structures his story in terms of two great personages in Scripture, the archetypical prophet Moses (the first third of the gospel) and the archetypical king David (the last third), with an interlude of passage from the source of the Jordan at Caesarea to the mouth of the Jordan at Jericho in which the implications of Jesus' baptism and death are laid out (the middle third). Contrast these features with Homeric parallels to the same elements: the journey as Odysseus's journey home is not nearly so evident as the Exodus way in Mark; the way is brilliantly portrayed in reverse, from the Jordan (cf. Psalm 114) to the Passover. The shift from Odysseus to Hector as the referent for Jesus is not nearly so evident as the distinction between Moses and Israel on the way and David in Jerusalem, marking the first and third blocks of Mark. The shrewd Jesus in Jerusalem is the astute "Davidic" prophetic monarch, even as Mark critiques the Davidic pretensions of the Jerusalem church.

Besides plot elements, every significant theme in Mark has a clear and compelling scriptural basis. In the first fifteen verses of Mark's account, for starters, there are at least sixteen Scripture passages clearly cited, referred to, or alluded to, and virtually all of these help to introduce fundamental themes that are sig-

---

[18] This is the problem dealt with in George W. E. Nickelsburg, "Tobit, Genesis, and the *Odyssey:* A Complex Web of Intertextuality," in MacDonald, ed., *Mimesis and Intertextuality*, 41–55. Treating Tobit as related to Genesis, *Jubilees,* and *Odyssey* (the last on the basis of MacDonald's argument), Nickelsburg asks pertinently what is the relationship among these three sources, a valid question that MacDonald deflects, saying of Nickelsburg (*Mimesis and Intertextuality,* 7): "N. agrees with my claim that the author of Tobit used the beginning of the *Od,* but he shows that this dependence was not exclusive, for the author also used the legend of Ahikar, the story of Job, and especially the patriarchal narratives of Genesis [partly by way of *Jub.*]. N. also suggests that ancient authors may not have been conscious of their imitations. . . . This proposal of multiple literary models lying behind Tobit is consistent with ancient mimetic practice, which often was consciously eclectic. Authors frequently disguised literary dependence by employing as many as five models." Thus MacDonald shifts the focus of Nickelsburg's essay to the multiplicity of models rather than the relationship of the models.

nificant throughout Mark.[19] They bring Mark, like other New Testament writers, into the larger stream of engagement with longstanding exegetical issues,

[19] Isa 40:3; Exod 23:20; Mal 3:1; Mal 4:5 [MT 3:23]; 2 Kgs 1:8; Zech 13:4; 2 Kgs 2:1-18; Exod
14:1–15:20; Josh 3:1–5:15; Psalm 114; Gen 8:10-12; Gen 22:2; Ps 2:7; Isa 42:1; 1 Kgs 17:4-6; 1
Kgs 19:4-9. MacDonald compares the beginnings of the *Odyssey* and Mark in an appendix to *Homeric Epics,* 194–97, where he gives passing recognition to a single Scripture reference, "the prophecy
of Isaiah." MacDonald suggests that the prophet Isaiah is Mark's muse, whom the gospel writer "in-
vokes . . . as a witness to Jesus' ὁδός, 'journey' or 'way.'" MacDonald notes that this "way" is a significant theme throughout Mark and sees it as imitative of Odysseus' νόστος—in itself a potentially
telling comparison despite the absence of the word νόστος in the New Testament. However, ignor-
ing the fact that the opening quotation in Mark—Mark's unequivocal "starting point" (ἀρχή)—
comes not only from Isaiah but from Exodus and Malachi as well, MacDonald takes no account at
all of the extraordinary importance of the "way" in the Torah, Isaiah, and Malachi, as well as Joshua
3–5 and 2 Kings 2, which also figure prominently in the beginning of Mark. See, for example, Joel
Marcus, *The Way of the Lord: Christological Exegesis of the Old Testament in Mark* (Louisville:
Westminster John Knox, 1992); Willard M. Swartley, *Israel's Scripture Traditions and the Synoptic
Gospels: Story Shaping Story* (Peabody, Mass.: Hendrickson, 1994). The other grand comparison
made here by MacDonald is between Telemachus and Jesus: "The epic and the Gospel both begin
with a young man learning of his paternity [as son of the ruler] by means of a flying messenger. In
both stories, other characters are present, but the communication comes to the hero alone. Both
young men gain courage from a god to confront their foes: Telemachus confronted the suitors, and
Jesus withstood Satan." A footnote points out that, like Jesus, Telemachus is called ἀγαπητός. Several of the weaknesses permeating MacDonald's book are illustrated in this short summation. Parallels are often phony: the spirit in Mark is not, like Athena, a messenger (and John, who does not fly
like a bird, *is* Mark's "messenger"); Telemachus does not "learn" that Odysseus is his father in the
same way Jesus learns that God is his father. Characters paralleled tend to shift at random: first
Athena is the spirit, then God; Jesus is usually Odysseus but here is Telemachus; the suitors are usually the Temple authorities but here are Satan. Parallels sometimes assume too much: how do we
know that, like Telemachus, Jesus "gained courage" from God, the spirit, or John? Multiple terms
for a parallel end up leaving the basis for comparison vague: Jesus "gains courage," is "emboldened,"
and is "empowered" by the "heavenly messenger" (all on p. 196). There is an unrecognized redundancy: that "both Telemachus and Jesus . . . staked out their claims to kingdoms as only sons of
their royal fathers," a comparison that is repeated several times in the appendix, adds little to the acknowledged starting point of the entire argument for Homeric influence in Mark, that the *Odyssey*
and Mark share a notable set of plot rudiments. The main event—in this case Jesus' baptism—is left
unaddressed by supposed parallels. The most serious fault illustrated here is again the failure to recognize the all-encompassing importance of the scriptural bases of the text. As universally recognized, the voice from the sky quotes Genesis 22 (including ἀγαπητός), Psalm 2, and Isaiah 42. These
are all exceedingly important for scriptural and Jewish themes developed by Mark as a whole, all
with characteristic irony: Jesus as the new Isaac (for which see the brilliant treatment in Jon D. Levenson, *The Death and Resurrection of the Beloved Son: The Transformation of Child Sacrifice in Judaism and Christianity* [New Haven: Yale University Press, 1993]); Jesus as the royal "son of God";
and Jesus as the suffering and redeemed royal and prophetic "servant of the Lord" portrayed by Isaiah. MacDonald concludes the appendix with an answer to the possible objection that he might be
implying that the writer of Mark "contrived the entire account" in literary imitation rather telling

as has been discussed in the burgeoning literature on the use of the Scriptures in the New Testament in the last fifteen years.[20]

As an illustration of the competing claims of Scripture and Homer, let us look at Mark 9:2-10, the subject of Chapter 11 of *Homeric Epics*.[21] MacDonald treats this as a recognition scene (an essential component of the traditional return story) indebted mainly to *Od.* 16.167-307, Odysseus' transfiguration before Telemachus. The scriptural background is usually thought—for very good reasons—to include Exod 24:12-18, where Moses is summoned by God to the mountain, sets out "with his servant Joshua/Jesus," ascends to the top of the mountain enveloped in a cloud, from which God, appearing like a devouring fire,

---

what actually happened; this diverts from the larger question looming over the entire endeavor: how does Mark's supposed use of Homer relate to Mark's patent use of Scripture?

[20] "Much of the Bible is fundamentally elliptical. It says much in a few words, in words that point beyond themselves, for the canonical writings are literature of inheritance, being deliberately interactive and full of allusive reciprocal discourse. . . . The [Dead Sea] scrolls drive home the lesson that the New Testament is not a linguistic island . . . but instead the offspring of parental texts, which it understands through the Jewish tradition and honors through consistent interaction and allusion" (Dale C. Allison, *Scriptural Allusions in the New Testament: Light from the Dead Sea Scrolls* [North Richland Hills: Bibal, 2000] 4, 66). There are now hundreds of significant books and articles on the use of the Scriptures in the New Testament. See Richard Hayes, *Echoes of Scripture in the Letters of Paul* (New Haven: Yale University Press, 1989)—MacDonald cites this, 207 n. 32; Willard M. Swartley, *Israel's Scripture Traditions*; Craig A. Evans and W. Richard Stegner, eds., *The Gospels and the Scripture of Israel* (Sheffield: Sheffield Academic Press, 1994); Craig C. Broyles and Craig A. Evans, eds., *Writing and Reading the Scroll of Isaiah: Studies of an Interpretive Tradition* (Leiden/New York: Brill, 1997); Craig A. Evans and James A. Sanders, eds., *Early Christian Interpretation of the Scriptures of Israel* (Sheffield: Sheffield Academic Press, 1997); idem, *The Function of Scripture in Early Jewish and Christian Tradition* (Sheffield: Sheffield Academic Press, 1998); Craig A. Evans, ed., *The Interpretation of Scripture in Early Judaism and Christianity: Studies in Language and Tradition* (Sheffield: Sheffield Academic Press, 2000); Dale C. Allison, Jr., *The Intertextual Jesus: Scripture in Q* (Harrisburg: Trinity Press International, 2000); Steve Moyise, ed., *The Old Testament in the New Testament: Essays in Honour of J. L. North* (Sheffield: Sheffield Academic Press, 2000); Steve Moyise, *The Old Testament in the New: An Introduction* (New York: Continuum, 2001); Donald H. Juel, "Interpreting Israel's Scriptures in the New Testament," in Alan J. Hauser and Duane F. Watson, eds., *A History of Biblical Interpretation*. Vol. 1: *The Ancient Period* (Grand Rapids: Eerdmans, 2002); James L. Kugel, *The Bible As It Was* (Cambridge, Mass.: Harvard University Press, 1997). For examples of the rich complexity of that use see, e.g., James A. Sanders, "From Isaiah 61 to Luke 4," in Jacob Neusner, ed., *Christianity, Judaeans, and Other Greco-Roman Cults: Studies for Morton Smith at Sixty.* Part I: New Testament (Leiden: Brill, 1975) 75–106; Joel Marcus, *The Way of the Lord*; Jon Levenson, *The Death and Resurrection of the Beloved Son*; Dale C. Allison, Jr., *The New Moses: A Matthean Typology* (Minneapolis: Fortress, 1993); William Loader, *Jesus' Attitude Towards the Law: A Study of the Gospels* (Grand Rapids: Eerdmans, 2002). For Mark, in addition to Marcus: Thomas R. Hatina, *In Search of a Context: The Function of Scripture in Mark's Narrative* (Sheffield: Sheffield Academic Press, 2002).

[21] MacDonald, *Homeric Epics*, 91–96.

after six days calls to Moses, with among other things instructions for building an elaborate tent shrine. MacDonald is not entirely convinced this passage lies behind Mark 9, but grants that "It is quite possible that the giving of the Torah on Mount Sinai provided Mark with the setting upon a mountain, the presence of a cloud, a heavenly voice, and other details. After all, Mark's Jesus speaks with Moses and Elijah, both of whom were related to Mount Sinai."[22] This concession reveals both an unwarranted skepticism and a misunderstanding of the way the writer as exegete works with his scriptural sources. The gospel writer is not simply looking for motifs and details to show a connection. Believing, apparently, that this is indeed all the gospel writer is after, MacDonald is quick to identify "other details in the story" that "Jewish antecedents cannot explain." MacDonald recognizes that the passage is a type scene of an epiphany: "Epiphanies were common in ancient literature, and several of these motifs [supposedly not found in the "Jewish antecedents"] are topoi, such as luminescent clothing, trembling, and offering gifts or establishing cult."[23]

Other similarities, however, are distinctive and point, in MacDonald's view, unambiguously to Mark's dependence on the *Odyssey*. "Odysseus and Jesus both wear clothing whitened by a heavenly launderer, Telemachus and Peter both err in ascribing divinity to mere mortals, and those who witness both transfigurations must be silent about what they saw."[24] Dazzled by these comparisons, MacDonald fails to see more compelling scriptural parallels, such as that the disciples' fear might recapitulate the reaction of the Israelites at seeing the glory of God at Sinai. Peter's suggestion regarding the provision of tents has nothing to do with "establishing cult" or "ascribing divinity" in Mark's account, and much to do with Israel dwelling in tents on their military trek to conquer the land, as the ensuing discussion of the significance of Elijah's coming makes clear (cf. 2 Sam 20:1; 1 Kgs 12:16). With characteristic sleight of hand he makes washed garments and fulled and bleached garments comparable in such a way that "luminescent" covers both, thus obscuring the possible influence the church's practice of baptism may have had on Mark's description of the whitened garments.[25] The voice from the cloud declaring Jesus to be God's son whom the disciples are to heed is indebted not only to the scriptural account of

[22] Ibid. 96, cf. 92.

[23] Ibid. 95.

[24] Ibid.

[25] MacDonald addresses the issue of baptismal symbolism in his consistently insightful discussion of the role of the νεανίσκος (*Homeric Epics*, 162–68, especially 166). The chief flaw in his treatment is his interpretation of the νεανίσκος, who ends up dressed in white like Jesus on the mountain, as a negative figure, indebted to Homer's Elpenor (ibid. 127–30), rather than a positive figure, which precludes accepting the figure's baptismal significance.

Sinai but equally, as others have pointed out, to Deut 18:15-18, in order to legitimate Jesus' succession to the prophetic authority of Moses and Elijah. As a reprise of Jesus' baptism to royalty in Mark 1, it has no more to do with ascribing divinity to Jesus than Peter's declaration that Jesus is the "anointed one" in Mark 8:29.

What the gospel writer is concerned with when he references Scripture as he does in Mark 9 are such extremely important issues as what remains of the status of Moses, given the rulings on Mosaic law that Jesus has made in the course of the gospel to this point and will continue to make, or how the conception of baptism on which Mark is structured relates to the scriptural hopes for the vindication of Israel. Moreover, the writer is concerned to address interpretative issues raised by the collocation of related passages of Scripture in a way that furthers his own narrative points. In the story of Jesus' metamorphosis on the mountain and the *connected* sequel as he comes down the mountain the narrative resumes its interpretation of the opening mélange from Exodus 23, Isaiah 40, and Malachi 3, in each case dealing with the larger context of each of those passages. Exod 23:20-23: "I am going to send a *malʾāk*—an angel/messenger/commander—in front of you, to guard you on the way and to bring you to the place that I have prepared. Be attentive to him and listen to his voice . . . . If you listen attentively to his voice . . . then I will be an enemy to your enemies and a foe to your foes." The connection with Mark 9 goes beyond the order to obey the *malʾāk*. The passage, addressed to Moses, raises the question, who is this *malʾāk* ? When combined with Exod 24:13 the question becomes both more urgent and more specific. Moses was supposed to be alone on the top of Sinai, and Elijah makes this motif explicit by claiming to be the lone prophet left when he also appears alone on Horeb. But what about the Joshua/Jesus who went with Moses? Why did Moses not tell him, as he had the others with him, to remain behind? Was Joshua/Jesus still with Moses on the mountain? Is Jesus the *malʾāk*?

Quite possibly—but other passages complicate the question. The voice of God's *malʾāk* is heard in Isaiah 40 in Mark's reading, a prophecy clearly fulfilled in Mark in the first instance by John, who is Elijah returned. This is confirmed not just by John's guise but also by the similar passage from Malachi, which discloses that the *malʾāk* will appear prior to the Lord's march on his temple, and the *malʾāk* is Elijah. So what, these passages require the writer to explain, is the relationship among the *malʾāk*, Moses, Elijah, and Jesus? The story in Mark 9:2-13 explains precisely this, and furthermore connects the answer to a concern basic to Mark, the significance of baptism for the vindication of Israel. Seeing Jesus in baptismal glory taking counsel with Elijah—who before his reappearance at the Jordan was last seen at the same place in a whirlwind, with chariot and horses of fire—and with Moses, the leader of Israel marching in force to the Jordan and the promised land, Peter reasonably infers that God's war against Israel's enemies and foes is about to begin and, as his lord's chief lieutenant, he is both terrified and exhilarated. The implication, prefigured and confirmed by Moses and Elijah standing right in front of him, is that the dead shall be raised. Coming down the mountain, then, the disciples are nonplussed by Jesus' instruction to say nothing until he has risen from the dead. Doesn't the *mal'āk*'s coming, at the Jordan and again on the mountain, signal the rising of the dead rather than the making of more dead, Jesus included? Otherwise, what would be the point of the scribes saying, in line with Malachi, that Elijah must come first? Jesus answers by referring to the end of Malachi—Elijah must indeed "restore" all things—but, like Mark, he combines Malachi's pronouncement with the rest of Isaiah's account of the servant prophet/king to reiterate the central teaching of the middle third of Mark, that the servant must suffer and be rejected. And in any case Elijah has already come and the same thing happened to him that is about to happen to the servant.

Clearly, the gospel writer makes use of his scriptural source for more than isolated details and motifs. Not only is Scripture rather than Homer primary, but also the supposed uses of Homer tend to be not only random but superficial, not in the sense of trivial necessarily, but shallow, without the depth of connection with either the main Markan themes or the rich background in Jewish exegesis that Mark often builds on.[26] This critique could be made of most of MacDonald's twenty chapters comparing parts of Mark with Homer, where there seems to be at work a determined disinclination to recognize one of the greatest gains

[26] A study that might have been of use to MacDonald is Jeffrey H. Tigay, "On Evaluating Claims of Literary Borrowing," in Mark E. Cohen, Daniel C. Snell, and David B. Weisberg, eds., *The Tablet and the Scroll: Near Eastern Studies in Honor of William W. Hallo* (Bethesda, Md.: CDL Press, 1993) 250–55. A work more recent than *Homeric Epics* presents an extended argument for the improbable thesis that the *Odyssey* influenced the writing of the entire book of Genesis: Thomas L. Brodie, *Genesis as Dialogue: A Literary, Historical, and Theological Commentary* (New York: Oxford University Press, 2001) 447–94. Like MacDonald, Brodie develops his own criteria for evaluating literary borrowing (ibid. 421–32), having failed to find any other: "One would imagine, given the central difficulty in recognizing sources, and given the modern deluge of dissertations and publications, that there would be numerous systematic studies for dealing with the problem, numerous guides setting out comprehensive criteria for establishing literary dependence. Apparently there is none. At least, the present writer, despite prolonged searching in good libraries, has failed to locate one" (ibid. 423). (Brodie heard an oral presentation by MacDonald in 1996 offering five criteria that MacDonald said "needed refinement" [ibid. 423].) Brodie describes the relationship between the *Odyssey* and Genesis, despite its extensiveness, as a "secondary" one (ibid. 449), acknowledging that there were other and often more significant sources.

in New Testament scholarship of the last fifteen years, an understanding of the density, richness, and complexity of all four gospel writers' use of Scripture.[27]

Scholars have rightly been at pains to point out the importance of the Hellenistic cultural environment of the early churches,[28] so a reminder of possible non-scriptural allusions in the gospels may be helpful. But since the vast use of Scripture is indisputable, a writer's use of non-Jewish texts cannot be treated in a vacuum. It is important not to lose sight of the primacy of the Jewish Scriptures in the early church, a primacy that has recently been shown to apply even to the heavily philosophical Greek and Latin patrology.[29] As a writer of his time, Mark indeed practiced the Hellenistic art of mimesis, that is, mimesis of Jewish Scriptures.

The biggest challenge now facing the project of finding Homer in Mark is to show how imitation of Homer, invisible though it was, contributed to the wider array of Mark's interconnected themes. How would the audience's conscious or unconscious recognition of Jesus as a transvalued Odysseus have enhanced their apprehension of Mark's message? How does this imitation relate to Mark's use of what was, unlike Homer, his "primary literary inspiration," the Jewish Scriptures? This is a challenge that proponents of the primacy of Homer in Mark appear at present disinclined to take up, since they find themselves quite unconvinced of the importance of the Scriptures for the New Testament.[30] A second challenge is the one that also faces any literary treatment

---

[27] There are significant exceptions to this tendency. MacDonald begins his analysis of the story of the Last Supper, Mark 14:17-52, with this concession: "As it now stands, this section of the Gospel is heavily indebted to Jewish scriptures." However, after listing examples, he concludes, "These scriptural antecedents . . . fall short of explaining most of the literary features of 14:17-52" (*Homeric Epics*, 125).

[28] See, e.g., M. Eugene Boring, Klaus Berger, and Carsten Colpe, eds., *Hellenistic Commentary to the New Testament* (Nashville: Abingdon, 1995). Luke's debt to the Aeneid has been superbly argued by another student of the Harvard doctoral program, Marianne Palmer Bonz, *The Past as Legacy: Luke-Acts and Ancient Epic* (Minneapolis: Fortress, 2000). For a brilliant analysis of the effect of the imperial cult and its texts on Luke-Acts see Allen Brent, "Luke-Acts and the Imperial Cult in Asia Minor," *JTS* 48 (1997) 411–38. Dennis MacDonald has himself made a rather convincing case for Luke's use of the *Odyssey* in "The Ending of Luke and the Ending of the *Odyssey*," in Randal A. Argall, Beverly A. Bow, and Rodney A. Werline, eds., *For a Later Generation: The Transformation of Tradition in Israel, Early Judaism, and Early Christianity* (Harrisburg: Trinity Press International, 2000) 161–68.

[29] Robert Louis Wilken, *The Spirit of Early Christian Thought: Seeking the Face of God* (New Haven: Yale University Press, 2003).

[30] E.g., Gregory J. Riley, "Mimesis of Classical Ideals in the Second Christian Century," in *Mimesis and Intertextuality in Antiquity and Christianity*, 94–95, 100: "The substance and basic stance of Christianity cannot . . . be derived from the Old Testament. We might do better to attach the collected works of Plato to the front of the New Testament than to do as we do now. . . . we

of the gospels, the classic question of the oral traditional sources of the Gospel narrative. The place to start now with that question, particularly as regards Mark as a story of endurance and martyrdom, is Anne Wire's new work, *Holy Lives, Holy Deaths: A Close Hearing of Early Jewish Storytellers.*

---

would go much farther in understanding its basic message using Plato than we do using Moses and the Deuteronomists. Consider how different were David the warrior-king and Socrates the gadfly. Yet how much closer was Jesus, the Son of David, to Socrates in lifestyle, career, message, and death than he was to David! . . . How can one understand the cross of Christ and the willing martyrdom of so many Christians from the viewpoint of a book that curses the crucified and praises long life, peace and prosperity? . . . The substance of the Christian understanding of Jesus and proper discipleship fits more the pattern of Greek literature than that of the Old Testament. . . . keep in mind the notable examples from the New Testament . . . the Gospel of Mark, the life story of Paul as reflected in his letters . . . all of which depend heavily on Old Testament passages and images and are full of quotations and allusions from the Old Testament, but whose substance likewise is the call to endure with faithfulness to the death in language straight out of the Greek tradition." There is no gainsaying the importance of the Hellenistic and Roman contribution to early Christian ethics and ethos. Apart from the role of the Scriptures, Riley makes a significant point with respect to the church, especially for the second century and later. The understanding of the Scriptures, and of the nature of their resonance in the gospels and Paul, reflected in this statement, however, and particularly of the Prophets, is inadequate and mistaken. For a fuller treatment of Riley's reaction against what he sees as the "Judaism only" distortion of Christianity's background see his *The River of God: A New History of Christian Origins* (San Francisco: HarperSanFrancisco, 2001). See also the treatment in Stanley K. Stowers, "Does Pauline Christianity Resemble a Hellenistic Philosophy?" in *Paul Beyond the Judaism/Hellenism Divide*, 81–102.

The Life and Death of the Just One:
A Community Schism in Wisdom of Solomon

Barbara Green, O.P.

꩜

The prime occasion for this reflection is the celebration of the contribution of Antoinette Wire to her friends, colleagues, and students. Her life as a teacher spans many of the recent shifts in biblical studies, challenges she has taken creatively and in her stride. I first met Anne in the mid-1970s when she was working on form criticism and New Testament miracle stories. But my favorite sense of her rises from a view I had much more recently and for several weeks from my office window. Anne taught a small seminar class that met outdoors in a garden. I could see the students gather, take their places, and participate enthusiastically in discussion. But before they arrived their teacher came, accompanied by a large wicker basket she had carried from her house, several blocks away in the hilly region that enfolds the GTU neighborhood. Anne would carefully unpack the basket of its lovely cups, teapot, thermos, and so forth, so that she could provide refreshment and sustenance for her students as they learned. The consistent thoughtfulness, the blend of practicality and its opposite (much easier if students provide their own beverage in disposable cups), the beauty of the small table she set, the vigor with which I know the conversation proceeded, all give me a sense of Anne Wire as one of Sophia's friends and helpers. I am glad to be her colleague, pleased to offer a paper in her honor.

A second prompt was the occasion to reconsider the Sophia tradition when I had an opportunity to co-teach a seminar on Wisdom of Solomon and the Gospel of John. I wrote an M.A. thesis on those two books in the mid-1970s, concentrating on their common understanding of immortality/eternal life.[1] But

---

[1] Barbara Green, "A Study of Theological Relationships between the Concept of Immortality in Wisdom of Solomon and Eternal Life in the Gospel of John" (M.A. thesis, Jesuit School of Theology at Berkeley, Graduate Theological Union, 1976). My recent study of the book is found in

203

my interests shifted, and years went by while I paid little fresh attention to the book, even when I occasionally taught it in the midst of a general course on Wisdom Literature. Biblical studies has changed substantially in the past twenty-five years, most markedly in questions of method and reading strategy. Sophia studies have come into their own as well, freshly animating issues on which I had previously worked somewhat abstractly. Finally, I have lived another quarter century of life and face new challenges. The issues of how we "grow" our biblical traditions—and they us—are urgent for me. As we live, confronted by a more complex world and by a more discriminating sense of what is of enduring religious value, how do we read our ancient canonical documents so that they remain vital to us in both senses of the word: alive and crucial? How is our reading of Scripture both assisted by and responsive to our own transformation toward a deeper participation in the life of God? Insofar as our desire is to move into an ever-deeper relationship with God and the community of believers and to do so faithfully, responsibly, and creatively, can we find in our revelatory texts cues to that same process? Can we glimpse our forebears struggling to make a similar move, granted their own circumstances?

My specific question involves a re-sketching of a plausible context for Wisdom of Solomon, generated in some way by the particular circumstances affecting its community at the time of writing. But a text, especially one as discreet as Wisdom, is not simply a window onto those circumstances. Consequently, the circumstances need to be intuited, hazarded, hypothesized, and constructed, rather than confidently retrieved. Nor is narrative simply a product of social factors, important though we have come to see that those are. A biblical text like Wisdom is also a site where certain beliefs of a community, argued out in the particular genre of the work, are made clear not only for its originating community but to later readers as well.

My thesis for this brief article is that what is clear in the Gospel of John is also discernible in Wisdom of Solomon: The narrative of the life, death, and Life of the innocent just man (Wisdom 2–5) rehearses, though anonymously, the same events that so challenged and reshaped all Jewish communities from the mid-first century C.E. Consequent choices for the community are presented starkly as well (chs. 11–19), offering the first readers multiple occasions to find themselves on the side of Wisdom or to scorn her, choosing for Life or Death. The crucial hermeneutic for the Wisdom community is the capacity both to identify with the strength of their heritage and also to reshape it profoundly enough so that it can continue to facilitate survival, to offer Life to its

"The Wisdom of Solomon and the Solomon of Wisdom: Tradition's Transpositions and Human Transformation," *Horizons* 30 (2003) 41–66.

readers, whose circumstances differ so from those of the earlier generations whose exodus experience is the ostensible subject of the recital.

The discourse of Wisdom of Solomon rehearses not simply a struggle of insiders versus outsiders, raises not only the challenge of coping with hostile external opponents. It deals with urgent intra-Jewish questions as well, specifically gifts made available as a result of God's workings among the just and the pattern of refusal that has characteristically been present in encounters between the righteous and the ungodly. In the case of the Just One who dies at the hands of his co-religionists and about whom profound but provocative claims are then made, the challenge involves how to name God. How will Judaism and certain Jews of the Alexandrian community understand and articulate God's role when the innocent suffer? What is the appropriate understanding of death, and of life beyond death? Can the role given to Sophia, intimate of both God and creation, provide a useful bridge across the abyss that confronted Jews of the mid-first century?

John's story of the man born blind (ch. 9) can specify the key issue, which is how both a community and an individual come to believe in Jesus and begin to appropriate all that he offers—or refuse to do so (a process visible elsewhere in the gospel as well). Mature scholarly work on the Johannine material helps make more visible a similar, comparable dynamic in Wisdom of Solomon, where God's agency in the shape of Sophia saves believers into immortality, a process resisted by others. That the life, death, and Life of Jesus occasioned a major rearticulation of Jewish tradition in John's gospel is utterly clear, as is opposition to such a re-visioning. The identity of Wisdom's righteous man who died untimely is not quite so clear, nor is it generally considered good practice for modern interpreters to see Jesus lurking in Old Testament texts; but I will sketch the plausibility of it here. Though the reinterpretation of classic images into fresh insight runs throughout the book, it can be glimpsed efficiently in Wisdom 2–5 and 17:1–18:4. In somewhat differing circumstances both the Wisdom and Johannine communities and narratives struggle to rearticulate their traditions in fidelity to their core beliefs while pushing deeper as well. And in both processes, the Sophia role is crucial.

IMPLICATIONS OF THE LIFE AND DEATH
OF THE JUST ONE: THE JOHANNINE COMMUNITY

At its surface John 9 reads as an episode in the life of the historical Jesus, distinctively but not uniquely told in John, relating how the cure of a blind man brought to a head controversy about the significance of Jesus. Issues of how he observed Judaism, how he might be ascribed various traditional roles (e.g., prophet, messiah, Son of Man) seem the coin of the realm in debates between Jesus and the religious authorities of his day.

A more nuanced awareness of the importance of the circumstances of a text's production alerted scholars to additional possibilities and authorizes the following scenario:[2] Between the death of Jesus (in the 30s) and the completion of the written gospel (the 90s), as its narratives were gradually taking shape, community members carried on contentious dialogue primarily with other Jews over the claims that must/must not be made about Jesus. Among these were how he is messiah, and eventually, how he is uniquely related to God. The crucial need was to understand classic thought, terminology, and images both faithfully and profoundly afresh. An artistically subtle narrative like John 9 articulates not so much the issues of the 30s but those of a later generation (perhaps the 60s). The textual opponents of Jesus become "the Jews," those who in his absence contest what the Johannine tradition claims about Jesus. The rift between those who understand Jesus, as John ultimately presents him, and those who refuse such insight, for whatever reasons, widens across time, so that the narrative allows us to trace splits that have become final. This reconstruction suggests that Johannine advocates of certain claims about Jesus became unwelcome in the synagogues and were eventually expelled.

The gospel shows traces of the transpositions of tradition by which believers remain faithful to their commitments while radically widening and deepening them. The central unnamed figure who has been cured of blindness is pressed not so much on that matter as on the identity of the one who gave him sight. In a text shaped by the rich symbolism of sight and blindness, the issues argued out include whether or how Jesus can be understood—seen—as messiah, whether or how he lives the tradition acceptably and fruitfully, whether he is in fact not a or "the" prophet but a deceiver (cf. Deut 13:6), and what is the significance of his signs. J. Louis Martyn suggests that the way forward for the evangelist on Jesus' significance is not so much from precise, logical, verbal argument or from the standard Moses/Jesus typology. Interlocutors whose basic faith stance has become quite different are not liable to persuade each other by such tactics, since the key is not in verbal formula but in the grasping of experience through language. A more radical move is wanted.

A Johannine scholar of the next generation, female and Jewish, has repositioned the work of Martyn and Brown, reflecting in the process both advances

---

[2] See Raymond E. Brown, *The Gospel According to John I–XII* (Garden City, N.Y.: Doubleday, 1966) 369–79, with further detail about stages of redaction and the community in idem, *The Community of the Beloved Disciple* (New York: Paulist, 1979); see also J. Louis Martyn, *History and Theology in the Fourth Gospel* (2d ed. Nashville: Abingdon, 1979), Chapter 6. Each scholar makes his case throughout the work; Brown has summary charts on pp. 166–69.

in redaction criticism and implications of situated and intentional reading. Summing up the work of Martyn and Brown, Adele Reinhartz concludes that the texts they cite are not so neatly reduced to historical/redactional ciphers for a later situation.[3] Her preference is to see narratives like John 9 as reflective of a spectrum of ways in which various Jews become believers in Jesus or do not. The narratives, specifically the dialogues, make the component issues apparent: the identity of Jesus in relation to God, the process of receiving his gift of light and Life, the processes of refusing it.[4] Without denying that the gospel makes visible certain circumstances of the late first century, Reinhartz widens the more orderly and simple dichotomization of issues (into the 30s, 60s, 90s) into something less historically precise and more ideologically complex, hypothesizing that the voice of the narrator is sorting a range of issues that were, over time and in various renditions, controversial about Jesus in the Johannine community:

> These observations alert us to the possibility that the ecclesiological tale that may be pried from the Gospel narrative is itself shaped not only or perhaps not even primarily by the historical experience of the community but by the ideological agenda of the Beloved Disciple himself, by his strong convictions concerning the central christological message that Jesus is the Christ and Son of God, and/or by his desire to keep his followers from turning their backs on the gift that they have accepted.[5]

Hence she makes the discussion encoded in John 9 not so much "us versus them" or about how "they threw us out" as it is an intra-communal struggle of Jesus-believing Jews who, if pressured, must resist going back "there."

Sandra Schneiders is concerned to widen the reference in certain other ways. She urges us to discern dissent and rivalry within as well as persecution from without the group, and not only intra-Jewish but inter-Christian community differences.[6] And she asks not only how the Johannine narrative articulates

---

[3] Adele Reinhartz, *Befriending the Beloved Disciple: A Jewish Reading of the Gospel of John* (New York: Continuum, 2001) 37–49.

[4] See ibid. 71–78 for her excellent discussion of the portrayal of Jesus' Jewish opponents in the gospel and for some of the problems attached to compliant reading.

[5] Ibid. 53.

[6] The seminar that revived my interest in Wisdom was co-taught with Sandra Schneiders, whose work on the Fourth Gospel and on hermeneutics and spirituality have been immensely stimulating for me, nowhere more than on the topic of Wisdom. Her most apt general contribution to the present topic is *Written That You May Believe: Encountering Jesus in the Fourth Gospel* (New York: Crossroad, 1999), specifically here Chapter 2; more specific is her "To See or Not To See: John 9 as a Synthesis of the Theology and Spirituality of Discipleship," in John Painter, R. Alan Culpepper, and Fernando F. Segovia, eds., *Word, Theology, and Community in John* (St. Louis: Chalice, 2003) 189–209.

the community's sociohistorical circumstances but also how it mediates a profound religious experience into language, thus giving shape to Martyn's sense that John's gospel offers a new hermeneutical key. How is the gospel, ch. 9 in particular, a place for later believers to continue that same process of experiencing commitment to Jesus? For Schneiders, then, the gospel mediates a diverse set of possibilities for continuing to understand, articulate, live, and be transformed by the reality of who Jesus is in relation to God, to Sophia, to other believers: "John 9, more clearly perhaps than any narrative in the Gospel, fuses the horizons of the pre-Easter Jesus, the post-Easter Johannine community, and the readers of the Gospel."[7] Explored there are both the reality of receiving sight and the choice of refusing that gift—i.e., the difference between curable and terminal blindness. The man who starts blind and is given sight traces the journey of a believer moving to affirm Jesus as a man, a prophet, from God, Son of Man, and finally Lord.[8] In fact the man's fundamental choice, which Schneiders says is to bear witness to the truth of his experience regardless of the consequences, helps us see him as resembling Jesus, who at his trial and throughout his life speaks the truth.[9] The man born blind who sees, thanks to his encounter with Jesus, becomes an instance of the presence of Jesus in the world.[10]

Opponents are characterized not so much by ethnicity (though they are labeled Jewish in John) as by their basic stance of refusal of the truth, ". . . the congenital incapacity for divine life that must be overcome through birth anew/from above by water and the Spirit . . . ."[11] The encounter between these two characters sharpens the profound mystery of how God and human beings cooperate in the drama of Life, demonstrating in the man born blind a synergistic blend. The Fourth Gospel describes the basic sin as perverse refusal, the misclassifying of good and evil, the seeking after one's own glory rather than ascribing it to God.[12] The pericope renders very stark the choice for John's community and any later reader wishing access to what the evangelist describes: to receive sight and life accordingly or to refuse to acknowledge it, with consequences implied. The dynamic is most sharply presented in a final later exchange between Jesus and the authorities over who is blind and who sighted, who is sinfully responsible (9:40-41).

---

[7] Schneiders, "To See or Not To See," 192–93.

[8] Ibid. 193–99, noting shifts at John 9:11, 17, 33, 38.

[9] Ibid. 201.

[10] Ibid. 196.

[11] Ibid. 190.

[12] Ibid. 199–201.

In this progression of interpretations the quest widens beyond a search for historical referents in the passage to envision a process in which persons of every era may participate. To use other language: The worlds behind and within the text collaborate to open before the text, demonstrating how believing and refusing function to transform both tradition and its many participants. The narrative of the encounter between Jesus and the man (within his community) makes present for readers the dynamic of choice: to share Jesus' Life or not. The choice to receive sight moves one into closer relationship and even unity with Life's source. Where Jesus goes, those will follow who profess belief in him, articulating their experiences in ways both ancient and fresh. Something quite similar is afoot in Wisdom of Solomon.

IMPLICATIONS OF THE LIFE AND DEATH OF THE JUST ONE: THE WISDOM OF SOLOMON COMMUNITY

The Solomonic setting of the Old Testament text is not remotely persuasive to modern scholars, whose attention consequently has been focused on historical and sociopolitical issues in the first centuries B.C.E. or C.E. for backdrop to Wisdom of Solomon. Such concerns have been found plausibly within the contentious social circumstances that shifted for the Jews in Alexandrian Egypt as the various Romans, Greeks, and Egyptians coped with their altered power positions during the reigns of the first five Roman emperors.[13] Standard criticism and exegesis on the book shows how its ideas and language both dialogue and dispute with various philosophies and theologies of the non-Jewish Hellenistic world. Wisdom's "Solomon" can colonize "foreign" concepts and then trump them and their matrix belief systems. In such scholarship the book of Wisdom is typically the work of a beleaguered community, struggling both to keep its civic identity, status, and position and also to encourage its young that the Jewish tradition is second to no Hellenistic philosophy. In fact, Jewish thought is shown to hold its own among the medley of philosophical discourses those young are imagined to hear on the streets and in the schools of Alexandria. The

---

[13] Much excellent recent work done on diaspora Judaism highlights the complexity and relevance of local situations rather than assuming that what we know must be generally pertinent. See John M. G. Barclay, *Jews in the Mediterranean Diaspora from Alexander to Trajan (323 BCE–11 CE)* (Edinburgh: T & T Clark, 1996) 1–9; Peder Borgen, *Early Christianity and Hellenistic Judaism* (Edinburgh: T & T Clark, 1996) 2. For specifics on Alexandria consult Barclay (Chapter 2); Borgen (Chapter 3); John J. Collins, *Jewish Wisdom in the Hellenistic Age* (Louisville: Westminster John Knox, 1997), Chapter 8; Lester L. Grabbe, *Wisdom of Solomon* (Sheffield: Sheffield Academic Press, 1997), Chapter 5; and Erich S. Gruen, *Heritage and Hellenism: The Reinvention of Jewish Tradition* (Berkeley: University of California Press, 1998).

book exhorts fidelity to those tempted to abandon Judaism for something more politically expedient. To such interpreters syncretism and assimilation are the danger, or perhaps their offspring, nonobservance and freethinking.[14]

Assuming those useful hypotheses, I wish to read with something slightly different in mind, to pose a second urgency. The book's underlying dynamic need not consist exclusively in the struggle between what is foreign/pagan and what is Jewish but may include as well issues able to be constructed as primarily intra-Jewish.[15] Wisdom first narrates the encounter between the Just One and his co-religionists (Wisdom 2–5) and then moves on to offer a disquisition on the cosmopolitan character of Wisdom (6–9), explored in a midrash on the Exodus that strains to include new insight (11–19). Even the book's stress on "alien" worship practices—ascribed to "the others" (13–15)— revisits cultic lapses from Israel's own past and thus places centrally into discussion the question of how God is to be appropriately approached within the Jewish tradition. The work's driving problem involves the way in which the God of Israel/of Judaism can be understood, named, and worshiped in the community's existential circumstances. We can call this the struggle of monotheism in shorthand, though that is ultimately misleading. Better to investigate what language prompts us to say about God's oneness and capacity for relationality. How to move the edges of orthodoxy always provokes a crisis within, whatever is going on "without." David Seeley suggests: "Precisely because the tradition has broken down the origin and destiny of the community must be retold in a new and compelling manner."[16] Old external foes become internal, the agency of God needs to be extended, and the community needs to revision what is on offer: light, life, friendship with

---

[14] Louis H. Feldman, *Jew and Gentile in the Ancient World: Attitudes and Interactions from Alexander to Justinian* (Princeton: Princeton University Press, 1993), Chapter 2, specifically pp. 63–83. The question of persecution is not about whether there was violence against the Jews in mid-first century Alexandria; there was. Less clear is whether the text makes visible that persecution or hints at something else. Collins (*Jewish Wisdom in the Hellenistic Age*, Chapter 10) thinks the persecution discussion is more philosophical than actual; Grabbe (*Wisdom of Solomon*, 90) appraises that the writer and first readers of the book do not very obviously suffer actual persecution.

[15] See Lester L. Grabbe, "Hellenistic Judaism," in Jacob Neusner, ed., *Judaism in Late Antiquity, Part 2: Historical Synthesis* (Leiden: Brill, 1995) 53–83, for a good discussion. Gruen's study of multiple transpositions of the Exodus narrative provides another way to appreciate how fluid the tradition remained, even so late (see his Chapter 2). Gruen holds that the Exodus story was central for Jewish self-concept and identity, and its multiple details allowed for considerable reshaping that would have been stimulating for community appropriation and resist easy polarization into faithful or unfaithful use.

[16] See David Seeley, "Narrative, the Righteous Man and the Philosopher: An Analysis of the Story of the *Dikaios* in Wisdom 1–5," *JSP* 7 (1990) 55–78, for certain Hebraic and Hellenistic texts that help compose these sentiments.

God. The book shares these matters with both the general Wisdom tradition in and outside Judaism and also with "young Christianity," seeking ways to talk about Jesus. Made prominent as well is how to refuse such gifts.

The Just One is dealt with in the first half of the book (not, we may note, in the second half, chs. 10–19, where unnamed biblical heroes are easily identifiable). So key is he that testimony regarding him falls into four segments (2:12-20; 2:21–3:9; 3:10–4:20; 5:1-14). His opponents, the ungodly, first describe him—unsympathetically—in 2:12-20: He knows God, is a servant of God, claims God as father, remains nonviolent under attack. These are elaborated in quite another key by the "royal" narrator (in 2:21-24, continuing into 3:1-9), who maintains that such as this innocent one remain in the hand of God, untouched by torments, at peace, accepted by God, abiding with God in love. Then, continuing to ruminate upon the discrepancy between how things may seem and how they are—the basic contention of this discourse on the righteous sufferer—the narrating voice discourses rather upon those who die early and those who die childless (3:10–4:9), or both. In other words, before the impious weigh in again the narrator describes those loved by God who are taken up early—apparently untimely, unfruitful—because they are pleasing, not displeasing, granted their early departure is not understood by all who know of it (4:10-15).[17] And Wisdom 4 concludes with a judgment scene, confronting the first startled and then speechlessly dishonored opponents with some inkling about the one(s) they have persecuted. The final quoted discourse of the ungodly (5:4-14) confirms that they have learned that they were wrong about what they said previously. In that speech they revisit their former views to pronounce them wholly misguided. Somewhat in the manner of Paul, who selects rather minimally from gospel tradition when talking about its central figure, "Solomon" emphasizes only what is most salient: fundamental opposition from within, innocent and committed suffering in which the community of the sufferer is implicated, vindication for the innocent and survival beyond death, and dreadful consequences for the opposing group. The description suits the figure of Jesus (and of course others as well, known to us within and without the Bible, or perhaps unknown to us).[18]

The opponents of God's purposes are characterized at length and consistently. In Wis 1:6-15 we are introduced to them summarily; their wicked

---

[17] Robert J. Miller, "Immortality and Religious Identity in Wisdom 2-5," in Elizabeth Castelli and Hal Taussig, eds., *Reimagining Christian Origins: A Colloquium Honoring Burton L. Mack* (Valley Forge, Pa.: Trinity Press International, 1996) 199–203, makes an excellent case for links between suffering experienced by the righteous and the importance of immortality for consolation.

[18] For helpful discussion about other possible identities of the unnamed hero consult Jane Schaberg, "Major Midrashic Traditions in Wisdom 1:1-6, 25," *JSJ* 13 (1982) 75–101.

words—lies, deceit—signify. There are several descriptors of their behavior, which include testing and distrusting God, practices that entrap not God but themselves. Worse, they invite Death closer, thinking him a friend; this is the first of the cardinal perceptual errors that run throughout the book: the mistaking of what is lethal for what is life-bearing. In Wis 2:1-10 the ungodly testify to the brevity of the human lifespan and its apparent end. They move on to their own inferences for how to act: Seize enjoyment, which leads to oppression of the righteous. From such a move comes their next deed, which is testing out what will happen to the innocent object of their oppression, what he will do and what God will do. So we have come, by example, full circle back to the sin of testing God. Such discourse, the narrator has already suggested, will "count"; such words will testify, not be hidden or go their way without result. In 5:4-14 the ungodly speak in direct discourse again, exposing some reversal of insight. They have witnessed something, at least so far as articulation goes. Redescribing what they had earlier seen, they enunciate their error, respeak their own behavior in negative terms, acknowledge what is basically wrong: They have not known God. Their mistake is "idolatry," a commitment to nonreality, vanishment, and tracelessness (described with various imagery in 5:9-14). Arresting and sobering is that their insight is also without trace. It does the ungodly no apparent good to have fresh and chastened thoughts, but they testify in any case for the sake of readers, who must make their—our—choice. The dynamic is similar to the gradual hardening of position of the incurably blind in John 9.

Resonance with John 9 can also be felt in Wis 17:1–18:4, one of several elaborate comparisons where an anonymous group (discernibly the Hebrews enslaved in Egypt and liberated into wandering) is contrasted with its unnamed oppressors. The discourse explains how God saves one group into immortality while the other chooses to perish. The royal narrator spends some twenty-five verses exploring the contrast between light and darkness, most of it in the realm of death.[19] The unjust, supposing themselves in control of their slaves, are described as "captives of their own darkness and prisoners of long night . . . exiles from eternal providence" (Wis 17:2). Thinking themselves unseen and their sins secret, they are nonetheless exposed by the narrator: alarmed by sudden terrors of darkness, appalled by unexpected flashes and noises, these hal-

---

[19] David S. Winston (*The Wisdom of Solomon*. AB 43 [Garden City, N.Y.: Doubleday, 1979] 303) and James M. Reese (*Hellenistic Influence on the Book of Wisdom and Its Consequences* [Rome: Biblical Institute Press, 1970] 141–43) point out the intricate intertwining of the physical, psychological, and moral realms implicit in darkness/light symbolism.

lucinations magnified by fear and guilt.[20] The artifices on which they had counted lie humbled and useless, and the ungodly perish obdurately, brought down by their rejection of hope and help. They surrender to forces of night and Hades that "Solomon" calls impotent, ". . . for with one chain of darkness they were all bound" (17:7). Only a few words describe the others: dwelling where light illumines brightly, led by a pillar of fire (17:20; 18:1, 3).

Both John and Wisdom present a fundamental problem that splits their communities. An individual: controversial, resisted, misunderstood, opposed, rejected, persecuted, and finally put to death, is nonetheless vindicated into Life. The opposition to him is not incidental but profound, placing into radical contestation appropriations of the tradition that appear to sustain each side. The main struggle is not with outsiders but with those who share the heritage. The imagery of light and darkness and the role of an unseen helper work the dynamic of life and death here. Fundamental is the choice posed by each work: sight or blindness, light or darkness, acceptance of the vindication of the Just One, acceptance of the unseen saving Presence—or not. A final issue to visit quickly is the role of Sophia in each work.

THE ROLE OF SOPHIA IN WISDOM OF SOLOMON AND JOHN

Again more suggestively than definitively, it remains to sketch the manner in which the figure of Sophia works in these transformations of faith commitment and appropriation of tradition. Sophia's contribution is similar in Wisdom and John, and comes primarily when she allows the God of the Jewish people to be more deeply articulated and extend to creatures the gift of Life (immortality/eternal life). In Wisdom, Sophia is characterized as an agent: not independent of God, but not subordinate; not worshiped separately, but not subsumed into "YHWH alone."[21] Martin Scott summarizes: "Just as Yahweh is an expression of the one God *(male),* so too Sophia is an expression of the one God *(female);*" she is "God herself at work in the life and salvation history of Israel."[22] James D. G. Dunn's sense is that monotheism is not compromised by such creativity; rather, ancient and reliable language is given fresh tasks.[23]

---

[20] For the verbal links between this passage and the idolatry sections see Winston, *The Wisdom of Solomon,* 305.

[21] For careful detail and argumentation consult James D. G. Dunn, *Christology in the Making: A New Testament Inquiry into the Origins of the Doctrine of the Incarnation* (Philadelphia: Westminster, 1980) 172–74; Martin Scott, *Sophia and the Johannine Jesus* (Sheffield: Sheffield Academic Press, 1992) 46–49 and 74–78.

[22] Scott, *Sophia and the Johannine Jesus,* 80, 78.

[23] Dunn, *Christology in the Making,* 169–70.

The Gospel of John utilizes the same tradition, following Wisdom of Solomon rather than the thought of Paul, Matthew, Luke, or the Letter to the Hebrews (which relate Sophia and Jesus, but differently). John's prologue, using *logos* language, introduces the phenomenon of pre-existence: "The Logos is simply Sophia taking on flesh . . .";[24] but then, dropping *logos* language and utilizing the Sophia themes of the book of Wisdom, John makes the case for Jesus as Sophia: primordial intimacy with God, collaboration with the creator and interaction with all creation, imagery of light and life, the seeking out of those made friends of God, the presence of signs, and so forth. Scott concludes: "Jesus Christ is none other than Jesus Sophia incarnate."[25] The traditional language of Wisdom is stretched in both portrayals to speak profoundly of God's capacities to offer Life.

If we can see traces of the tradition transposing and transforming within the two biblical texts, assisted to do so by the presence and agency of Sophia, there is no need to suppose the process stops there. My attempt has been to suggest that Wisdom of Solomon, roughly contemporary with John's gospel and other early Christian writings, can be read as responsive to the same urgent issues: the oneness and simultaneous richness of God, the capacities of God to extend life beyond death, the immense faith-and-imagination-challenge to both cling to and push deeper into traditional language. As the various Jewish communities struggled to shape their own experience of God's saving actions and the language of their sacred traditions, the figure of Sophia, long ubiquitous in the "neighborhood" and variously understood, emerged as a way to see and speak. Her characterization is deeply traditional but also capacious. Two communities faced the challenge of the life, death, and Life of God's just one: the Alexandrian community, caught also in questions of its own survival as a polity, and the Johannine community, struggling to situate itself in relation to the synagogue as well as to its other matrices. For each, in substantially similar ways, and granted clear differences as well, the figure of Sophia allows and invites fresh insight into God's gifts available to creatures. The need to discern God at work within every part of the cosmos surely continues strongly in our day. This interpretation, which constructs Jesus present in a First Testament text, is a bold reading. Bold may be just what is needed.

---

[24] Scott, *Sophia and the Johannine Jesus*, 105. See pp. 88–165 for his detailed presentation of the case.

[25] Ibid. 170.

ΑΓΝΕΙΑ as a Sublime Form of ΕΡΩΣ in the *Acts of Paul and Thecla*

Eung Chun Park

જી

Juxtaposing competing values can be a powerful device for developing a plot in a literary work that has narrative elements. For example, in Sophocles' *Antigone,* King Creon's strict injunction that no one in Thebes should give a proper burial to Polyneices' corpse presents Antigone with a terrible dilemma of having to choose between obeying the decrees (τὰ κηρύγματα) of the king and honoring the "unwritten and unfailing laws of gods (ἄγραπτα κἀσφαλῆ θεῶν νόμιμα)."[1] Determined to abide by the latter, Antigone gives her brother a ritual burial. Enraged, Creon punishes Antigone by locking her in a cave, but she, in defiance, hangs herself. She is finally avenged by the gods, who punish Creon by having his son and his wife successively commit suicide in protest against his cruelty toward Antigone. Thus, over the course of the series of dramatic turns of events the initial tension is resolved with one value gradually prevailing over the other.

In the *Acts of Paul and Thecla* there is a juxtaposition of two competing values that runs throughout the story: carnal affection vs. sexual abstinence.[2] Traditionally the story of Thecla has been interpreted mainly from the perspective of Thecla's instant conversion to the Christian message of ἀγνεία and

---

[1] Sophocles, *Antigone,* 450.

[2] Recent scholarship on the *Acts of Paul and Thecla* tends to acknowledge that the story has its origin in oral traditions. See, for example, Dennis R. MacDonald, *The Legend and the Apostle: The Battle for Paul in Story and Canon* (Philadelphia: Westminster, 1983) and Willy Rordorf, "Tradition and Composition in the Acts of Thecla: The State of the Question," *Semeia* 38 (1986) 43–52. This does not mean that the written text lacks literary artistry. This essay assumes that there was a final redactor who shaped the narrative world according to the literary conventions of the time so that the text had literary integrity of its own.

her continuing struggle to protect it against all hardships.³ This essay tries to appreciate another motif that runs counter to the theme of ἁγνεία, that is, the romantic/erotic feelings Thecla has for Paul. On the surface these two motifs, ἔρως and ἁγνεία, seem to be in opposition to each other and as such they provide a major plot device for the actions of the protagonist, Thecla, and the various antagonists in the *Acts of Paul and Thecla*. At a deeper level, however, the two can be viewed as different stages of the same pursuit, that is, ἔρως. Here I will attempt to read the story of Thecla in light of the metamorphosis of her carnal affection, which is one form of ἔρως, into a more sublime form of the same, that is, ἁγνεία as love for Christ. The Platonic idea of the gradual upward intellectual journey of a philosopher in pursuit of ἔρως from carnal desire for a beautiful body to a vision of the Form (εἶδος) of Beauty itself, which is acclaimed as the ultimate goal of philosophy in the *Symposium,* will be used as a key reading strategy in this interpretation.

By using Plato's work as an interpretive tool I do not suggest that the author of the *Acts of Paul and Thecla* was aware of Plato's theory of Form and self-consciously applied the idea of different stages of love in the *Symposium* to her/his story.⁴ Historically speaking, the *Acts of Paul and Thecla* may or may not have been intertextually dependent on the *Symposium*. If it was, this could be with or without authorial intention. The most this essay can claim is that it makes sense to read the story of Thecla from the perspective of the Platonic idea of gradual change from one form of ἔρως to another. There are aspects of the story of Thecla that cannot be adequately explained by the Platonic theory of ἔρως. I will try to account for such aspects in terms of the gender issue that plays an important role in the *Acts of Paul and Thecla*.

1. MULTIPLE STAGES IN THE PURSUIT OF ΕΡΩΣ IN PLATO'S *SYMPOSIUM*

The *Symposium,* which is regarded as one of the "middle" dialogues of Plato, purports to be an oral report by Apollodorus to his companions on what

---

³ For the early history of interpretation of the Thecla story see Léonie Hayne, "Thecla and the Church Fathers," *VC* 48 (1994) 209–18.

⁴ By "the author" I do not mean the Asian presbyter Tertullian refers to in *De Baptismo* 17 as the author of the Thecla story. First of all, the historical veracity of Tertullian's statement cannot be established. Also, even if it is historically accurate information it is not certain whether it refers to the one who wrote the Thecla story alone or the final editor of the *Acts of Paul,* which includes the Thecla story. It is even possible that it refers to some other document than the Thecla story as we know it. For instance, Stevan L. Davies, "Women, Tertullian and the Acts of Paul" *Semeia* 38 (1986) 139–43, argues that it refers to a (now lost) pseudepigraphical letter attributed to Paul. In this essay I use the term "author" to mean the one who wrote the final text of the Thecla story (out

he heard from Aristodemus about a συμπόσιον that had taken place at Agathon's house in 416 B.C.E., during which eminent Athenian intellects took turns offering an encomium on Love (τὸν λόγον τὸν περὶ τοῦ Ἔρωτος).[5] The *Symposium* is also one of the major sources for Plato's renowned theory of Form (εἶδος), together with the *Phaedo,* the *Republic,* and the *Phaedrus.*[6] In fact ἔρως, as the subject of the discourse, and the theory of Forms as the philosophical frame of reference for it are closely woven together in the *Symposium.* Either the theory of the Forms is worked out in the course of explaining the different stages of pursuing ἔρως or vice versa. Whichever came first, the combination of these two in the *Symposium,* i.e., the theme of ἔρως and the theory of Forms, is germane to the Platonic idea of the so-called "one and many."

The speech of Socrates, which marks the climax of all the discourses in the *Symposium,* comes last among the six. In this particular speech, however, Socrates does not speak in his own voice, which is very unusual. Instead, the Platonic Socrates cites the Mantinean woman Diotima as the source of everything he knows about love. Because of this rather remarkable deference by Socrates to an otherwise unknown female figure, Diotima, as the source of his learning, scholars speculate that Plato at this point moves beyond the historical Socrates and articulates his own philosophical ideas through the voice of a fictitious character called Diotima.[7] In the citation by Socrates, Diotima begins by refuting the popular notion, which had just been reiterated at length in Agathon's speech (*Sym.* 195a) and which Socrates implies he himself once held, that ἔρως is the paragon of surpassing beauty. Then she declares that ἔρως, being neither beautiful nor good (ὡς οὔτε καλὸς εἴη . . . οὔτε ἀγαθός, *Sym.* 201e), *desires* the very things he is lacking, that is, beauty and goodness (*Sym.* 202d).[8] It is in this desire of his for beauty and goodness that ἔρως is an inspiration for all lovers of wisdom (φιλόσοφοι), who seek the same.

Having defined ἔρως as the symbol for the pursuit of beauty, Diotima proceeds to argue, in accordance with the typical Platonic motif of "ascending" as

---

of imagination or from pre-existing oral traditions), whether or not s/he is identical with the one who put together various stories of Paul into what was later known as the *Acts of Paul.*

[5] Citations of the Greek text of the *Symposium* in this essay are from W.R.M. Lamb, *Plato: Lysis, Symposium, Gorgias.* LCL 166 (Cambridge, Mass.: Harvard University Press, 1925).

[6] Kenneth Dorter, *Form and Good in Plato's Eleatic Dialogues: The Parmenides, Theaetetus, Sophist, and Statesman* (Berkeley: University of California Press, 1994) 21–23.

[7] For example, Thomas A. Szlezák, *Reading Plato* (London and New York: Routledge, 1999) 100–01. For a recent discussion of this issue see Louis A. Ruprecht, Jr., *Symposia: Plato, the Erotic, and Moral Value* (Albany: State University of New York Press, 1999) xiii.

[8] This particular nature of ἔρως is called "in-between-ness" by Ruprecht, *Symposia,* 57. As such it coheres well with the motif of journey in the *Symposium.*

a metaphor for a philosopher's advancement in knowledge,[9] that there is an upward movement in the well-guided journey of a seeker of wisdom in his *(sic.)* experience of ἔρως.[10] According to Diotima, a seeker's first encounter with ἔρως is his *(sic.)* love for a particular body (ἑνὸς αὐτὸν σώματος ἐρᾶν, *Sym.* 210a) that is beautiful in appearance. Needless to say, this bodily love is, in the *Symposium,* in the form of homoeroticism, especially carnal desire of an adult male for an adolescent boy παιδεραστεῖν, *Sym.* 210b). The next stage is for him to recognize that the beauty attached to one particular body is the same as the beauty that belongs to any other and, by comprehending this truth, to become a lover of all beautiful bodies (καταστῆναι πάντων τῶν καλῶν σωμάτων ἐραστήν, *Sym.* 210b).

Then the next advancement is for him to regard the beauty of souls (τὸ ἐν ταῖς ψυχαῖς κάλλος) as higher than that of bodies.[11] Diotima is not very specific as to how the transition from the latter to the former can be accomplished. She simply lays it out as a stage that must be visited on the way to the higher goal.[12] This is where the lover of wisdom (φιλόσοφος) moves from mere observation to the realm of knowledge (ἐπιστήμη), in which he may finally be able to "see" (κατόψεται)[13] the vision of something wonderful and beautiful in nature (τι θαυμαστὸν τὴν φύσιν καλόν, *Sym.* 210e). This is called "the very thing that is beautiful (αὐτὸ ὃ ἔστι καλόν)" and also "the beauty itself (αὐτὸ τὸ καλόν)" (*Sym.* 211d). Ever existing and neither becoming nor perishing (ἀεὶ ὄν καὶ οὔτε γιγνόμενον οὔτε ἀπολλύμενον, *Sym.* 210e), this "αὐτὸ τὸ καλόν" is the *"Form* (εἶδος)" of beauty, even though the word εἶδος is not used in this particular section. Having seen this eternal truth, the philosopher becomes truly immortal, which is a superior mode of attaining immortality to the ordinary way of mimicking it by procreation. This is what ἔρως ultimately desires and

[9] Szlezák, *Reading Plato,* 61.

[10] Catherine Osborne, *Eros Unveiled: Plato and the God of Love* (Oxford: Clarendon Press, 1994) 89. Osborne makes an observation that the motif of Apollodorus' uphill journey in the narrative frame of the *Symposium* coincides with the motif of ascent in Diotima's lecture on love in Socrates' speech. She points out the parallel usage of the verbs meaning "going up": ἀνιών for Apollodorus (*Sym.* 172a) and ἐπανιών for Diotima's description of the philosopher's advancement (*Sym.* 211b).

[11] Earlier in his speech Socrates quotes Diotima as saying that begetting can be done in two ways: κατὰ τὸ σῶμα καὶ κατὰ τὴν ψυχήν (*Sym.* 206b). Ton H. C. van Eijk calls them "two ways of being ἐρωτικός," in "Marriage and Virginity, Death and Immortality," in Jacques Fontaine and Charles Kannengiesser, eds., *Epektasis: Mélanges Patristiques* (Paris: Beauchesne, 1972) 210.

[12] G.R.F. Ferrari, "Platonic Love," in Richard Kraut, ed., *The Cambridge Companion to Plato* (New York: Cambridge University Press, 1992) 248–76; see p. 257.

[13] For the Platonic concept of "seeing" as a metaphor for intellectual perception see J.C.B. Gosling, *Plato* (London: Routledge, 1983) 120–25.

therefore it is still περὶ τῶν ἐρωτικῶν. That is why, in Plato's dialogues, ἔρως includes sexuality but involves more than body.[14] In other words, pursuing carnal desire and beholding the Form of Beauty itself are two different stages of experiencing τὰ ἐρωτικά, the former being the starting point and the latter the ultimate goal. They are not necessarily in opposition to each other. Rather, they are "qualitatively homogeneous."[15]

2. CARNAL DESIRE AND SEXUAL ABSTINENCE IN THE *ACTS OF PAUL AND THECLA*

The *Acts of Paul and Thecla* is an early Christian novel about Thecla's love journey.[16] If Chariton's genre designation of his own work as a story of πάθος ἐρωτικόν in the prologue of *Chaereas and Callirhoe* is apt, it would also fit the character of the *Acts of Paul and Thecla,* which contains many typical elements of ancient Greek love romances.[17] When the heroine Thecla appears for the first time in the story she is introduced as θέκλα τις παρθένος betrothed to a man named Thamyris (*APTh* 7).[18] By that time Paul, who is not exactly a hero in this story, has already been introduced. Unlike Chaereas and Callirhoe in Chariton's novel, or Habrocomes and Anthia in Xenophon's *Ephesiaca,* neither Paul nor Thecla is depicted as possessing superhuman beauty.[19] However, just as for the two young couples mentioned above, there is the typical "love at first sight" between Thecla and Paul, at least on the part of the former. When Thecla first sees Paul preaching she becomes instantly lovestruck, and for three days and three nights she does not leave Paul, neither eating nor drinking but "looking intensely (at Paul) as if on some joyful spectacle" (ἀτενίζουσα ὡς πρὸς εὐφρασίαν, *APTh* 8).[20] When she sees other women around

---

[14] Ruprecht, *Symposia,* 80.

[15] Martha C. Nussbaum, *Love's Knowledge: Essays on Philosophy and Literature* (New York: Oxford University Press, 1990) 113–17.

[16] For a discussion of the nomenclature for ancient novels see Thomas Hägg, *The Novel in Antiquity* (Berkeley: University of California Press, 1983) 1–4.

[17] For a list of features in the *Acts of Paul and Thecla* that are common in ancient novels see ibid. 160.

[18] Citations of the Greek text of the *Acts of Paul and Thecla* (henceforth *APTh* when used as a reference) in this essay are from Ricardus Lipsius and Maximilianus Bonnet, eds., *Acta Apostolorum Apocrypha,* Vol. 1 (Hildesheim and New York: Georg Olms, 1972).

[19] The narrator's description of Paul's appearance in the beginning of the novel (*APTh* 3) is rather unflattering. Thecla is once called 'beautiful (καὶ σὺ εὔμορφος)" by Paul (*APTh* 25) and she does attract suitors wherever she goes. But her physical beauty is not raved upon in the story.

[20] Hägg (*The Novel in Antiquity,* 160) says this reaction of Thecla "is reminiscent of the purely physical manifestations of awakening love in, for instance, the *Ephesiaca*."

Paul she becomes extremely jealous (*APTh* 7). Thecla has just been awakened to love, and it is not with the right person but with a stranger (ξένον, *APTh* 13). Thus begins Thecla's tumultuous love journey.

Thecla's mother, alarmed by this, sends to Thamyris, Thecla's fiancé, and informs him of the whole incident. Thamyris immediately goes to Thecla and tries to woo her back, but neither he nor Thecla's mother is able to detach Thecla from her newly found man, Paul. Thamyris, in his desperation, keeps looking for those who gather around Paul, when he encounters the two dubious characters Demas and Hermogenes. These inside opponents of Paul advise Thamyris to have Paul prosecuted on the charge that he is influencing the young not to honor the convention of marriage. They also argue that the resurrection Paul talks about has in fact already taken place in the children people beget (*APTh* 14). Interestingly enough, this is exactly what Diotima says about begetting as one of the means of achieving immortality in the *Symposium*. Begetting children is indeed the easiest form of simulating immortality among ordinary people. It is τόκος ἐρωτικὸς κατὰ τὸ σῶμα, and as such it is inferior to τόκος ἐρωτικὸς κατὰ τῆν ψυχήν (*Sym.* 206b). In the *Acts of Paul and Thecla* the idea of achieving immortality through begetting children, coming as it does from the mouths of the antagonists, will be refuted in the rest of the story.[21]

What is peculiar about Thecla's falling in love with Paul is that she is attracted to his words (*APTh* 7), not to his appearance, as is the case with most ancient love romances.[22] Moreover, the subject of Paul's preaching that she is drawn to is predominantly ἁγνεία. In other words, it is almost paradoxical that Thecla falls in love with Paul in the first place. Erotic feeling toward a man should not arise in Thecla's mind once it has embraced the message of ἁγνεία. When it happens nonetheless in the story it signals an ensuing conflict between carnal desire and sexual renunciation, and the implied reader may anticipate a gradual resolution from the former to the latter.

The first episode that shows the carnal side of Thecla's affection for Paul takes place when Paul is put in prison by the city proconsul because of the charge brought by Thamyris. The night Paul is imprisoned, Thecla goes to the prison and by bribing the gatekeeper and the jailer gains access to the cell

---

[21] It is fascinating to compare this statement with 1 Tim 2:15, in which the "orthodox" theology teaches that women will be saved through childbearing!

[22] There is, however, an interesting remark by the narrator that Thecla had not seen Paul's figure (χαρακτῆρα Παύλου) before but heard of his word only (*APTh* 7). In other words, Thecla had heard about Paul's preaching before and it had not attracted her until she actually saw him in person. So the text gives a mixed message on this matter. On the surface it clearly says Thecla is attracted to Paul's message, but there is also an implication that *seeing* him made her fall in love with him.

where Paul is kept. There in the "privacy" of the prison chamber Thecla meets Paul in person for the first time. She sits at his feet, listens to what he says, and kisses his bonds (καταφιλούσης τὰ δεσμὰ αὐτοῦ, *APTh* 18).[23] Here the text says "Her faith increased" (κἀκείνης ηὔξανειν ἡ πίστις), but what really increased is her erotic feeling for Paul. Later the gatekeeper and the jailer will testify that she was bound by affection (συνδεδεμένην τῇ στοργῇ, *APTh* 19) while she was with Paul in the prison cell.

When this secret encounter is made known to Thamyris he stirs up the city officials and they have Paul dragged out of prison to the tribunal. Thecla remains in the prison cell and rolls herself (ἐκυλίετο) on the ground where Paul was sitting (*APTh* 20), as if it could give her a feeling of physical contact with him. Certainly Paul's message of ἀγνεία would have created a tension in Thecla's mind, which has just been kindled with love for Paul, but obviously it has not deterred her from desiring physical contact with Paul and even simulating it in his absence. The beginning of the Thecla saga is characterized by a tension that has tilted toward carnal desire.

Shortly after this episode Thecla is also brought to the tribunal. When she is interrogated by the governor about her refusal to marry Thamyris she does not even answer his question. Instead, undaunted by implied threats, she stands by Paul, looking at him intensely (ἡ δὲ εἰστήκει Παύλῳ ἀτενίζουσα), just as lovers often do with each other.[24] A striking contrast is found in Paul's behavior. In spite of Thecla's unrelenting affection for him, Paul is completely unresponsive. When he is released after being scourged he simply goes away, leaving Thecla behind, even though she has been sentenced to be burned to death. Unaware of Paul's departure, Thecla keeps searching for him, "as a lamb searches for a shepherd in the wilderness" (ὡς ἀμνὸς ἐν ἐρήμῳ περισκοπεῖ τὸν ποιμένα, *APTh* 21). Thus Paul is depicted here as a bad shepherd who leaves his lamb in danger and flees away.

In that light the Christophany scene that immediately follows Paul's disappearance from Thecla is highly symbolic. In the midst of life-threatening danger she *sees* the Lord sitting as if he were Paul (εἶδον τὸν Κύριον καθήμενον ὡς Παῦλον, *APTh* 21). That is, at a critical moment Christ the good shepherd appears to Thecla, even though she mistakes him for Paul. This Christophany and Thecla's confusion of it with Paul are highly suggestive of the direction this narrative is going to take. That is, the current erotic feeling Thecla has for Paul

---

[23] Cf. In Xenophon's *Ephesiaca* the heroine Anthia also visits her lover, Habrocome, in prison and kisses his bonds.

[24] Ἀτενίζουσα is exactly the same word that was used earlier to describe how Thecla was fixing her gaze upon her newly found love (*APTh* 8).

is something she will have to move past in order to advance toward the ultimate love for Christ, which will be symbolized by a life of ἀγνεία, a loftier form of ἔρως in this narrative.

In that sense this *"vision"* of Christ in the *Acts of Paul and Thecla* is the climax of the story, and as such it proleptically makes a striking parallel with the *"vision"* of the Form of Beauty that an ἔρως-stricken philosopher ultimately sees at the end of his journey in the *Symposium*. The only difference is that in the *Symposium* seeing the vision is identical with understanding the eternal truth,[25] whereas in the *Acts of Paul and Thecla* the vision induces proper understanding with an implied time gap.[26] This is probably due to the fact that in the *Acts of Paul and Thecla* the vision is not Thecla's own intellectual achievement but a revelation from above. Regardless of how she gets there, what is important is that she sees the vision and eventually understands it.

After Thecla is miraculously saved from the fire she once again goes to look for Paul. When she is finally taken to him she hears him pray to God for her, "Stand by her, because *she is yours*" (πάρεσο αὐτῇ ὅτι σή ἐστιν, *APTh* 24).[27] Even after Thecla hears this remark by Paul, which makes it clear where her heart should belong, she still thanks God for saving her so that she may see Paul again. Then she says to Paul, "I will cut my hair and follow you wherever you may go." Is Thecla trying to overcome her erotic feelings for Paul by removing the symbol of her female beauty?[28] Or is she volunteering to cut off her hair simply as a practical tactic she believes would allow her to stay close to Paul? At this point in the story the text remains ambiguous. What is not ambiguous, however, is that Thecla is now trying to move past her romantic feelings for Paul. The upward journey of ἔρως is progressing in Thecla's mind.

Paul refuses to grant Thecla's petition, referring to her beauty as the reason for his refusal. However, in the next scene Paul goes to Antioch, taking Thecla along with him. A certain Alexander sees Thecla and immediately falls in love with her. When he tries to bribe Paul for Thecla, Paul disowns her by saying, "I don't know her, nor is she mine" (οὐδὲ ἔστιν ἐμή, *APTh* 26). Then, in spite of Thecla's desperate search, Paul disappears from the scene again, leaving her in great peril at the hands of this foreign man, Alexander, who intensely desires her. Whether or not this episode works as a catalyst for Thecla's growth beyond her erotic feelings for Paul, she becomes a completely differ-

---

[25] For the concept of knowledge as vision see Gosling, *Plato*, 120–39.

[26] This kind of time gap between a vision and a proper understanding of it is also found in the story of Peter's vision in Acts 10.

[27] This statement of Paul is matched with his later comment to Alexander that Thecla is *not his:* οὐκ οἶδα τὴν γυναῖκα ἣν λέγεις, οὐδὲ ἔστιν ἐμή (*APTh* 26).

[28] Cf. MacDonald, *The Legend and the Apostle*, 20.

ent person from this point on. No transition is explicitly narrated, but the change is dramatic.

From this point to the end of the story Thecla no longer harbors or expresses erotic feelings for Paul. She is no longer emotionally dependent on him. Instead, she now sees herself as a servant of God (τὴν τοῦ θεοῦ δούλην) in her own right (*APTh* 26), and in that capacity she offers an intercessory prayer to God for Tryphaena on behalf of her deceased daughter (*APTh* 29). This marks her first act of ministry as a servant of God, and it happens shortly after Paul has left her, both physically and symbolically. This is not a coincidence in the story. Detachment from erotic desire for a single person is a significant step toward maturity both in the *Symposium* (201b) and in the *Acts of Paul and Thecla,* maturity in the love of wisdom (ἐν φιλοσοφίᾳ, *Sym.* 210d) in the former and maturity in the love of Christ in the latter.

By removing Paul from Thecla the narrative creates for the latter a new environment in which she can pursue ἀγνεία, which is required for the more sublime form of Christian ἔρως, that is, love for Christ, independently of Paul, who was simply a medium for delivering the message of ἀγνεία to her. In order to maintain her ἀγνεία Thecla has to endure many hardships in the ensuing episodes, but now she no longer looks around seeking to find Paul for help as she did in the earlier part of the story. Instead she prays for those who mourn for her suffering and faces the tribulation with courage.

As she is thrown into the arena to fight with wild beasts she performs the baptismal ritual for herself (*APTh* 34), which functions as a critical sign of her independence in the story. It makes a stark contrast with an earlier scene in which Thecla begs Paul to baptize her and take her along, but he refuses (*APTh* 25). When she is miraculously spared from the wild beasts she declares to the amazed governor, "I am a servant of the living God" (ἐγὼ μέν εἰμι θεοῦ τοῦ ζῶντος δούλη), and she makes a confession that she believes in the Son of God, whom she identifies as the "substance of immortal life" (ζωῆς ἀθανάτου ὑποστασίς). Having seen the vision and understood the true source of immortality, Thecla is now entitled to be a servant of God in her own right.

Finally, this change in Thecla's feeling from carnal affection to ἀγνεία, which is neither accidental nor insignificant to the story line, can also be shown at the level of literary structure by observing the two parallel cycles of hardships she goes through.

Cycle 1: Hardships of Thecla and disappearance of Paul (*APTh* 21–22)
     Re-encounter of Paul and Thecla (*APTh* 23–25)
Cycle 2: Hardships of Thecla and disappearance of Paul (*APTh* 26–39)
     Re-encounter of Paul and Thecla (*APTh* 40–41)

In the first cycle Thecla's concern about her chastity is not expressed overtly. Instead, we have a picture of Thecla desperately seeking Paul as a bereaved lover looks for her lost love. In the second cycle, however, there is no description of Thecla seeking Paul. Instead, her only concern is to keep her ἀγνεία intact. For example, in sections 26, 27, and 31 all that Thecla entreats Alexander and the proconsul for and all that she prays to God for is her ἀγνεία. By the same token, in the first cycle Thecla asks Paul's permission to change her appearance into that of a male figure, but in the second she is already dressed in male attire when she goes to Paul. The transition from carnal desire for Paul to love for Christ through ἀγνεία is completed in Thecla. It has been a successful upward journey from a lower form of ἔρως to a higher form of the same.

3. ΕΡΩΣ, ΑΓΝΕΙΑ, LIBERATION AND REDOMESTICATION OF WOMEN

An interesting aspect of the metaphor of a philosopher's upward journey in the pursuit of the Form of Beauty through various stages of erotic experiences in Plato's *Symposium* is a recognition of carnal desire, whether it is heterosexual or homosexual, as a legitimate form of τὰ ἐρωτικά. It is certainly a lower form of ἔρως, but it is still important because it is a starting point of the journey. Therefore it is never denigrated as negative in the *Symposium*. That is why Socrates, even at the level of his philosophical maturity, is still unabashedly attracted to the physical beauty of a young man, Alcibiades.[29] In other words, the popular notion of the so-called *amor platonicus* as something completely devoid of carnal affection is a misconception.

Carnal desire in the *Acts of Paul and Thecla* is more ambiguous than in Plato's dialogues. Just like the philosopher in the speech of Diotima in the *Symposium,* Thecla starts from there. She falls in love with one living person, Paul. She fixes her gaze upon him, yearns for his touch, kisses his feet, and tries to feel his body warmth by rolling herself on the ground where he was sitting. The love story of Thecla's intense desire for Paul and her unrelenting devotion to him is sympathetically narrated throughout the first half of the story. In that sense carnal affection *per se* is not portrayed negatively in the *Acts of Paul and Thecla* either. It is a starting point and it eventually turns into a higher form of

---

[29] In the *Gorgias* 481d Socrates says he is in love with two things, Alcibiades, son of Cleinias, and philosophy. In the *Protagoras* 309a Socrates is teased by someone for his flirting with Alcibiades, which was obviously well known in the Socratic circle. In the *Symposium* 213cd Socrates jokingly tells Agathon how he has been constantly pestered by Alcibiades' jealousy since the moment he fell in love with him.

love in the second half of the story, just like the Platonic upward journey of a philosopher in pursuit of ἔρως in the *Symposium.*

However, unlike the accomplished philosopher who has seen the ultimate *vision* of the Form of Beauty in the *Symposium,* Thecla, who in our story also has seen the *vision* of the Lord and has achieved the highest form of love for Christ, should keep herself from any other form of τὰ ἐρωτικά. Eros does not require exclusive love of his followers in the *Symposium;* Christ does in the *Acts of Paul and Thecla.* That is why Thecla sheds her sexuality by sewing her tunic into a cloak "in the fashion of men" (σχήματι ἀνδρικῷ) before she goes to Myra to see Paul. This act of Thecla in putting on male attire is not about her attempt at becoming male, as if maleness were required for the life of a servant of God. It is rather an unimaginative way of depicting Thecla's symbolic act of becoming asexual. Carnal desire as the starting point should ultimately be done away with in the *Acts of Paul and Thecla* not because it is intrinsically bad, but because the love of Christ does not allow room for it.

The message of absolute ἁγνεία, because of its necessary requirement of sexual abstinence, is functionally, if not intrinsically, antisocial. It denies the convention of marriage and procreation. Since society, with its patriarchal family structure, was fundamentally androcentric, the antisocial message of ἁγνεία would have meant partial undoing of the inequality imposed on women in the conventional family system. Liberation of women from male dominance in the most basic unit of society would have been a corollary, if not the purpose, of the Christian message of ἁγνεία. The story of Thecla ends on that note.

However, realities would have been more complex. If all men and women in early Christianity had embraced and practiced the message of absolute ἁγνεία it would have been a utopian community in terms of gender equality, but as a celibate community it could not have lasted long! The canonical, "orthodox" version of early Christianity in the second century C.E. opted for compromising the notion of ἁγνεία as marital chastity, allowing sexual relationships for the purpose of procreation, as 1 Tim 2:15 clearly indicates. If anyone had bothered to compare, this "orthodox" modification of the notion of ἁγνεία would have been partially but conveniently compatible with the Platonic idea/practice of ἔρως, at least in the *Symposium,* if not in the *Republic.* In any case, this revised notion of ἁγνεία served the theology of love-patriarchalism of "orthodox" Christianity, reaffirming the conventions of the society. As long as the conventions of marriage and family were upheld in their traditional forms the message of ἁγνεία was no longer good news of liberation for women. Rather, it was a means of redomesticating them. The original message of liberation of women that came as a corollary of the notion of absolute ἁγνεία was done away with. Tertullian's statement about the Thecla story in *De baptismo* 17 unambiguously testifies to this phenomenon.[30]

Even though Diotima is a female teacher, the philosopher in her teaching, cited by Socrates in the *Symposium,* is exclusively a male figure. There is no indication that this figure is meant to be representative of both genders. However, in the fifth book of the *Republic* Plato unambiguously makes the ideal state inclusive of both genders at the level of its guardians.[31] The implication is that the pursuit of ἔρως for the ultimate vision of the Form of Beauty can be undertaken by both male and female with varying degrees of success depending on their intellectual abilities. At least in theory, gender equality is suggested. Apart from the fact that the picture of gender equality in the *Republic* is only partial and ambivalent and that Plato generally believes that the female is an inferior gender,[32] the ideal state of the *Republic* is precisely that, i.e., an ideal state in the sense that it is not realistic.

Unfortunately, inspiring a loftier form of ἔρως without denigrating human sexuality and at the same time making the journeys of the lover of wisdom or the lover of Christ gender inclusive on equal terms is something that neither the *Symposium* nor the *Acts of Paul and Thecla* was able to achieve. Plato made an additional attempt in that direction in the *Republic* and ended up revealing further ambiguities and inconsistencies in his notion of gender equality. Nevertheless, one can reasonably say that both the Athenian Academy in the fifth century B.C.E. and the unknown early Christian community of the *Acts of Paul and Thecla* (if there was one) in the second century C.E. respectively witnessed to a remarkable idea that went beyond the conventional wisdom of their times. Yet neither Plato, with the female wisdom teacher Diotima of the *Symposium* and the famous fifth book of the *Republic,* nor the less celebrated author of the *Acts of Paul and Thecla* was able to make a lasting impact on the realities of longstanding gender inequality, whether such a change was part of the authorial intent in each case or not.

---

[30] "If those who read the writings that falsely bear the name of Paul adduce the example of Thecla to maintain the right of women to teach and to baptize, let them know that the presbyter in Asia who produced this document, as if he could of himself add anything to the prestige of Paul, was removed from his office after he had been convicted and had confessed that he did it out of love for Paul" (*CSEL* 20, p. 215 as cited in Edgar Hennecke and Wilhelm Schneemelcher, eds., *New Testament Apocrypha.* Vol. 2, *Writings Relating to the Apostles, Apocalypses and Related Topics* [Philadelphia: Westminster, 1965] 323).

[31] Plato, *Republic* 454e, 455de, and 456a.

[32] For example, the Platonic Socrates says in the *Timaeus* 90e that all men who lived as cowards and wasted their lives in wrongdoing were reborn as women in their second incarnation.

Rendezvous with Thekla and Paul in Ephesos: Excavating the Evidence

Ruth Ohm Wright

ༀ

The discovery of a fresco in Ephesos depicting three main characters from the *Acts of Thekla (AThl)*[1] rekindles the question of the *AThl*'s audience and reception. The purpose of this essay is to consolidate select material and textual evidence relevant to the charismatic figures of Paul and Thekla in order to illuminate issues raised by the unanticipated yet pivotal discovery of Thekla in Ephesos. Some of the questions prompted by the fresco's discovery include: What was the artist trying to evoke in the painting? What social factors shaped this particular sign of devotion in Ephesos, a city not otherwise recognized as central to Theklan piety? What aspects of Thekla's activities became prevalent in visual culture?

THE ACTS OF THEKLA

Thekla's account can be found in two primary documents. It is widely accepted that the *AThl* originally circulated together with the *Acts of Paul (APl)* at least until the early second century;[2] Tertullian (155–ca. 220) refers to Thekla's self-baptism (*AThl* 34), names the *"Acta Pauli,"*[3] and identifies the

---

[1] *AThl* is used throughout to indicate the section of the *Apocryphal Acts of Paul* that tells the story of Paul and Thekla. The English translation can be found in Edgar Hennecke and Wilhelm Schneemelcher, eds., *New Testament Apocrypha.* Vol. 2 (London: S.C.M., 1974) 353–64. *APl* denotes the entire text of the *Acts of Paul*, including the Theklan episodes.

[2] Willy Rordorf summarizes the main evidence in "Tradition and Composition in the *Acts of Thecla:* The State of the Question," *Semeia* 38 (1986) 43–52.

[3] Against this manuscript reading Stevan L. Davies gives priority to another manuscript that reads *"scripta Pauli."* He argues that Tertullian refers to a letter written pseudonomously, and not the *APl* (Stevan L. Davies, "Women, Tertullian, and the *Acts of Paul,*" *Semeia* 38 [1986] 139–44). On the question of the relationship between the *Acts of the Apostles* and the *APl*, particularly as

227

author as a presbyter from Asia.[4] A significant feature of recent scholarly discussion has been the question of audience and authorship of the *AThl*. While the content of their arguments differs in detail, many believe that the *AThl* embrace traditions that circulated and were handed down by women.[5]

The *AThl* closes with Thekla making her final stop in Seleucia. The end of this narrative was revitalized in the mid-fifth century with the writing of the *Vie et miracles de Sainte Thècle (Life and Miracles of Thekla the Holy Apostle and Martyr of Christ)*, which reports wonderful stories of Thekla's final residence.[6] Attributed to pseudo-Basil, the text clearly promotes Theklan devotion in Seleucia and provides the basis for her cult. The narrative also acts as a lively testimony to the theological debates of this period with its considerable emphasis on the Trinity and dogma, as declared by Thekla herself.[7] Thus, woven into this expansion of Thekla's story is the articulate proclamation of theological attitudes that are difficult to conceive for second-century dogmatic development.

DESCRIPTION OF THE EPHESIAN CAVE

While the existence of the so-called Grotto of St. Paul in Ephesos has long been documented, it was not until 1995 that the cave was re-examined; in 1998

---

they may relate to the exposition of Paul's activities in Ephesos, see Willy Rordorf, "In welchem Verhältnis stehen die apokryphen Paulus-akten zur kanonischen Apostelgeschichte und zu den Pastoralbriefen?" in Tjitze Baarda et al., eds., *Text and Testimony: Essays on New Testament and Apocryphal Literature in Honour of A.F.J. Klijn* (Kampen: Kok, 1988) 225–41. Rordorf argues that the *APl* did not know of the *Acts of the Apostles*. One of the fundamental differences, he contends, is that the *APl* presumes more or less settled communities and emphasizes chastity, whereas *Acts of the Apostles* deals with the formation of communities and focuses on the Jewish opposition. Consequently he contends that the *APl* must be dated into the mid-second century (236).

[4] Tertullian, *De Baptismo* 17.

[5] It is beyond the scope of this essay to review the growing literature on the *AThl;* only a slice of the research is noted here. To name a few: for a European perspective on Thekla research see Anne Jensen, *Thekla—Die Apostolin* (Freiburg: Herder, 1995). An informative overview and commentary is offered by Sheila McGinn, "Acts of Thekla," in Elisabeth Schüssler Fiorenza, ed., *Searching the Scriptures: A Feminist Commentary* (New York: Crossroad, 1995) 800–28. For women as the authors of the *AThl* and members of an ascetic group of widows see Stevan L. Davies, *Revolt of the Widows* (Carbondale: Southern Illinois University Press, 1980); Dennis Ronald MacDonald, *The Legend and the Apostle* (Philadelphia: Westminster, 1983); Virginia Burrus, *Chastity as Autonomy* (Lewiston, N.Y.: Mellon, 1987).

[6] Gilbert Dagron, ed., *Vie et miracles de Sainte Thècle* (Brussels: Société des Bollandistes, 1978). Dagron's publication comprises an expansive "Introduction" (exploring aspects of the cult of Thekla, manuscript tradition, authorship, etc.), and the text and translation (French) of two documents: "The Life of Saint Thekla" and "The Miracles of Saint Thekla." Hereafter I will refer to each of these separately as "Introduction," *"Vie,"* or "Miracles."

[7] See especially Dagron, *"Vie,"* 26 (Dagron, "Introduction," 270–75).

the marvelous fresco program inside was unveiled.[8] Situated approximately 80 meters above sea level on the north side of Mount Bülbül, the cave is positioned in a section outside the enclosed excavation area of Ephesos. From the site of the cave one has a view over the western, lower city of Ephesos and the harbor area. The entire complex consists of a larger cave, a smaller, unfinished cave, and an architectural structure built on the terrace anterior to the caves. The primary, larger cave measures circa 15 meters in length, 2.10 meters in width and 2.3 meters in height. It stretches more or less straight back into the mountain, slightly widening at the end into a circa 2.7 meter space.

The walls were hewn from natural rock and bear several layers of plaster with paintings; at some later point the paintings were covered with whitewash. Almost three hundred inscriptions cover large portions of the top, youngest plaster layer. Nearly all the inscriptions have the characteristic form of acclamations or short prayers, such as ΠΑΥΛΕ / ΒΟΗΘΙΤΟΔΟΥΛΟCΟΥ / NIK . . . ("Paul, help your servant Nik . . ."), and ΚΥΡΙΕΒΟΗΘΙΤΟΥΔΟΥΛΟΥCΟΥΤΙΜΟ-ΘΕΟΝΚΕΒΟΗΘΗ . . . ("Lord, help your servant Timothy and help . . ."). Two arcosolia niches and three wall recesses are carved into the eastern cave wall.

A delightful fresco cycle was almost fully uncovered on the western wall near the entrance of the cave, and belongs to the middle layer of plaster.[9] We see the upper portion of a female figure with raised right arm and in a crimson *maphorion,* as well as the identification ΘΕΟΚΛΙ[to the left of her head. She is turned toward a seated figure at her right, who is clearly identifiable through the inscription ΠΑΥ / ΛΟC as well as his familiar features, though here he models a split-beard. He likewise has his right hand raised; a codex lies open on his left thigh, and he is turned toward a small house with a tree. From an

[8] First mentioned in the excavation report by Otto Benndorf, *Forschungen in Ephesos* 1 (1906) 105; rediscovered by W. Mondrijan in 1955 and some inscriptions published by Fritz Gschnitzer, *Skizzenbuch* (1955) nos. 2605-2621, as well as Dieter Knibbe, *Inschriften von Ephesos* 4 (Bonn: Habelt, 1980) 155–58 and nos. 1280 and 1285. The grotto underwent a more formal excavation by Franz Miltner, "Vorläufiger Bericht über die Ausgrabungen in Ephesos," *Österreichische Jahreshefte* 43 (1956–1958), Beiblatt 54–58, fifty years after its initial discovery! For discussion of the grotto's history of research and a detailed excavation report see Renate Pillinger, "Neue Entdeckungen in der sogenannten Paulusgrotte von Ephesos," *Mitteilungen zur Christlichen Archäologie* 6 (2000) 16–29.

[9] Additional paintings belonging to a younger plaster layer were uncovered at the cave's termination, on the southern and western walls. These depicted three male figures with nimbi (southern wall); the alpha and omega and aureole surrounding the middle figure clearly suggest Christ. On the southern end of the western wall one figure and two heads were uncovered. Their later dating and subject matter call for a separate treatment. A donor inscription, as well as another (unidentified) bearded figure wielding a sword were also painted. Renate Pillinger, "Neue Entdeckungen in der sogenannten Paulusgrotte von Ephesos," 22–23.

opening or window in the house peers a second female figure in a similar crimson *maphorion*. To her right are the letters ΘE, which, with the identity of the other two figures, can easily be completed to ΘEKΛA. This middle plaster layer with the Thekla cycle has been dated to the fifth or early sixth century.

Thus we have here, exquisitely preserved and complete with identification, a fresco depicting Theoklei[a] and the apostle Paul in front of a house, with The[kla] peering out from a window. It expresses a unique iconographic rendition of the legend handed down in the *AThl*. The scene depicted can be found in the Greek version of the *AThl;* Paul is situated in front of a house, preaching, while Thekla sits spellbound at the window listening to the apostle. Her mother Theokleia looks on with no small dismay since Thekla has already been betrothed to the desirable young man Thamyris *(AThl 7)*.[10]

MATERIAL EVIDENCE OUTSIDE EPHESOS

Late antique images of Thekla are not lacking, though a number of these cannot be tied to a specific locale dedicated to Theklan veneration.[11] The primary site for the cult of Thekla is a city near the coast of southern Asia Minor, called Seleucia (modern day Silifke, Turkey). While this geographical center of her cult leaves no preserved images, it is rich in structural witness. Two other sites of Theklan devotion can be traced to Egypt.[12] Thekla is paired with Saint Menas of Phrygia on pilgrim flasks from Mareotis; the necropolis of El-Bagawat, located at the Kharga Oasis in Egypt's western desert, preserves Thekla in two intriguing fresco programs.

---

[10] The corresponding section from the *AThl* reads: (5) And when Paul entered into the house of Onesiphorus there was a great joy, and bowing of knees and breaking of bread, and the word of God concerning continence and the resurrection, as Paul said . . . (7) And while Paul was thus speaking in the midst of the assembly in the house of Onesiphorus, a virgin named Thekla—her mother was Theokleia—who was betrothed to a man named Thamyris, sat at a nearby window and listened night and day to the word of the virgin life as it was spoken by Paul; and she did not turn away from the window, but pressed on in the faith rejoicing exceedingly . . . (8) Since however she did not move from the window, her mother sent to Thamyris. [Theokleia describes her plight to Thamyris, then encourages him to intervene] (9) Thamyris, this man is upsetting the city of the Iconians, and your Thekla too; for all the women and young people go in to him, and are taught by him. "You must," he says, "fear one single God and live chastely." And my daughter also, who sticks to the window like a spider, is [moved] by his words [and] gripped by a new desire and fearful passion; for the maiden hangs upon the things he says, and is taken captive."

[11] A complete discussion and reassessment of the known material and textual evidence surrounding the devotion to Thekla is beyond the scope of the present work.

[12] Textual evidence suggests devotion to Thekla also in Alexandria and the Nile Delta. For a discussion of these see Stephen J. Davis, *The Cult of Saint Thecla: A Tradition of Women's Piety in Late Antiquity* (Oxford: Oxford University Press, 2001).

Two historical figures attest to the prominence of the site in Seleucia. Circa 375, Gregory of Nazianzus affirms the popularity of Thekla's sanctuary.[13] Egeria's travel report bears witness that by 384 the shrine to Thekla was established and known in Seleucia.[14] Egeria describes her visit to the shrine: "At the holy church[15] there is nothing but countless monastic cells for men and women . . . . [Marthana] governs these monastic cells of *aputactitae,* or virgins . . . . There are many cells all over the hill, and in the middle there is a large wall which encloses the church where the shrine is. It is a very beautiful shrine . . . . Having arrived there in the name of God, a prayer was said at the shrine and the complete Acts of Thekla was read."[16] The later expansion of Thekla's story in the *Vie et Miracles* describes how she was swallowed up by the earth in the very place of the divine and holy table of the liturgical celebration (ἐν ὧπερ τόπῳ ἡ θεία καὶ ἱερὰ καὶ λειτουργικὴ πέπηγε τράπεζα).[17]

On the site are the remains of two churches, one of which is the Basilica of St. Thekla; the second is a church of unknown dedication. Underneath the fifth-century structure traditionally associated with Thekla are the probable remains of a small church connected to a cave crypt.[18] The fifth-century colonnaded and richly-decorated basilica[19] may be the same commissioned by Emperor Zeno sometime after 476. The correlation of Zeno with the building of this church is known through the sixth-century church historian Evagrius, who writes that the emperor dedicated a church to Thekla in gratitude for her intercession on his behalf.[20]

---

[13] Gregory of Nazianzus, *In Laudem Athanasii, Orat.* 22; *Carmen de Vita Sua* 1.547; cited in Davis, *The Cult of Saint Thecla,* 77.

[14] *Egeria: Diary of a Pilgrimage*, trans. George E. Gingras. *Ancient Christian Writers* 38 (New York: Newman, 1970).

[15] According to Egeria this is situated just "fifteen hundred feet from the city to the shrine of Saint Thekla" (*Egeria* 23.2).

[16] Ibid. 23.4.

[17] Thus also presupposing a church there. Dagron, *"Vie,"* 28.9-10 (Dagron, "Introduction," 281; cf. Davis, *The Cult of Saint Thecla,* 37).

[18] Dated to the end of the third or fourth century, the church has three aisles and an apse, possibly flanked by two smaller chapel structures. Ernst Herzfeld and Samuel Guyer, *Monumenta Asiae Minoris Antiqua.* Vol. 2: *Meriamlik und Korykos: Zwei christliche Ruinenstätten des Rauhen Kilikiens* (Manchester: Manchester University Press, 1930) 38–46.

[19] Archaeological remains suggest a structure eighty meters long, with three aisles, narthex, a portico on the southern side, and a semicircular apse flanked by two chapel-like pastophoria at the eastern end. Decoration is attested by capitals, a possible choir-screen fragment, mosaic floor laid out with geometric and animal designs in the nave, and *opus sectile* in the lateral aisles.

[20] Dagron, "Introduction," 61–63. Its identification as the Basilica of St. Thekla is not without some difficulty, however. Guyer remarks that it exhibits few characteristics of this period's Byzantine structures. In addition one might expect an architecture more characteristic of the imperial

Photos by N. Gail; Austrian Archaeological Institute (Oesterreichisches Archaeologisches Institut).

In contrast to the scarcity of buildings, images of Thekla abound. For the most part these fall into variations of two categories: Thekla pictured with Paul and Thekla's trials. A subclassification of these comprises (1) Thekla inside her mother's house, listening to Paul preaching; (2) Thekla sitting facing Paul, writing or being taught; (3) Thekla as an orans, in some examples standing between two lions;[21] (4) Thekla standing in the flames of the pyre;[22] (5) Thekla tied to a stake, between a lion and a bear at her feet and wild oxen at her hips.[23] Since the first two image types in this categorization are clearly most relevant to the fresco in Ephesos, the remaining image types are only briefly reviewed.

Of the 263 funerary chapels in the necropolis at El-Bagawat, the Chapel of the Exodus (chapel 30) and the Chapel of Peace (chapel 80) include paintings of Thekla.[24] In the Chapel of the Exodus, dated to the mid-fourth century, a roughly drawn Thekla stands among licking flames evoking the scene of her condemnation by the governor of Iconium. Thekla is poised with raised arms while a cloud of rain pours from overhead, delivering her from the fire (*AThl* 22, "*Vie*" 12).

In the Chapel of Peace, dated to the fifth or sixth century, a more polished fresco depicts Thekla and Paul seated cross-legged on stools and facing one another. Thekla holds a stylus and is writing in a book or writing tablet *(diptychon?)* on her lap. Paul gestures to the book she holds.[25] A depiction of

---

capital in a basilica dedicated by the emperor. He suggests that Evagrius may be referring to the monumental domed basilica situated just to the north. On the other hand, Guyer notes that Byzantine period architecture has a variety of influences, so that it might not be feasible to identify a strictly Byzantine conformity. Herzfeld and Guyer, *Monumenta Asiae Minoris Antiqua,* 32.

[21] Found on a pendant, Coptic comb, ring, miniature of Symeon Metaphrastes, and an oil lamp; usually one lion is in attack position and the other licks at Thekla's feet; in one example the *manus divina* reaches from above with a wreath (Claudia Nauerth, "Nachlese von Thekla-Darstelllungen," in Guntram Koch, ed., *Studien zur spätantiken und frühchristlichen Kunst und Kultur des Orients*. Göttinger Orientforschungen 2:6 [Wiesbaden: Harrassowitz, 1986] 16–17).

[22] Chapel of the Exodus in El-Bagawat. The texts describe Thekla as naked (*AThl* 22; Dagron, "*Vie*," 12 [Dagron, "Introduction," 218]); in the fresco she is wearing a tunic. Also found on a gold-glass medallion in the British Museum, Coptic textile fragment, and elsewhere. See Claudia Nauerth and Rüdiger Warns, *Thekla: Ihre Bilder in der frühchristlichen Kunst*. Göttinger Orientforschungen 2:3 (Wiesbaden: Harrassowitz, 1981) 22–24.

[23] Here she is often paired with Saint Menas on pilgrim ampulles. Menas ampulles have been found all around the Mediterranean, attesting to the popularity of his cult in the fourth to sixth centuries. See Kurt Weitzmann, ed., *Age of Spirituality* (New York: Metropolitan Museum of Art, 1979) 575–78. For discussion on the pairing of Thekla and Menas see Davis, *The Cult of Saint Thecla,* 120–26; also Nauerth, "Nachlese von Thekla-Darstelllungen," 14–15; and Nauerth and Warns, *Thekla,* 35-42.

[24] Ahmed Fakhry, *The Necropolis of El-Bagawat*. Service des antiquités de l'Égypte: The Egyptian Deserts (Cairo: Government Press, 1951).

[25] Paul may be gesturing with a pointing stick (or stylus?) he holds in his right hand. The fresco is damaged.

Adam and Eve is immediately to the left of Thekla, while Mary with a dove (the Annunciation) is to Paul's right.[26] All figures are identified with inscriptions above their heads.[27]

It is noteworthy that the figures hold writing instruments instead of a scroll or codex. Claudia Nauerth and Rüdiger Warns interpret this as a teaching scene, observing the close iconographic parallel to images of the evangelists writing the gospel message into a book, scroll, or diptych.[28] The same authors correlate the image with Thekla's commissioning by Paul in Myra (*AThl* 41).[29] In the later expansion of the *AThl* this moment is magnified by Thekla's appointment as an apostle (*"Vie"* 26; cf. 28).[30]

Originally from Rome and now housed in the British Museum are three enchanting early-fifth-century ivory plaques from a casket.[31] All panels depict two scenes; two of the plaques focus on Peter, one on Paul. In the Pauline plaque Thekla's torso is visible at the tower (gate?) of a fortress-like structure; her head rests on her hand and her gaze points downward.[32] Paul sits, though not on a stool but on some kind of block. His eyes do not explicitly read from the scroll he holds in his lap; rather he looks straight ahead.[33]

DISCUSSION OF THEKLAN PORTRAYALS

With this compact survey of images associated with Thekla's story, we can now highlight some aspects of the larger thematic context of Theklan lore. For example, both Paul and Thekla have episodes with lions in their *Acts* and both

---

[26] The biblical figures and scenes depicted here include: Adam and Eve, the sacrifice of Isaac, Daniel between the lions, Jacob, Noah; other figures include Peace (EIPHNH), Righteousness/Justice (ΔΙΚΑΙΟΣΥΝΗ), Prayer (EYXH).

[27] Chapel 25 in the necropolis preserves a badly damaged fresco that may depict another Paul and Thekla scene. Two figures sit facing one another; the right hand figure, perhaps a female (veiled?), holds a rectangular object in her hands. The male at the left has a scarf or hood thrown over his shoulders and holds an object in his hands. A square structure is painted to the right of the female; since it spans the corner of the west and north walls, it may connect to another scene. A large cross *(ankh)* is painted slightly above and between the two figures. Fakhry, *The Necropolis of El-Bagawat*, 80, 87.

[28] Nauerth and Warns, *Thekla,* 10.

[29] Ibid. 10–11.

[30] Dagron, "Introduction," 274; cf. 280.

[31] Weitzmann, *Age of Spirituality*, 507–08; see also Pillinger, "Neue Entdeckungen in der sogenannten Paulusgrotte von Ephesos," 26–27. Interestingly, the scenes meld together stories from the canonical *Acts of the Apostles* and the apocryphal *Acts of Peter* and *Acts of Paul*.

[32] Note that Thekla is not seated at a window.

[33] Nauerth and Warns, *Thekla, 2–3,* suggest that this does not represent the scene in the text of Thekla's first encounter with Paul; instead it represents Paul preaching from prison (*AThl* 17).

are delivered from a gruesome battle with beasts by the aid of lions. On his journey from Damascus to Jericho, Paul encounters a lion who requests to be baptized.[34] In Ephesos, when Paul is condemned to fight with the beasts, he encounters the same lion in the stadium (*APl* 7; cf. 1 Cor 15:32; 2 Tim 4:17). The two recognize each another and briefly converse. A miraculous hailstorm kills all the other beasts and archers sent out against the two, and soon afterward both the lion and Paul leave the scene unhindered. For Thekla, the lion incident takes place in the stadium at Antioch (*AThl* 3.28-33). The lioness to whom Thekla is tied during a procession licks her feet; the next day the same lioness licks her feet again, and dies while protecting Thekla from a number of other attacking beasts. Interestingly, despite the vogue of "the lion's tale" in antiquity,[35] Paul's episode with the lion clearly made little, if any, impact on material culture. In contrast, Thekla's story of the lion was wildly popular, as evidenced by the numerous representations of Thekla standing between lions.[36]

The overlap of female cultic figures with Thekla is especially important in situating the saint in the context of virgins: Artemis and Mary are most pertinent to Thekla's religious and cultural panorama.[37] In the case of the pagan goddesses the issue revolves around the authority of a local divine protector. Thekla acts the part of the newcomer who must assert herself as the vehicle of a greater divine truth and power.

We see this especially in later writings on Thekla's life. One manuscript version of pseudo-Basil's *Life* narrates how Thekla's power of healing and ex-

---

[34] The story of the first encounter with the lion is preserved in Ethiopic and Coptic texts; Tamás Adamik holds that these derive from a Greek original. For translations of the versions and summary of arguments see Tamás Adamik, "The Baptized Lion in the Acts of Paul," in Jan Bremmer, ed., *The Apocryphal Acts of Paul and Thekla*. Studies in the Apocryphal Acts of the Apostles (Kampen: Kok Pharos, 1996) 2:60–74. The translation of Paul's second encounter with the lion is included in Hennecke and Schneemelcher, *New Testament Apocrypha*, 251–54.

[35] The three known variants of the Pauline episode, as well as the resemblance between the lion rescues here and the legendary rescue of Androclus, attest to the popularity of lion scenes in antiquity (Adamik, "The Baptized Lion in the Acts of Paul," 65–70). Consider also the wide visual distribution of Daniel and the lions in the Roman catacombs and elsewhere (Weitzmann, *Age of Spirituality,* nos. 371, 377, 386–87, 421, 436). See the excellent discussion in Robin Margaret Jensen, *Understanding Early Christian Art* (London and New York: Routledge, 2000) 64–93.

[36] See n. 21 above.

[37] The textual tradition of Thekla's *Life* in Seleucia shows Thekla certifying her authority over the city's indigenous cults. Her first four miracles demonstrate how she establishes her superiority over against local deities such as Sarpedon, Zeus, and Aphrodite. The goddess who seemingly has the foremost role in the Seleucian environs, and hence the most difficult to supplant, is Athena (also known as a virgin goddess). Dagron, "Miracle 2" (Dagron, "Introduction," 293); cf. Dagron, *"Vie"* 27.56-61 (Dagron, "Introduction," 278–79); discussion in Dagron, "Introduction," 84–89, and Davis, *The Cult of Saint Thecla,* 75–77.

orcism adversely affects the Seleucian physicians' business prospects. The physicians attribute her power to her virginity, believing that this pure state enables Artemis to hear and respond to her.[38] Indeed, Artemis' key attribute and role is the protection of virgins—she is known to young women as "παρθένος with eternal παρθενεία"—and she is revered as savior, providing safety and protection to the city.[39] While her cult was spread throughout Asia Minor,[40] Artemis is unquestionably important for an Ephesian audience. As the patron goddess of the city with an acclaimed temple and a yearly festival in her name, Artemis is intimately united with Ephesos. Indeed, the apocryphal *Acts of John* depicts the centrality of Artemis; one of John's telling moments is the destruction of the idol temple through the mediated power of the true God.[41]

Thekla's overlay with Mary and Ephesos represents a complex enmeshment with several governing factors. To the extent of the evidence thus far, Mary plays no obvious visual role in the Ephesian fresco, yet her influence in this period of late antiquity, especially as it pertains to Ephesos, is hardly insignificant. As we shall see, Mary's status in the city is intertwined with theological, ecclesiastical, and political circumstances.

Three aspects of Mary play a role here. First, Ephesos boasts of the tradition that Mary fled with John to the city after Christ's death and lived there for her remaining days.[42] Mary's final resting place, however, proved to have a competitive market historically, and evidence suggests that the legend of Mary's domicile in Ephesos may date as late as the fourth or fifth century. Second, Mary appeared as a cultic model for virginity quite late. The first consequential external witness we see is Ambrose (d. 397), who in his treatise on virginity presents Mary as a quintessential model. Notably, Thekla also appears

[38] Fleeing from their plot to defile her virginity and make her powerless, Thekla is "saved" when the earth swallows her, leaving her pursuers with only a piece of her cloak. This episode appears in a manuscript tradition related to that of the expansion of the *AThl*, and presumably has an etiological function for her martyr cult. See Dagron, "Introduction," 48; and Davis, *The Cult of Saint Thecla*, 42–44.

[39] Rick Strenlan, *Paul, Artemis, and the Jews in Ephesus* (Berlin and New York: Walter de Gruyter, 1996) 48–52. Artemis devotion in Ephesos persisted well into the fourth and fifth century, even as Christians were claiming victory (ibid. 68–82; also Stefan Karwiese, *Gross ist die Artemis von Ephesos* [Vienna: Phoibos, 1995] for the changing face of Ephesos over the centuries).

[40] Herzfeld highlights the connection between Artemis as healing deity and Thekla, as well as Athena as an important local deity in Seleucia (Herzfeld and Guyer, *Monumenta Asiae Minoris Antiqua*, 3–4).

[41] *Acts of John* 37-44, in Hennecke and Schneemelcher, *New Testament Apocrypha*, 152–212).

[42] Even today this tradition is respected in the celebration of her feastday at the site of her supposed residence at Meryem Ana, just outside the city of Ephesos.

in this writing, though Ambrose exhibits her as a model for honorable death.[43] Third, less than a century later we see Mary featured strongly in theological doctrine when the heated subject of her title as *theotokos*—really more a question of Christ's divinity and humanity—is debated at the Council of Ephesos (431). From documents of the sessions we know that the meeting was assembled "in the great church called Mary"[44] (ἐν τῇ ἁγίαι ἐκκλησίαι τῇ καλουμένῃ Μαρίαι).[45]

The relationship between these three factors and the fresco is as follows. In the early to mid-fourth century Constantinople embarked on a program to legitimate its sovereignty through its see and ecclesiastical channels. On account of Empress Pulcheria's Marian devotion, the legend of Mary's death in Jerusalem as well as the transfer of her relics to Constantinople displaced Mary from Ephesos. This factor, coupled with Ephesos' declining status—at this time it fell under the jurisdiction of Constantinople's patriarchate—ended in a loss for the city as an ecclesiastical and political figurehead in the East.[46] Why might this be relevant to the cave fresco? Ephesos sustained a significant blow on account of such ecclesiastical and theological politics. Since the city had been divested of several important points of notoriety, it is noteworthy that the fresco in the cave re-emphasizes the apostolic tradition for which Ephesos was previously known. Further, one cannot ignore the possibility of devotion to Thekla as a precursor and model for the (then) rising cult of Mary. Interesting also is the

---

[43] *On Virginity* 2.6-21, cited in Anne Jensen, "Auf dem Weg zur Heiligenjungfrau," in Elisabeth Gössmann and Dieter R. Bauer, eds., *Maria—für alle Frauen oder über allen Frauen?* (Freiburg: Herder, 1989) 48. Jensen notes that Mary as the eternal virgin exists as early as Origen (d. 254), but Basil the Great (d. 379) dismisses this as an intellectual opinion only (ibid. 48–49).

[44] Recently the question of whether the Church of Mary cited in the textual sources indeed refers to the basilica currently known as such has been under debate. For the excavation report and arguments see Stefan Karwiese, *Die Marienkirche in Ephesos. Erster vorläufiger Grabungsbericht 1984–1986* (Vienna: Österreichischen Akademie der Wissenschaften, 1989).

[45] The Acts of the Council and Cyril's correspondence. This is also one of the pieces of evidence used to verify the claim that Mary resided in Ephesos with John (Edward Schwartz, ed., *Acta Conciliorum Oecumenicorum: Concilium universale ephesenum* [Berlin: Walter de Gruyter, 1922] I.1.2.3]). Cyril writes in a letter home, "I am letting you know that the holy council met in Ephesos on the twenty-eighth day of the month of Pauni in the city's great church, dedicated to Mary, the Mother of God . . ." (ἴστε τοίνυν ὅτι κατὰ τὴν ὀγδόην καὶ εἰκάδα τοῦ Παυνὶ μηνὸς ἡ ἁγία σύνοδος γέγονεν ἐν τῇ μεγάλῃ ἐκκλησίαι τῆς πόλεως, ἥτις καλεῖται Μαρία θεοτόκος . . .) (ibid. I.1.1.117-18).

[46] For a detailed exposition of this phenomenon coupled with the rise of the cult of Mary see Vasiliki Limberis, "The Council of Ephesos: The Demise of the See of Ephesos and the Rise of the Cult of the Theotokos," in Helmut Koester, ed., *Ephesos: Metropolis of Asia* (Valley Forge, Pa.: Trinity Press International, 1995) 321–40.

historical association of the cave as κρυφὴ Παναγία, traceable to a local tradition of successors to ancient Ephesian Christians in the neighboring town of Şirince.[47]

As noted above, a survey of non-Ephesian witnesses to Thekla's narratives and imagery offers a reflection of contemporary sociocultural perspectives and particularly highlights the diversity of interpretations of the "essence" of Thekla. In the second century the North African Tertullian, for example, emphasizes the false authorship (read: authority) of certain Pauline writings and the illegitimacy of the right of women to teach and baptize. From the female side, Thekla's dedication to Paul's message and consequential decision to evade marriage is understood to be a model for female monasticism. Macrina, the sister of Gregory of Nyssa (335–394) and Basil the Great (ca. 330–379), is eulogized for her commitment to an ascetic life and perpetual chastity.[48] Thekla apparently acted as a source of inspiration and role model to Macrina. Though she did not leave her mother and home, Macrina's commitment to this lifestyle attracted other virgins, and their household took on the character of a monastery.[49]

A number of later church Fathers render Thekla as an example of paradigmatic virginity.[50] Indeed, one factor linking certain aspects of the evidence is the theme of virginity; examples include Paul's mini-treatise on virginity in the *AThl,* the fact that virginity played such a central role in the stories surrounding women, and the tendency of fourth- to sixth-century ecclesiastical figures to praise Thekla as a model for the chaste female life. Indeed, on the basis of the number of references to her in the fifth- and sixth-century writings of the church Fathers, this was the peak of her popularity.

As early as the turn of the fourth century we see that an aspect of Thekla's character that drew disproportionate praise was her dedication to chastity. Methodius of Olympus (260–312) sets the stage for a comprehensive exposition on the topic with a banquet whose featured guests includes ten virgins, each offering an address.[51] In addition to a lengthy recitation on chastity, Thekla leads the guests in a concluding hymn to Christ as the Bridegroom. Dennis

---

[47] Written record of this tradition dates from 1892. Pillinger, "Neue Entdeckungen in der sogenannten Paulusgrotte von Ephesos," 17.

[48] Gregory of Nyssa, *Vita Macrinae.*

[49] For the question of Thekla as a precursor to female monasticism see Ruth Albrecht, *Das Leben der heiligen Makrina auf dem Hintergrund der Thekla-Traditionen* (Göttingen: Vandenhoeck & Ruprecht, 1986).

[50] Notice that in the Ephesian fresco both Paul and Theokleia stand in relationship to Thekla, thus putting her—or her representative virginity—at the figurative center of the scene.

[51] *Ante-Nicene Fathers,* vol. 6 (Grand Rapids: Eerdmans, 1996–2001).

MacDonald and Andrew Scrimgeour seek to determine features of the saint's icon from a pseudo-Chrysostomian sermon on Thekla. Clearly pointing to the icon during the delivery of his panegyric, this fifth-sixth century author sings Thekla's praises.[52] Pseudo-Chrysostom introduces the icon: "On one side it depicts the crown she won against pleasures [i.e., her virginity], and on the other the crown she won against dangers [i.e., her martyrdom]."[53] From here the author launches into a long discourse on virginity, entirely leaving aside the theme of her martyrdom except to describe how her "qualities of virginity . . . [are] a kind of great martyrdom before martyrdom."[54] Others who also exalt Thekla as a model for the chaste life include Gregory of Nyssa (335–394), Epiphanius of Salamis (315–403), Ambrose (ca. 339–397), and Isidore of Pelusium (360?–435).[55]

If we shift the focus to an appreciation of the Ephesian fresco's visual composition, several noteworthy points arise. First of all, compared with that of Paul and Thekla, Theokleia's portrait gives the impression of being larger in scale. Why is she so prominent? One explanation may be that Theokleia, acting as the (pagan) advocate against conversion, is designed to represent opposition to Christianity in a pagan environment. Is this the predicament of Christians in Ephesos at this time? Regarding the depiction of Thekla in the fresco, it is noteworthy that her portrayal virtually takes a back seat to that of her mother and Paul. Rather than capturing the dynamism of Thekla otherwise visible in *AThl*, here she is shown smaller in scale and enclosed. Perhaps this is meant to accentuate her at the moment just prior to her conversion. The painting emphasizes a transitional point in Thekla's life. She is yet on the inside, both in physical and "enlightenment" terms, but with the illumination of Paul's teaching she will be on the outside in both senses as well.

Let us review the different contents of Thekla images: In the El-Bagawat necropolis paintings the only items associated with Paul and Thekla are the stools they sit on and writing instruments; Thekla is shown in a teaching or writing pose with Paul. The depictions of Thekla in trial situations thoroughly resonate with the vigor we associate with the saint as she lives out her zeal for

[52] Dennis R. MacDonald and Andrew D. Scrimgeour, "Pseudo-Chrysostom's Panegyric to Thecla: The Heroine of the *Acts of Paul* in Homily and Art," *Semeia* 38 (1986) 151–60.

[53] Ibid. 154.

[54] Ibid. Similarly noted by Monika Pesthy, "Thecla among the Fathers of the Church," in Bremmer, ed., *The Apocryphal Acts of Paul and Thekla,* 172.

[55] Gregory of Nyssa, *Homilies on the Canticle of Canticles* 14; Epiphanius of Salamis, *Panarion sive Adversus haereses;* Ambrose, *Ad Vercellensem ecclesiam;* Isidore of Pelusium, *Epistolarum* 1.87. These and additional citations may be found in Pesthy, "Thecla among the Fathers of the Church," 164–78.

mission and faith in the *AThl*. In comparison to these, the "addition" of Theokleia in the Ephesos scene dramatically shifts the focus and message. The Ephesian image showing Thekla at the initial stages of her conversion portrays her at her most passive, albeit at a pivotal juncture. Where the other images offer *Thekla* as a lucid visual and thematic focus, the Ephesian fresco subordinates the character to her "virgin" or social status. As we have seen, this is consonant with a number of church Fathers, who praise Thekla for guarding her virginity, not for her teaching and missionizing. This raises again the question of intended viewership, or what the artist or donor wished to convey.

For the most part the emphasis has been on Thekla; what would change about our thinking if we were to shift the focus? It is significant that we have a tradition of Paul in Ephesos, yet no extant reference has placed Thekla in Ephesos until the unveiling of this painting. If we assume that the emphasis was not exclusive to Thekla, then what is the significance of an image of Paul in the cave? We have noted, for example, that the layer of graffiti and the paintings are coterminous. Why, then, is there no inscription addressed to Thekla in the graffiti, but several inscriptions—though not exclusively—to Paul?[56]

We must likewise consider the role of Theokleia in the fresco. In the *AThl* Thekla's mother orchestrates the greatest clamor against her daughter's decision.[57] My research thus far registers the mother's image in one other example, namely the thirteenth-century Tarragona altar from Spain.[58] There she is shown trying to inhibit Paul's influence, albeit unsuccessfully. Additionally, Theokleia is by no means as imposing a central figure in the altar's iconographic design as she is in the Ephesos painting. Does the inclusion of the disapproving mother in the fresco intend to underscore the clear authority Paul enjoys, both historically in Ephesos and as a figurehead of Christianity at large?

---

[56] The inscriptions are addressed to: God, (Jesus) Christ, Lord, and Paul (Pillinger, "Neue Entdeckungen in der sogenannten Paulusgrotte von Ephesos," 21).

[57] In the story Thekla's fiancé Thamyris comes off as quite a secondary figure to the protest. This fact in itself is exceptional in comparison to other apocryphal Acts (*Acts of Andrew* with Maximilla). Even within the *AThl* the husband of Artemilla and Eubula have more to say than Thamyris. Why is it at all the case that in the *AThl* Thekla's conversion stands in larger relationship to her mother?

[58] The altar in Spain's Tarragona cathedral appears to be drawing upon earlier traditions. The scene of Paul and Thekla parallels that on the ivory plaque (see n. 31 above) as well as the Ephesos fresco. On one of the altar's panels Thekla is shown inside her fortresslike house, peering out from the window. A crowd of men below direct their attention to Paul, some in approval (hands open) and some in dismay (finger pointing at Paul). Paul's left hand points to Thekla (who does not gaze at him directly); in his right he holds an opened book. An adjacent panel shows Theokleia holding back men whose fingers point up to Thekla. See Nauerth and Warns, *Thekla*, 85–91.

With respect to the larger vista of Thekla iconography, we must also address the relative rarity of images of Thekla and Paul from this narrative scene. Portrayals of Thekla suffering her trials fit within the common iconographic emphasis of Christians enduring persecution, thereby pointing to God's power in deliverance. Yet the grouping of Paul, Thekla, and Theokleia in an image is less common, and therefore less readily understood. Perhaps the subject expressed in the painting—rather than, or in addition to, the weight of the characters—is less an illustration of narrative and more an expression of desired action. Did the painter hope to inspire the viewer to conversion? Is the subject meant to be used as paraenesis, calling viewers to an ethic of imitation of Thekla or Paul?[59]

[59] Thanks are owed to Judith Bishop, Therese DesCamp, and Christopher Wright for their thought-provoking conversation and editorial comments.

List of Contributors

MARVIN L. CHANEY is Nathaniel Gray Professor of Hebrew Exegesis and Old Testament at San Francisco Theological Seminary, and a member of the core doctoral faculty of the Graduate Theological Union, Berkeley, CA.

MARY P. COOTE is Associate Professor of Biblical Greek, Associate Dean for Student Life, and Registrar at San Francisco Theological Seminary.

ROBERT B. COOTE is Professor of Old Testament at San Francisco Theological Seminary and a member of the core doctoral faculty of the Graduate Theological Union, Berkeley, CA.

MARY THERESE DESCAMP is a Doctoral Candidate at the Graduate Theological Union, Berkeley, CA, and an ordained minister in the United Church of Christ.

JOANNA DEWEY is Academic Dean and Harvey H. Guthrie, Jr., Professor of Biblical Studies at the Episcopal Divinity School, Cambridge, MA.

BARBARA GREEN, O.P., is Professor of Biblical Studies at the Dominican School of Philosophy and Theology and a member of the core doctoral faculty of the Graduate Theological Union, Berkeley, CA.

HOLLY E. HEARON is Assistant Professor of New Testament at Christian Theological Seminary, Indianapolis, IN.

GINA HENS-PIAZZA is Professor of Biblical Studies at the Jesuit School of Theology and a member of the core doctoral faculty of the Graduate Theological Union, Berkeley, CA.

HISAKO KINUKAWA is Adjunct Professor at the Lutheran Theological Seminary, St. Paul Graduate School, and International Christian University in Tokyo, Japan and an instructor in the D.Min. program of San Francisco Theological Seminary.

ARCHIE CHI CHUNG LEE is Professor of Old Testament Studies, Asian Biblical Hermeneutics, and Contextual Interpretation of the Bible in the Department of Religion at the Chinese University of Hong Kong.

LINDA M. MALONEY is Academic Editor at the Liturgical Press and a priest in the Episcopal Church.

RUTH OHM WRIGHT teaches in the field of Biblical Studies and Archaeology at the Graduate Theological Union. She has worked together with Professor Dr. Renate Pillinger, Director of Christian Period Excavations in Ephesos at the Austrian Archaeological Institute, since 1998.

EUNG CHUN PARK is Associate Professor of New Testament at San Francisco Theological Seminary and a member of the core doctoral faculty of the Graduate Theological Union, Berkeley, CA.

RICHARD ROHRBAUGH recently retired from Lewis and Clark College (Portland, OR), where he was Paul S. Wright Professor of Christian Studies.

LUISE SCHOTTROFF is Visiting Professor of New Testament at Pacific School of Religion, and a member of the core doctoral faculty of the Graduate Theological Union, Berkeley, CA.

ELISABETH SCHÜSSLER FIORENZA is the Krister Stendahl Professor of Divinity at the Harvard Divinity School, Harvard University, Cambridge, MA.

HERMAN WAETJEN recently retired from San Francisco Theological Seminary, where he was Robert S. Dollar Professor of New Testament, and served as a member of the core doctoral faculty of the Graduate Theological Union, Berkeley, CA.

SOJUNG YOON is a Doctoral Candidate at the Graduate Theological Union, Berkeley, CA.

List of Publications of Antoinette Clark Wire

Robert S. Dollar

Professor of New Testament
San Francisco Theological Seminary

و‍ب

Holy Lives, Holy Deaths: A Close Hearing of Early Jewish Storytellers. Atlanta: Society of Biblical Literature, 2002.

"Women's Work in the Realm of God," with Holly Hearon. In Mary Ann Beavis, ed., *The Lost Coin: Parables of Women, Work and Wisdom.* Sheffield: Sheffield Academic Press, 2002.

"Reconciled to Glory in Corinth? 2 Corinthians 2:14–7:4." In Adela Yarbro Collins and Margaret M. Mitchell, eds., *Antiquity and Humanity: Essays on Ancient Religion and Philosophy Presented to Hans Dieter Betz on His 70th Birthday.* Tübingen: Mohr Siebeck, 2001, 263–75.

"The Politics of the Assembly in Corinth," "Paul and Those Outside Power." In Richard A. Horsley, ed., *Paul and Politics Ekklesia, Israel, Imperium, Interpretation, Essays in Honor of Krister Stendahl.* Harrisburg, PA: Trinity Press International, 2000, 124–29; 224–26.

"Reclaiming a Theology of Glory from the Corinthian Women Prophets." In J. Shannon Clarkson, ed., *Conflict and Community in the Corinthian Churches.* New York: Women's Division, General Board of Global Missions, United Methodist Church, 2000, 36–51.

"Romans 3:21-30; also Acts 9:1-19; Galatians 1:13-17; 2 Corinthians 12:1-5." In Alan Falconer, ed., *Faith and Order in Moshi: The 1996 Commission Meeting.* Geneva: WCC Publications, 1998, 314–17.

"Lessons for North America from a Third-World Seminary." In Fernando Segovia and Mary Ann Tolbert, eds., *Teaching the Bible: The Discourses and Politics of Biblical Pedagogy.* Maryknoll, NY: Orbis, 1998, 352–61.

"Reading our Heritage: A Response," *Semeia* 83/8 (1998) 283–93.

245

"Touring for a Song: Visits with Christians in China," *Christian Century* 115 (July 1–8, 1998) 651–52.

"A North American Perspective [reply to M. Dube, D. Mbuwayesango, Y. Yoo, J. Chuh, M. Masenya, L. Guardiola-Sáena, M. Sibeko and B. Haddad, R. Bevera, J. Kim and E. Mouton]," *Semeia* 78 (1997) 145–49.

"Biblical Interpretation in Later Twentieth Century China" (in Chinese). In Xu Weixian and Wang Xiangbao, eds., *Contemporary Chinese Studies Overseas (Dangdai Haiwai Hanxu Yenjiu)*. Nanjing: Jiangsu Peoples Publishing House, 1997, 502–43.

"Li, Eusebeia, Torah: A Response to Towner and Yeo," *Jian Dao* 5 (1996) 143–47.

"Full Communion of Lutheran and Reformed Churches in the Light of Jesus' Story." In Harding Meyer and Antoinette Wire, eds., *Lutheran Reformed Theological Reflections on Full Communion*. Chicago: Evangelical Lutheran Church in America, 1996, 14–34.

"Christian Miracle Stories and Modernization" (in Chinese). In Gao Shiyu and He Guanhu, eds., *Christianity and Modernization* (Ji Du Jiao Wen Hua Yu Xian Dai Hua). Beijing: Chinese Academy of Social Sciences Publishing House, 1996.

"Songs of China's Rural Churches." In Judith A. Berling, ed., *With Faith We Can Move Mountains: Reflections of the GTU Asia Pacific Bridges Consultation in China, October, 1995*. Berkeley, CA: Graduate Theological Union, Asia Pacific Bridges, 1996, 51–62.

"Chinese Biblical Interpretation Since Mid-Century," *Biblical Interpretation* 4 (1996) 101–23.

"Some Stages in Wisdom's Long Journey" (in Chinese). *Nanjing Theological Review* 22–23 (1995) 37–43.

"A Reformed View of the Santiago Conference," in *Oikoumenika*. Patriarch Athenagoras Orthodox Institute at the Graduate Theological Union, Occasional Papers, No. 3 (1995) 37–43.

"The God of Jesus in the Gospel Sayings Source," In Fernando Segovia and Mary Ann Tolbert, eds., *Reading from this Place*. Minneapolis: Fortress, 1995, 1:277–303.

"Performance, Politics, and Power: A Response to R. Ward and A. Dewey," *Semeia* 65 (1994) 129–35.

"1 Corinthians." In Elisabeth Schüssler Fiorenza, ed., *Searching the Scriptures: A Feminist Commentary*. New York: Crossroad, 1994, 153–95.

"'Since God is one': Rhetoric as Theology and History in Paul's Romans." In Edgar McKnight and Elizabeth Struthers Malbon, eds., *The New Literary Criticism and the New Testament*. Valley Forge, PA: Trinity Press International, 1994, 210–27.

"Praying to the God Who Helps the Helpless," *Church and Society* 83 (1992) 22–32.

"Wisdom's Long Journey," *Pacific Theological Review* 24 (1991) 6–12.

"Gender Roles in a Scribal Community." In David Balch, ed., *Social History of the Matthean Community: Cross-Disciplinary Approaches.* Minneapolis: Fortress, 1991, 87–121.

Healing for God's World: Remedies from Three Continents. With Kofi Asare Opoku and Kim Yong-Bock. New York: Friendship Press, 1991.

The Corinthian Women Prophets: A Reconstruction through Paul's Rhetoric. Minneapolis: Fortress, 1990.

"God Overcomes Death with Life." In Jack Stotts and Jane Dempsey Douglass, eds., *To Confess the Faith Today.* Louisville: Westminster John Knox, 1990, 130–39.

"Introduction to NHC IX, 3: Allogenes." In Charles Hedrick, ed., *Nag Hammadi Codices XI, XII, XIII.* Leiden, New York, Copenhagen, Köln: Brill, 1990, 173–91.

"Prophecy and Women Prophets in Corinth." In James E. Goehring, Charles Hedrick, Jack T. Sanders, with Hans Dieter Betz, eds., *Gospel Origins and Christian Beginnings: In Honor of James M. Robinson.* Sonoma, CA: Polebridge Press, 1990, 134–50.

"The Chinese Christian Three-Self Movement: A Model of Solidarity for Women," *Union Seminary Quarterly Review* 43 (1989) 181–200.

"The Social Functions of Women's Asceticism in the Roman East." In Karen King, ed., *Images of the Feminine in Gnosticism.* Philadelphia: Fortress, 1988, 308–23.

"The Syrophoenician Woman: Mark 7:24-30," *Aidyatha,* Student Christian Movement of India, 3 (March 1988) 33–37.

"Introduction: Allogenes (XI/3)." Revised and extended. In James M. Robinson, ed., *Nag Hammadi Library in English.* 2d ed. Philadelphia: Fortress Press, 1988, 490–91.

"Ancient Miracle Stories and Women's Social World," *Forum* 2 (1986) 77–84.

"*Not* Male and Female," *Pacific Theological Review* 19 (1986) 37–43.

"Theological and Biblical Perspective: Liberation for Women Calls for a Liberated World," *Church and Society* 76 (1986) 7–17.

"Economics and Early Christian Voices," *Pacific Theological Review* 19 (1985) 15–24.

"In Memory of Her: A Feminist Theological Reconstruction of Christian Origins." [Article in a Symposium on Elisabeth Schüssler Fiorenza], *Anima* 10 (1984) 105–19.

The Parable is a Mirror. Atlanta: Office of Women, GAMB, Presbyterian Church (USA), 1983.

"The Miracle Story as the Whole Story," *South East Asia Journal of Theology* 22 (1981) 29–37.

"Alias James," with Robert B. Coote, *Pacific Theological Review* 12 (1979) 10–14.

"Structure of the Gospel Miracle Stories and Their Tellers." *Semeia* 11 (1978) 83–113.

"Introduction: Allogenes XI/3." In *The Nag Hammadi Library in English,* ed. James M. Robinson, 442. Philadelphia: Fortress Press, 1977.

Coordinator (with Norman Gottwald). *The Bible and Liberation: Political and Social Hermeneutics.* Berkeley: Community for Religious Research and Education, 1976.

Index of Ancient Writings

2:1-2	43 n.41
2:2	43 n.42
2:3-4	43 n.42
2:12	42
2:12-15	35
2:15	44, 220 n.21, 225
3:4	27
3:5	27
3:8	20
3:12	20, 27
4:3	44
4:6	36
4:7	45 (n.47)
5:3-16	42
5:13	43 n.42
5:17	27, 36
6:2-3	36

2 Timothy

1:15	45
1:15-18	45 n.47
2:17-18	45
3:6	45 n.47
4:2	36
4:3	36
4:10	45 (n.47)
4:17	236
4:19	37

Titus

1:9	36, 42
1:10-15	45 n.47
1:11	43 n.42
2:1	36
2:3-5	42
3:8	27 n.26
3:14	27 n.26

Philemon

10–17	26
18–19	23

Hebrews

5:12	36
6:4-6	167
10:26-29	167
13:7	166 n.31
13:9	36
13:17	166 n.31
13:24	166 n.31

James

3:1	36

1 Peter

2:12-13	43 n.41

2 John

9	36
10	36

Revelation

2:18-28	44
2:24	36

OLD TESTAMENT APOCRYPHA AND PSEUDEPIGRAPHA

4 Maccabees

6:26-30	166 n.29

Pseudo-Philo, *Liber Antiquitatum Biblicarum*

31	69
31:3	79 n.24, 80 n.25
31:7	81
33	82 n.28
44	70

Wisdom of Solomon

1:6-15	211
2–5	204, 205, 210
2:1-10	212